Politics, Economics, and Power

Politics, Economics, and Power

Ideology and Practice Under
Capitalism, Socialism, Communism, and Fascism

By

NATHANIEL STONE PRESTON
The American University

The Macmillan Company
Collier-Macmillan Limited, London

To Ravida

Third Printing, 1969

Library of Congress catalog card number: 67–18418

The Macmillan Company
Collier-Macmillan Canada, Ltd., Toronto, Ontario

Printed in the United States of America

Preface

A word should be said about the approach which I have taken in this book. Despite a personal predilection for capitalism, which I believe to be pragmatically and ethically superior to the other systems surveyed, I have not sought to plead its cause. Rather, I have attempted only to portray the choices of goals that certain men and nations have made in economic and political life, to show the means by which they seek to fulfill them, and to show some of the more important consequences of different ways of relating economic and political power. If I have tried to keep from intruding my own preferences into the description, that is by no means an invitation to others to refrain from making choices themselves. On the contrary, the invitation here is to make them with as much understanding of their nature as can be gained, and this book is offered as an introduction, but an introduction only, to the knowledge on which those choices may be based.

I have included somewhat more political, economic, and social history than is customary in a book of this sort, particularly in the introductory chapter, in the belief that it is useful as a setting against which to appreciate the meaning and purpose of the modern ideologies that are its central concern. Lord Bryce once wrote that ". . . the chief practical use of history is to deliver us from plausible historical analogies." * My purpose is partly that, especially in regard to analogies made between early economic development and that taking place in many parts of the world today. But it is also to serve as a reminder of the extent to which our current disputes are colored by feelings arising out of past experiences that may have lost their relevance to the problems with which we are trying to contend.

It is difficult to express acknowledgments to those who have assisted in one way or another during the long course of writing and preparing a manuscript

* James Bryce, *The American Commonwealth,* 2nd ed. revised (London: Macmillan & Co., 1891), I, p. 8.

for publication, without appearing in some way to be boasting about the perfection of the work itself. The list may take on the semblance of an honor roll of those associated with some great deed or event, when in fact it is intended as a humble expression of gratitude, and as the writer's admission of his helplessness without the unselfish aid of others. Certainly in my case I intend the latter interpretation, for I am indebted to many people, some of whose names I do not even know, for information, assistance, and counsel. Writing for the most part in Washington, D.C., I have had at my elbow a host of government and embassy officials willing to give extraordinary effort to answering my requests for specific items of information, most of which have not found their way onto these pages, but which have supplied me, I hope, with perspective in choosing those I have included. To these anonymous but invaluable and most generous benefactors, I wish to record my gratitude.

A number of persons were kind enough to read all or parts of the manuscript and to advise me on needed improvements. They cannot be held responsible for the result, but I here register my thanks for their help. Foremost among them is Professor Michael D. Reagan of the University of California, Riverside, whose unfailingly constructive criticism and frequent suggestions of sources from which I might profitably draw material could not have been more welcome. Secondly, I must name my father, Jerome Preston, whose influence upon this work is greater than I am sure he realizes, and who read the entire manuscript with such diligent attention to detail that it threatened at times to impair my filial devotion to him, but never my respect. Professor Edgar S. Robinson of The American University read four chapters under great pressure of time and at a real sacrifice of his own convenience, yet gave to his reading the meticulous care that characterizes him as a scholar. Professor James H. Weaver, also of The American University, saved me from some of my errors in statements of economic theory in the first two chapters, and Mr. H. F. B. Fane, Counselor (Labour) at the British Embassy, and Mr. Kai Lie, Secretary at the Norwegian Embassy, both in Washington, were good enough to review my analysis of socialism in Chapter 3.

Several others have shared their wisdom with me or allowed me to use their resources for information-gathering. Among them I would name Professor Charles K. Wilber of the Department of Economics at The American University, who aided me in the translation of Russian statistics and gave me a number of insights into Soviet welfare policies; Mr. Sidney H. Hebblethwaite, Counselor (Information) at the British Embassy, who saw to it that my every question was answered there; Professor John C. Scott, Acting Chairman of the Department of Sociology at The American University, who responded to countless requests for guidance on the subject of social class; Professor Allan G. Gruchy of the University of Maryland, who was so kind as to lend me the proofs of his text on comparative economic systems * so that my work could

* Allan G. Gruchy, *Comparative Economic Systems: Competing Ways to Stability and Growth* (Boston: Houghton Mifflin Company, 1966).

have the benefit of his painstaking research even before his book reached publication; Mr. Olaf Solli, Economic Counselor of the Norwegian Embassy, and Mr. Peter Hammarström, attaché of the Royal Swedish Embassy, who responded with great courtesy to my many questions; and Professor James D. Smith of the Department of Economics, The American University, who instructed me in the intricacies of statistical analysis of the distribution of wealth.

To these acknowledgments I should add my appreciation to Dean Earl H. De Long of the School of Government and Public Administration of The American University, who arranged for my release to half-time leave at a critical time in the writing of this book and kept to a minimum the miscellaneous demands for service on committees, and so on, that every dean must make on his faculty; to my editor at The Macmillan Company, Mr. Robert J. Patterson, whose patience with missed deadlines and gentle prodding were in perfect balance; and to Mr. Janis Athanassiadis, who helped as my graduate assistant in the work on the first two chapters. To Mrs. Marjorie M. Moomey I owe a special debt of gratitude for most accurate typing and cheerful willingness to work under almost constant pressure of time. Finally, my wife has shared so greatly in making this book possible—by reading, criticizing, helping me to test ideas, joining in the tiresome labor of proofreading, and not least by helping our children endure the almost constant inaccessibility of their father while the work was in progress—that I can find no more fitting response than to dedicate it to her in appreciation and deep affection.

N. S. P.
Holderness, New Hampshire

Table of Contents

Chapter 3 / Socialism

List of Tables and Figures

1 / Introduction

The Nature of This Study

This book is about a debate—a debate that has dominated much of the political discourse of the past century and that is still with us today—concerning the proper place of government in the economic life of nations. In its most intense form it is the contest between the great ideologies of capitalism, socialism, communism, and fascism.[1] In its milder version it arises regularly in policy struggles over public power, welfare, public housing, and many of the other issues that make up the substance of political controversy.

Is it a real debate—are the alternatives posed in it meaningful? Is there an essential difference, say, between socialism and capitalism as they are practiced today? Has capitalism given way to "creeping socialism," as some would assert, and is the "welfare state" the symbol of its surrender? What of the often-heard claim that we have reached the "end of ideology"? When we speak of socialism, of capitalism, or of communism are we mouthing only "myths" that no longer carry real conviction? [2]

Perhaps we cannot answer all these questions, but neither can we disregard them. They confront us almost daily in the political choices we must make, and the fact that they do warrants both an inquiry into the foundations of ideological controversy and an effort to define the issues involved. As citizens we often differ about the proper role of government in economic life. We need

---

[1] Because there are few active and vocal supporters of fascism at present, it could be considered to have dropped out of the debate. Its historical importance in the present century, however, and the possibility of its resurgence are arguments for its continued inclusion.

[2] This last is a view that has important scholarly support. See Robert A. Dahl and Charles E. Lindblom, *Politics, Economics, and Welfare* (New York: Harper & Row, Publishers, 1953), pp. 3–18.

1

to know whether our differences rest on disagreements about facts, or whether they arise from a divergence among the values or goals we seek to fulfill through political and economic activity. And we need to understand what our choices imply for the political system itself, for lying near the center of the controversy is one of the age-old questions of politics—political power. In approaching this subject, then, we are undertaking a most important part of the study of government, and it is from that point of view that we shall proceed.

To the student of government, the proper delimitation of his field of study may prove to be one of the most difficult problems he faces. Even though he knows that his focus is on those aspects of human activity that revolve around the making of authoritative decisions for or in the name of society as a whole, he must realize that he cannot ignore those patterns in the total culture that confer position and power in the making of authoritative decisions. Furthermore, he cannot remain indifferent to the content of the decisions themselves —that is, to the actual policies adopted and their effects. Economic decisions of government present both sides of this problem, first, because they are policy decisions, and secondly, because the results of these decisions may be to make some people more or less powerful in society, and ultimately in the political realm, thus giving them a larger or smaller voice in future political action. But more of this later; suffice it to say that an investigation from this approach is justified, not merely in terms of one type of political system, such as democracy, but in terms of the political power relationships generated in economic life and of the economic power that finds its source in politics.

Some Definitions. To approach the study of government and economics, or economics and politics, we ought first to define the area of our concern. We are dealing, in essence, with two aspects of human organization that are a part of the total complex of organizational relationships making up society. Since the beginning of recorded history, and undoubtedly before, man has employed organization to meet two principal problems: his relation to his environment and the relations among individuals. Man has organized in order to worship or placate the God or gods whom he believed ruled him or his environment; he has organized to draw sustenance from nature and to divide or distribute the produce thereof; he has organized for recreation; for procreation; for education; for peaceful communal existence; and for war. Each such act of organizing orders the relationships among individuals—assigning tasks and often establishing rights and duties—but more than one of the functions listed can be performed by the same organization. Society is a network of relationships arising out of the various ways that men are organized within it. One cannot merely designate one set of individuals within society and say, "These are engaged in politics," and take another set and say, "These are engaged in economics," for the same people may be engaged in both, to a greater or lesser degree. In discussing economics and politics, therefore, we are referring to the economic aspect (or *order,* in the terminology we shall use) and the political aspect (or *order*) of society, recognizing that, however clearly we may distinguish them analytically, they are seldom, if ever, found existing as wholly separate organizational entities.[3]

We shall define the economic order as consisting of those relationships among men in society that arise out of the production and distribution of goods and services. Examples of these are the relationships between buyer and seller, hiring agent and job-seeker, corporate directors and management, and regulatory commissions and the industries they regulate. The term, *order*, does not imply that there is unified control over the economy, or even that economic activity is especially orderly. It only suggests a structure of relationships centered on some common activity.

Correspondingly, the political order consists of the relationships in society that arise out of or are concerned with the making of authoritative decisions for or in the name of the whole society, such as those between voter and candidate, senator and senator, ruler and subject and, of course, regulatory commissions and the industries they regulate.

As parts of the web of human relationships in society, these two orders affect each other, overlap one another, and, as suggested in the examples, may coalesce at points. Where economic decisions are made authoritatively for a society, as they are in most primitive societies and in modern communism, the economic order becomes a part of the political order. When a government agency regulates prices, the relationship between the agency and the regulatee is political, because the regulation is authoritative; it is also economic, because the production or distribution of goods and services is thereby affected. The political order in societies throughout history has had some economic functions, but the range of functions to be performed and the consequences of their being so performed are the stuff of the current discussions about welfare programs, medical care, elimination of poverty, and even the reservation of lands for parks or wilderness. They are also, and most importantly, central elements of the larger contest of ideologies—points of dispute between communism, fascism, socialism, and capitalism. In consequence, ideological issues very often become mingled with policy questions and inject an emotional flavor into the debate on the latter, especially when neither the values underlying the ideology nor the economic and political effects of the policy decision are clearly understood.

To give but one example of the erratic nature of the mingling of ideological and policy questions, a government decision to reserve an area for recreational

[3] For a more rigorous discussion of the relationship between the two orders, which includes also the other aspects of human society, see Talcott Parsons and Neil J. Smelser, *Economy and Society: A Study in the Integration of Economic and Social Theory* (Glencoe, Ill.: The Free Press, 1956), especially pp. 46–84. On the philosophical question of the relationship between the disciplines of economics and political science, see Joseph Cropsey, "On the Relation of Political Science and Economics," *American Political Science Review*, LIV (March, 1960), pp. 3–14.

purposes is an economic decision—it prevents the land from being mined to extract the wealth that may lie below the surface or being tilled to grow food and directs it to the production of recreational services instead. This decision also affects the distribution of recreational benefits, for it makes them available to the whole community, rather than to the few who might have owned the land before; it has an equalizing effect. Yet this is rarely called socialism, whereas a proposal to use government funds to build a hydroelectric project, damming a river and drowning out a wilderness area, usually is. Both divert production; both provide some equalization of benefits (the latter through a preferential or beneficial rate structure for the electricity produced). Both are involvements of the political in the economic order, yet if one is socialism, why is not the other?

The Question of Power. The effect of the two orders on one another is not found only at the points of actual invasion. Of equal or greater importance is the fact that, because both orders fix relationships among human beings, establishing rights and duties, both confer positions of power and influence in society. Social power is a curious phenomenon. It is an ability to cause others to do what we wish, or at least to modify their activity in a direction favorable to our desires.[4] It arises from a wide and, perhaps, infinite variety of sources. It may be derived from traditional habits of deference (as when younger members of society permit their elders to dominate decisions) or from the ability to reward or to punish by the giving or withdrawal of benefits. It may be a consequence of love or of a half-remembered fear developed in childhood. It may be highly specific and limited to the relations of a particular pair of persons in respect to a single subject, such as a friend accepting his companion's guidance on voting; or it may be the generalized rule of a tribal chieftain, applicable to all members and on all matters of consequence. Because the web of personal relationships in society is so intertwined, power is often transferable from one subject to another.

In a modern industrialized society, economic and political power are frequently interchangeable, or translatable from one order into the other. The interchange in one direction is disclosed by contemporary studies of community power structure in the United States, which regularly identify the economically powerful as participants in political power as well. In the other, the ability of American Presidents to force industry reconsideration of prices even in the absence of a price-control law and (to take a more trivial instance) the power of political leaders to exact favors from businessmen have been too well doc-

---

[4] The reader should note that the word *power* is defined here somewhat in the manner that a physicist defines it—as a tendency that may be very great or very small. When we use the term in ordinary discourse, we tend to have in mind only very great power— the power of organized labor or business, for example—and to forget that there are degrees of power running all the way down to the power of a friend of a city councilman to get his traffic ticket "fixed" and beyond.

umented of late to require elaboration. The translation is not perfect, of course. In a very class-conscious society, for example, a newly rich man may find that he is given less respect and attention by government officials than is provided to a man of aristocratic lineage whose fortune has all but vanished; in this case economic power has proved less easy to convert into political power than was the power represented by traditional respect.

Economic power, however, is not merely a matter of possession of wealth. Wealth by itself is of limited utility as a source of power unless it either confers respect, which is a more general basis of social power, or can be used to purchase compliance, through bribery, for example. In most societies respect is given to the holders of wealth, but bribery is subject to such severe social and legal sanctions as to be of relatively little use for most purposes. In a democratic polity that permits or requires political campaigns to be privately financed, wealth may be used to assist the election of favored candidates or to place elected officials under obligation by the generous provision of campaign funds. But this, too, is limited in its effectiveness by the fact that, to win an election, candidates need not only money, but votes. The wealthy are few; the poor are many. The real basis of economic power is more often the ability to direct the performance of economic functions; the basis is *organizational,* not pecuniary. Economic power is at the disposal of managers of enterprises who can determine what will be produced, how much, and at what price to offer it. It is held also by labor-union leaders who can bring production to a halt by ordering a strike.[5] Both of these types of power become directly employable in the political order when the cooperation of their holders becomes desirable for the purpose of some governmental policy as, for example, when a government in pursuit of an anti-inflationary policy asks both labor and management to "hold the line" on wages and prices. In such circumstances there may exist an opportunity to exact other favors from government in return for the exercise of restraint. In the most general case, economic power resolves itself into social and political power through the habitual respect, consideration, and obedience given to those who command large organizations of men. They may be consulted as a matter of course on important policy decisions,[6] they may join in associations—"pressure groups"—in order to make

[5] These examples are oversimplified for convenience in illustrating the point. Obviously both the manager and the labor leader do not "possess" power in the sense that they need not concern themselves about the willingness of their subordinates or union members to obey their direction. Their power is based not only on their organizational positions, but on the relationship between them and those whom they direct or lead. For more on this, see Robert A. Dahl, "The Concept of Power," *Behavioral Science,* II (July, 1957), pp. 201–215. This article includes an interesting (although unsuccessful) attempt to measure power. Economic power as power to *withhold* is discussed in John R. Commons, *Legal Foundations of Capitalism* (Madison: University of Wisconsin Press, 1957), ch. III.

[6] This may result also because of their control of information needed by others—a control that again arises from organizational position rather than from wealth.

themselves heard, or they may threaten to use their influence with their followers to sway votes in elections, and thus demand the attention of political officials. Through all of these devices, economic power—and by this is meant the power of any kind of economic organization: labor union, private company, nationalized enterprise, or cooperative—can find expression in the political order.

Clearly, for each, different forms of action are more suited for the effective exercise of power than others, and the degree of organization and attention given to the effective use of the available weapons will greatly influence the amount of power exerted. There may also be limits to the amount of economic power that can be translated into social and political power in a given society. Americans, for example, tend to be suspicious of too massive a concentration of economic pressure on the political order. It was not without reason that one study of the political activities of the National Association of Manufacturers had for its title a question: "NAM: Influential Lobby or Kiss of Death?" [7] There is no precise rate of exchange of power between the two orders.

However imperfect it may be, the implications of the interchange between political and economic power are important in evaluating the competing ideologies of our time. There has been some tendency on the part of the proponents of each to ignore one or another of the possibilities of power acquisition and transfer. Those who favor capitalism give scant attention to the political consequences of privately held economic power, while decrying the economic and social consequences of concentrated political power. They fear the growth of government more than they do the growth of large business enterprises. Socialists substantially reverse this, or used to before they had a chance to try out their system, and have been inclined to overlook the compounding of political and economic power that results when the political order is placed in charge of the economic order. They have tended to forget that the transfer of a business from private to public ownership does not rob its managers of their power, but may actually increase it. Communists, finally, are compelled by their ideology to regard political power solely as an outgrowth of private economic dominance—an instrument for the suppression of those whom the economic system already exploits. To the communist all social power rests at bottom on economic power, and all injustice in the distribution of power will disappear once private economic power is destroyed.

Particular economic policies may have far-reaching effects upon political participation and on political power. This, too, is often lost sight of in the debate. When a government grants benefits to some economic group, we usually regard it as acting in response to an exercise of power by that group, but there are striking instances in which it is the grant itself that establishes and enlarges the group's power. The National Farmer's Union (NFU) in Great

[7] Richard W. Gable, *Journal of Politics*, XV (May, 1953), pp. 254–273.

Britain is today one of the most powerful interest groups in that country, encompassing some 90 per cent of the farmers in England and Wales. Although its more recent successes in gaining and maintaining subsidies and other benefits may be attributed to its political strength, its greatest growth in membership occurred after, not before, the introduction of subsidies.[8] An example of an interest group actually brought into existence as the result of public policy conferring benefits is the National Association of Small Business Investment Companies in the United States. The companies that are its members were created pursuant to an Act of Congress. The Association now has as one of its main interests the support and improvement of the legislation that made its existence possible! On a broader scale, it is suggested by available voting studies that voting itself increases in frequency as the welfare of a group improves. Widely distributed government assistance to the economically weak, therefore, may be a means of enlarging the number of persons who participate in political power through the electoral process.

All of this serves to illustrate the importance of the economic, as well as the political order to any theory of politics, be it democratic or otherwise. And this has been well recognized by some, but not all political theorists. James Harrington, in his justly celebrated *Oceana* provided for an "Equal Agrarian," or law that undertook to limit and stabilize political power by limiting the amount of land (economic power) that could be held by any one member of his Commonwealth. Plato recognized the problem in reverse, by denying private property to the holders of political power, his guardian class.[9] John Locke, a less able theorist, founded his system on property, but then failed to take full account of the inequalities of power that were the likely result. Certainly the dictator who sees in private control of the economy a challenge to his supremacy is right, and it is appropriate that the fascist states took good care to provide close political control over private enterprise, and that communist nations have taken over their economic systems entirely. Certainly the syndicalists of the late nineteenth and early twentieth centuries were at least correct in supposing that the economic power of labor could be transformed into political power through the medium of the General Strike, if only the workers could be mobilized for it. Madison, too, in stating the theory that underlay the Federal Constitution, perceived that the widening of the area governed by a single political system would tend to render any one economic power less significant and less likely to dominate in the contest of economic powers for the control of the political order.

[8] The great impetus to NFU growth was the program of government encouragement to agriculture during the Second World War—a program that arose from needs felt within the political order, rather than from demands posed by the farmers, however happy the latter may have been with the result. See Michael Tracy, *Agriculture in Western Europe* (New York: Frederick A. Praeger, 1964), pp. 253–254, 268–269.

[9] And, given the nature of the economic system of his time, his solution was as sound as Harrington's was for his time. Neither, of course, would be adequate today.

The Ideological Conflict. The conflict of ideologies today, aside from its expression in the form of national aspirations for power in the world of nation-states, is principally one concerning how the economic order should be run and what its relationship to the political order should be. This is true, at least, of the three to which we shall direct our main attention.[10] Socialism demands that the economic order be subordinated and made responsive to decisions made in the political order—that the latter be given precedence over the former. Communist theory of the "withering away of the State" looks ultimately to the elimination of the political order and the assumption of its few remaining functions by the economic order and by society as a whole. In its practice, however, it does substantially the opposite, and the economic order is so controlled by the political as to become a part of it. Capitalism asserts that the two should be as separate as possible, with the political order cast in a supplementary, corrective, and supportive role so far as economic decisions are concerned. All three are concerned with power, but this is by no means the reason for the conflict. For the subordination of one order to another, or their separation, is only viewed as a means to more important goals; and those are the realization of certain values and the achievement of certain types of relationships between men in society that are felt to be desirable and that can only be realized or achieved through the power arrangements envisioned. The goal or objective is some vision of the good life—of the ideal organization of society for the fulfillment of the purposes of man; the relationship of the economic to the political order is the means, the principle by which this goal is to be reached.

What are some of these goals? They include an abundance of material things, a full self-expression of the individual, a maximization of the "better" qualities of man—his industriousness, his cooperativeness, his sense of justice, his humane tendencies, his drive to learn, his adventuresomeness, his thrift, his generosity, and his versatility—and freedom from oppression which stultifies human and social growth. What distinguishes one ideology from another, however, is the order in which these goals or objectives are ranked, and sometimes the definitions attached to such words as *freedom, self-expression,* and *justice*. Some rank cooperativeness over adventure, and others industry over versatility, or freedom (as defined) over abundance.

Objectives and Principles. The distinction between objectives and principles (or means) is important, for it will help explain the debate and help us in determining where the areas of agreement lie. For there are points of agreement, especially in the realm of principles when they are stated as means: If

[10] Because fascism is not, in the main, directed to the solution of economic problems, it stands in a different relation to this question than the others. It demands complete subordination of the economic order to the political, but it does so not so much to improve the working of the economy generally as to direct it toward production for war and to ensure that economic power provides no challenge to the rulers of the state.

you do thus and so, such will be the result. Capitalists and socialists are in general agreement that government ownership will permit stronger control over an industry by the electorate than mere regulation. Capitalists simply disagree that this is desirable. They feel that government ownership leads to a failure to achieve the kind of freedom they envision for society and believe it tends to hamper production and innovation, both of which they value highly. Socialists, on the other hand, are not so sure that production and innovation will suffer (here there is a disagreement about the facts, which might be subject to checking). Besides, they feel that this is less important than the desirability, in basic industries at least, of having the productive forces directed by an agency responsible to the public, instead of controlled by persons who are guided only by their private judgment and their interest in personal gain.

Why are different objectives chosen by proponents of the various ideologies, and why do whole nations seem to range themselves on one side or another of the ideological conflict, accepting the goals and the slogans of one or another ideology? The answer appears to lie partly in historical accidents that limited the alternatives open to a nation at crucial moments in time, and partly in the great mystery of cultural choice, in the tendency of man to seek something more than mere existence—to find a deeper meaning in life. For men do dedicate their lives and their societies to purposes above the level of the beehive and the anthill; they seek glory, or the service of God, or progress, or beauty, or communion with, rather than just survival in nature. The choices that a society makes are modified through the centuries, and some bases of choice may well be lost in the darkness of prehistory. Contemporary studies of the cultures of both primitive tribes and modern societies reveal that there is a great range of goals from which a society must select only a few upon which to concentrate its efforts. A society organizes its life around these choices, developing more fully those functions that will tend to fulfill the objectives chosen and leaving unperformed functions that another society, with different goals, would regard as vital.

If the choice of a society is for a noneconomic goal, such as the worship or service of a god or gods, then the economic order will be organized to serve that goal and not merely economic ends in themselves. A classic example of this is given in Ruth Benedict's description of the Zuñi in the Southwestern United States:

> The Zuñi are a ceremonious people, a people who value sobriety and inoffensiveness above all other virtues. Their interest is centred upon their rich and complex ceremonial life. Their cults of the masked gods, of healing, of the sun, of the sacred fetishes, of war, of the dead, are formal and established bodies of ritual with priestly officials and calendric observances. No field of activity competes with ritual for foremost place in their attention. Probably most grown men among the western Pueblos give to it the greater part of their waking life. It requires the memorizing of an amount of word-perfect ritual that our less trained minds find staggering, and the perform-

ance of neatly dovetailed ceremonies that are charted by the calendar and complexly interlock all the different cults and the governing body in endless formal procedure.

Economic affairs are always . . . comparatively unimportant in Zuñi. . . . Like all the Pueblos, and perhaps in greater degree than the rest, Zuñi is rich. It has gardens and peach orchards and sheep and silver and turquoise. These are important to a man when they make it possible for him to have a [ceremonial] mask made for himself, or to pay for the learning of ritual, or to entertain the tribal masked gods at the Shalako. For this last he must build a new house for the gods to bless at housewarming. All that year he must feed the cult members who build for him, he must provide the great beams for the rafters, he must entertain the whole tribe at the final ceremony. . . . Riches used in this way are of course indispensable to a man of prestige, but neither he nor anyone else is concerned with the reckoning of possessions, but with the ceremonial rôle which he has taken. . . .[11]

The amount of human energy devoted to the noneconomic goals of a society may be immense—enough to raise the economic level of its population remarkably if turned to other purposes. Consider for a moment the choice that modern nations have made to preserve their separate identities as nation-states. The services of the economies of each of them are partly turned to the production of weapons and the maintenance of military forces, to the conduct of diplomatic relations, and to the maintenance of a degree of costly self-sufficiency in the economy itself. Additional effort goes for other goals: The building and maintenance of places of worship; the creation and housing of objects of art; the support of composers and performers of music; the discovery and preservation of the artifacts of prehistoric civilizations; the exploration of space; and so on. So it is also, even within the realm of matters we would call economic, that choices may be made that shape the operation of the economy to greater production, or wider and more even distribution, or more production in one field than another.

The Development of the Economic and Political Orders

If we turn from modern nations to consider the broad sweep of political and economic history, particularly in the West, we may gain some perspective on the present conflict over the role of government in the economy. For although the conflict is, and as we shall see could not be other than, a recent one, the nature of it can be understood better if we see what has happened over time to the relationship between things political and things economic. Politics and economics have not always been the separate categories that they are in men's minds today. It is, in fact, only relatively recently that the study of the two has been divided. As Robert Heilbroner points out in his clever and

[11] *Patterns of Culture*, Sentry ed. (Boston: Houghton Mifflin Co., 1959), pp. 59–60, 76–77.

most readable study of *The Worldly Philosophers*,[12] the world had to wait until the eighteenth century to develop the first true economists. It was not until the twentieth century that American universities largely abandoned the old designation of political economy and established departments of economics and departments of political science as separate entities. To be sure, political philosophers had dealt with economics through the ages—Plato devoted a great part of his *Republic* to the economic organization of his ideal city-state —but that is precisely the point; it was assumed that the political order would be controlling, and that it would regulate and direct human effort in the production and distribution of society's goods. Today the economic and political orders are both highly developed and reasonably distinguishable from other aspects of social organization, and we face the question of what their relationship should be. In ancient times they were hardly distinguishable at all, so the question could scarcely arise. The intervening period has been one of first slow, and then rapid differentiation of society into separate orders for political, religious, economic, and social activities, followed by an often fiercely fought reentry of government into the role of regulator, supervisor and, occasionally, performer of the economic function and sometimes of the others as well. In this process political and economic organizations both were shaped, and the goals of various societies developed and modified.

Three threads must be traced in reviewing the politico-economic history of the West. There is, first, the changing relationship of the political order to the rest of the social complex, including the economic order. Secondly, there is the shaping of the economic order through various forms of organization and varying, and an ultimately increasing productivity as Western society turned to placing economic goals high among the legitimate objectives of human effort. Third is the remarkable change of outlook of society when whole peoples, and not just the visionary few, came to believe that progress, if not perfectibility itself, was possible through conscious and intelligent effort— progress for the individual in bettering his own condition, and progress for society in creating a happier and more comfortable world in which to live and work.

Primitive Society. In primitive society, at least in the examples that anthropologists have been able to study at close hand in recent years, there was little or no differentiation of the members of the community for the performance of its various functions; all took part in the hunt or drive, in the raising of food (if it was an agricultural village), in the religious rites, and in social festivities, to the extent that they were not disbarred by age or sex. In some cases, there may have been "specialists" in certain skills, such as the Leopard-Skin chiefs of the Nuer, whose services were called for in the reconciliation of disputes, or the Antelope Shaman of the western Shoshoni Indians who was

---

[12] Rev. ed. (New York: Simon & Schuster, 1961), pp. 6–27.

supposed to bring success in the hunt.[13] These, however, were not heads of distinct organizations but only, as it were, officers of the general community. The social order, the political order, and the economic and religious orders were one. Political power, although it might command such small riches as the village afforded, did not set a chief off greatly from his followers, and the economy was not so productive that he could direct his people into the construction of great monuments to his glory or the maintenance of his court in sumptuous ease. The support of the economy was agricultural or pastoral, and it provided little beyond subsistence.[14] The role of the chief was far more likely to be one of ensuring the survival of his people by enforcing the rules of redistribution that kept all from starvation. If he maintained storehouses, it was to provide for those dependent on him in time of need and for the holding of festivals in which all shared. The whole picture of a primitive economy tended to be one of rules of division and of reciprocal giving that were a part of the fabric of social intercourse and were deeply involved in the magical and religious ritual around which the life of the community was built. The economy, lean as it was, was subordinated to the social relationships and religious strivings of the village. Although gaining a living occupied the greater portion of a man's lifetime, it failed to set either his or the community's goals. In outlook, the primitive was traditional. He did not look for his condition or his society to change, nor did he seek innovation other than as a means to ease the tasks of daily life. Customs directed his activity and guided him into his occupation, giving him little scope for grand ambitions. Unless a slave, he doubtless did not find his government, such as it was, oppressive. At its best, that government was his assurance of an adequate mobilization of effort to gain food and a fair distribution of the rewards of that effort.

The Ancient World. Remarkably complex and wealthy as were the great empires of the West—Egypt, Greece, and Rome—the civilizations of the Incas and Mayas of Central America, and India and China in the East, the production of riches was still subservient to the religious objectives and power

[13] For these see, respectively, Lucy Mair, *Primitive Government* (Baltimore: Penguin Books, 1962), pp. 41–43, and Julian Steward, *Basin-Plateau Aboriginal Sociopolitical Groups* (Washington, D.C.: Smithsonian Institution, Bureau of American Ethnology, 1938), pp. 34, 247. It must be acknowledged that the use of recent primitive tribes as analogous to prehistoric social organizations in the West is dangerous, but lacking (for obvious reasons) data on the latter, one must hope that the analogy will not be misleading, if not relied on too heavily.

[14] A possible indication of the slim margin available for diversion into accumulation of wealth is given in a recent study of Africa, where it is reported that agricultural productivity in 1960 was ". . . still so low that it takes anywhere from two to ten people —men, women, and children—to raise enough food to supply their own needs and those of one additional—non-food-growing—adult." George H. T. Kimble, *Tropical Africa* (New York: Twentieth Century Fund, 1960), Vol. I, p. 572. Kimble estimates the average to be 6 to 1 or worse.

strivings of these societies, and the enjoyment of the fruits of the economy extended only slightly below the level of the ruling elite. The size of the political unit had produced the emergence of government as a clearly definable institution, with the consequent creation of a bureaucracy and a ruling class of nobles (or briefly in Athens and Rome, citizens), military leaders, and priests. Government was in the hands of the few, who gained their right by birth. For the most part, society was regarded as a single unit for political, military, social, and religious purposes, and the economy, resting on a slave and peasant agricultural basis, was merely supportive of this structure. Until the rise of divergent religious sects in Rome, and again after the adoption of the Christian religion by Constantine, the religious community was united with the political community—the city's gods were the household gods. By the same token where the one or the other held primacy as the focus of civic life, it could command the total resources of the society. The wealth of the Incas was used in great ceremonies and sacrifices, that of the Greeks in nearly constant warfare. In the Greeks' use of the word, *polis,* which included not only the political entity of the city, but its social organization as well, the sense of unity could be observed.

The economies of these civilizations were often remarkably productive, and the surplus beyond that necessary to keep alive the working population was taken for the use of those whose functions represented the prime purposes of the society: the rulers or citizens, the military chiefs, and the priesthood. What had developed was, in the terms used by economic historians, an economy of *command* resting atop a basic economic organization governed by tradition. The peasant, the slave, and in most cases the artificer, were fixed in their trades by inheritance. Adam Smith records that in Egypt under the Pharaohs, "every man was bound by a principle of religion to follow the occupation of his father, and was supposed to commit the most horrid sacrilege if he changed it for another." [15] Personal striving for gain was regarded as degrading, not a fit activity for those in the upper strata, and not a means by which one could raise his station in society to become a part of the ruling elite. There were exceptions to this, of course, but the condemnation of working or trading for reward was most clearly evidenced in the systems that were considered democratic. Aristotle, in his discussion of the economy, distinguished between economic activity for use—household management and conservation of one's resources—and that for profit, with considerable disapproval of the latter. Cicero declared the wages of a hired worker "ungenteel and mean," found "nothing befitting a gentleman" in the work of an artisan, and disparaged retail trading in even sharper terms.[16] Incredible effort could be exacted from the laboring population, peasants and slaves, enough to build the great pyramids of Egypt and Central America, but this was at the command of the

---

[15] *The Wealth of Nations,* Book I, ch. VII.
[16] *De Officiis,* Book I, ch. XLII.

rulers and not for the reward of those who built them. The impressive trade carried on by the cities in many of these empires was also affected by the form of organization of society and the objectives pursued by it:

> Unlike the modern city which is not only a receiver of goods shipped in from the hinterlands, but also an important exporter of goods and services back to the countryside, the cities of antiquity tended to assume an economically parasitic role vis-à-vis the rest of the economy. Much of the trade which entered the great urban centers of Egypt, Greece, and Rome (over and above the necessary provisioning of the city masses) was in the nature of luxury goods for its upper classes, rather than raw materials to be worked and then sent out to a goods-consuming economy. The cities were the vessels of civilization; but as centers of economic activity, a wide gulf separated them from the country, making the cities enclaves of economic life rather than nourishing components of integrated rural-urban economies.[17]

Individuals could profit from this trade, and the working populations of the cities could find employment in it, but it did not produce a prosperity that was widespread or that penetrated to those upon whom the whole structure rested, the peasantry and the slaves.

Power in these societies was able to command wealth and found its own source in positions of leadership in politics, warfare, and religion. These positions, in turn, were conferred largely under traditional rules of inheritance or by suppositions about magical powers or endowments. The fruits of production were controlled by them through taxation, landholding, and slave labor. They, in turn, regulated the system of distribution to the nonproducing elements of society and to all the population in times of famine. In some instances, of which Egypt was an example, the system operated not unlike a greatly enlarged version of the patriarchal family.[18] Although there was an obvious emphasis on the building of great empires, and not infrequent philosophizing and code-writing designed to produce the best possible governmental system, the over-all impression given is one of stasis: Either each system was regarded as the best possible scheme (or the only one there could be), or it was felt that one single best could be constructed. The idea of continuous human progress was still absent. For the great mass of the people, all prospect of betterment was denied.

Medieval Europe. It has become increasingly dangerous to generalize about the feudal age in Western history, as more and more studies have revealed the diversity of patterns to be found in its political, economic, and social life. Nevertheless, it is essential to outline here some of the more widely

[17] Robert L. Heilbroner, *The Making of Economic Society,* p. 24. © 1962. Reprinted by Permission of Prentice-Hall, Inc., Englewood Cliffs, N.J.
[18] Karl Polanyi, *The Great Transformation: The Political and Economic Origins of our Time* (Boston: Beacon Press, 1957), p. 51.

encountered characteristics of this long (1,000-year) period, for from it sprang an utterly new form of economic organization whose development cannot be appreciated without knowledge of the immediately preceding conditions.

The collapse of the Roman Empire reduced the territorial size of effective political organization, while the lingering vestiges of the Holy Roman Empire and the still-broad sweep of the authority of the Roman Church produced an impressive battle of political ideas across the continent of Europe. Actual government existed under the manorial system, where the feudal baron was both landowner and ruler of the villeins, serfs, and peasants on his land and under his protection. A pyramiding of rule and reciprocal obligation reached upward from the baron to the King.[19]

In one sense, political power now followed economic power, represented by the ownership of land. In another sense the reverse was true, for with the break up of broad political authority and the consequent lack of law and order to protect the small peasant farmer from depredations by his stronger neighbors, it was not uncommon for a free peasant to place himself in the status of a serf in order to gain the security that the lord's power would give him. In the manor, the political and economic orders were conjoined in a system of mutual obligation in which the serf, and to a lesser extent the free tenant, gave a portion of his produce and his effort, along with various small fees and money duties to the lord, in return for the latter's protection in times of trouble, relief in periods of famine, and the use of tools and beasts of burden for his work. Social life, too, revolved around the manor and the occasional traveling fairs that brought in goods and people from other parts of the world.

Henry Adams, in his nostalgic musings on history, saw the person of the Virgin Mary as the central figure in medieval thought and devotion, and it was the Christian Church that set the moral objectives of society. A bishop or an abbot, or the Pope himself, might be a lord of the manor, or a secular ruler, but the Church had a larger function both in laying down moral prescriptions for life on this earth as a means for the attainment of a life to come and as an institution contending fiercely for separate identity apart from the political order. Beginning with Augustine and Gregory the Great, and continuing through Gelasius and Boniface, churchmen and popes fought with kings and emperors to establish the moral as well as the secular authority of the Church. The outcome of these struggles was a wealth of writing that holds an important place in political theory and the recognition for the first time of a society having two orders, the secular (political) and religious, each to a degree independent of one another. At a later date, the leaders of the eco-

---

[19] The identity of landownership and rule is evidenced by the attitude of William the Conqueror and his lawyers, who ". . . did not distinguish his property from his sovereignty. . . . He was both landlord and King." John R. Commons, *Legal Foundations of Capitalism* (Madison, Wis.: University of Wisconsin Press, 1957), p. 214, citing various sources.

nomic order were to claim a right and necessity for independence in their own affairs not so different, in many ways, from that claimed for the Church in this period.

The Church, both as landowner and as moral authority, was the recipient of a large portion of the production of the medieval economy. Both money and human labor were given to support the clergy and their courts and to build the great cathedrals and monasteries that were the objects of Henry Adams' admiration. The secular lords employed their exactions from their estates in the maintenance of a large corps of retainers and in sumptuous hospitality—uses which, as Adam Smith pointed out, did little to build up the wealth or increase the productivity of the economy. In both cases, the productive forces were directed, as they had been in times before, to moral and social ends defined on noneconomic grounds.

The manor and the church, however, did not constitute the whole of medieval life; there were also the towns. These had survived, although radically depopulated, from imperial times. In the course of the Middle Ages they grew gradually back to and beyond their original strength, and new ones were added. In them were carried on those manufactures that the manor could not support, and through them passed a trade that was later to play a large role in the transformation of economic and political society. At first local in nature, the trading in the towns became extended by the advent of traveling merchants in the eighth and ninth centuries whose open-air fairs outside the manor walls also gave the impetus to the creation of new towns and thus commenced the urbanization of Europe.[20]

It should not be thought that the manufacture and the trading of the medieval town were comparable to the competitive activity of the modern city. Both local and external trade were subject to extensive regulation by the burgesses of the towns to exclude outside competition and to hold down the price of goods purchased from the countryside.[21] Manufacturing was in the hands of guilds, whose organization was as much social and governmental as economic, providing insurance, organizing festivals, prescribing behavior and dress, and most importantly, regulating production, profits, wages, and apprenticeship. Through rules designed to preserve the traditional life and craft of the guildsmen, innovations were fought and not infrequently stifled, at least for a time. Yet these rules standardized quality and required sharing of bargains in raw materials, which served to protect the public also.[22] Additionally, the stern disapproval by the Universal Church of excessive profit-making, usury, and other evidences of too great attachment to the treasures of this earth tended to blight the enthusiasm of the medieval entrepreneur. Although great fortunes were made in trade, and active and thoroughly secular economic activity flourished in such cities as Florence and Venice, the eco-

[20] Heilbroner, *Making of Economic Society,* pp. 47–48.
[21] Polanyi, *op. cit.,* p. 64.
[22] Commons, *op. cit.,* p. 225.

nomic life was peripheral to the life of medieval Europe, even as those cities were peripheral to its geography. The social and economic organization of the towns did not fit the pattern of mutual obligation found in the manor. Consequently, the towns tended to be partly outside the feudal system politically as well. There were cities that were under the protection of feudal lords, and others that relied on their walls for protection. The government of the cities was in the hands of the burgesses who gradually worked their way out of the obligations of feudal law, establishing for themselves a "law of merchants" for their internal regulation.[23] This law, although not hospitable to free competition, was at least more oriented to secular economics than was the feudal law. In local government, at least, political power had begun to follow and support economic power.

Despite the seeds of change that were germinating in the towns, the medieval world was still in the spell of tradition, both economically and politically. When change came, it would be fought by all of the powers of society, the Church, the manor, and even, and most fiercely, by those already living in a partly economically oriented world, the merchants and manufacturers guilds. There was no optimism that the future would hold better things on earth (whatever might be the rewards in Heaven), and a future that brought change brought fear as well. And, indeed, there was cause enough for fear. Political power was soon to pass from the barons to the King and from him, incredibly, to the people. The One True Church would be rent and challenged by a heresy that would not be suppressed. But the common people would face the most alarming plight of all: Freed of both the oppression and the protection of their betters, they must find or make their own place in the world. No longer would the way be barred to riches or to power, but the path that led up would lead down as well, to the sweatshop, poorhouse, and debtors' prison.

The Transition from Feudal Society.   At this point, on the threshold of one of the most radical redirections of human effort that the world has witnessed, it would be well to pause to review what has been found so far. Up to approximately the fifteenth century, life for the vast majority was unchanging and unchangeable. A common man's prime interest was to fill his allotted task with the least disturbance possible. He neither participated nor hoped to participate in his own government or in his own earthly salvation, however much he might have striven for a salvation after death. Political power belonged to the few and was directed not to the improvement of the lot of the lowest orders of society, who were considered born to degradation, but at best to the benefit of those who were called citizens and usually to fulfill the goals set by an even smaller number, the secular rulers, the warriors, or the priests. Throughout his history, man had been tied for his sustenance to the soil. Upward of 75 per cent of the population had been engaged in agriculture, and

[23] Heilbroner, *Making of Economic Society,* p. 35.

other forms of economic activity had been mere decoration on an essentially agricultural cake. Most men had found their occupations fixed for them by traditional rules of inheritance, and these traditions had ensured that all of the necessary tasks were performed. For the lowest orders, work was a means of subsistence, and not of rising in the world. If some innovation could ease the task, the time thus saved would be taken for leisure, for wages were seldom given, and nothing could be gained by increased work. Whatever surplus could be wrung from agriculture had generally been directed under an economy of command into the service of those whose functions represented the chief aims of society—which were not economic, but religious, military, or political. Command, in fact, had been to this point the principal means by which the economy had been raised to the production of great works. Only through it could the necessary mobilization of effort be achieved and tasks assigned in a manner that would bring the work to a successful conclusion. In the future far vaster works were to be constructed under the impetus and guidance of a new technique for the organizing of the economic order: the market economy. How extraordinary the new economic system was to be is best told in the words of Robert Heilbroner:

> Because we live in a market-run society, we are apt to take for granted the puzzling—indeed, almost paradoxical—nature of the market solution to the economic problem. But assume for a moment that we could act as economic advisers to a society which had not yet decided on its mode of economic organization. Suppose, for instance, that we were called on to act as consultants to one of the new nations emerging from the continent of Africa.
>
> We could imagine the leaders of such a nation saying, "We have always experienced a highly tradition-bound way of life. Our men hunt and cultivate the fields and perform the tasks as they are brought up to do by the force of example and the instruction of their elders. We know, too, something of what can be done by economic command. We are prepared, if necessary, to sign an edict making it compulsory for many of our men to work on community projects for our national development. Tell us, is there any other way we can organize our society so that it will function success-fully—or better yet, more successfully?"
>
> Suppose we answered, "Yes, there is another way. Organize your society along the lines of a market economy."
>
> "Very well," say the leaders. "What do we then tell people to do? How do we assign them to their various tasks?"
>
> "That's the very point," we would answer. "In a market economy no one is assigned to any task. The very idea of a market society is that each person is allowed to decide for himself what to do."
>
> There is consternation among the leaders. "You mean there is *no* assignment of some men to mining and others to cattle raising? No manner of selecting some for transportation and others for cloth weaving? You leave this to people to decide for themselves? But what happens if they do not

decide correctly? What happens if no one volunteers to go into the mines, or if no one offers himself as a railway engineer?"

"You may rest assured," we tell the leaders, "none of that will happen. In a market society, all the jobs will be filled because it will be to people's advantage to fill them."

Our respondents accept this with uncertain expression. "Now look," one of them finally says, "let us suppose that we take your advice and let our people do as they please. Now let's talk about something important, like cloth production. Just how do we fix the right level of cloth output in this 'market society' of yours?"

"But you don't," we reply.

"We don't! Then how do we know there will be enough cloth produced?"

"There will be," we tell him. "The market will see to that."

"Then how do we know there won't be *too much* cloth produced?" he asks triumphantly.

"Ah, but the market will see to that too!"

"But what *is* this market that will do all these wonderful things? Who runs it?"

"Oh, nobody runs the market," we answer. "It runs itself. In fact, there really isn't any such *thing* as 'the market.' It's just a word we use to describe the way people behave."

"But I thought people behaved the way they wanted to!"

"And so they do," we say. "But never fear. They will want to behave the way you want them to behave."

"I am afraid," says the chief of the delegation, "that we are wasting our time. We thought you had in mind a serious proposal. . . ." [24]

A remarkable loosening and breaking up of the unity of society was needed to bring the market-run economy into being. What, after all, is this "market" that Professor Heilbroner's "team of advisers" failed so miserably to explain? It is a place where goods are exchanged either for other goods or for some token of purchasing power, called money. Its regulating mechanism is in the price and bargaining process by which the supply and demand for a good are brought into harmony. If a great demand exists for a product, the competition between potential buyers will raise the price to the point that more and more people will be induced to produce it. If the demand is slight and the supply great, the price will fall, cutting the profits of the producers to the point that they will seek other businesses instead, thus reducing the supply. But consider what this requires: First, all of the participants must be seeking to maximize their incomes or minimize their expenditures—sheer economic motivation for their economic behavior. Secondly, people must be free to change their occupations and not be bound in them by tradition. Thirdly, there must be freedom for competitive buying and selling. If the peasant must give his surplus to the lord of the manor, and to no one else, or if the guild regulates production and

[24] Robert L. Heilbroner, *The Making of Economic Society*, pp. 15–16. © 1962. Reprinted by Permission of Prentice-Hall, Inc., Englewood Cliffs, N.J.

the law supports it in excluding others from production or importation, competition cannot exist.

All of these required radical changes, but even more were necessary before the market rather than the political order could undertake control of the whole *economy,* for to do this, all of the elements that go into the production and distribution of goods and services had to be brought into the market and treated as if they were commodities to be bought, sold, and exchanged. The feudal tie that bound the serf to the land and consigned a portion of his produce to his lord had to be broken so that the former could offer his labor, not for protection and security, but for a price—wages—with which he might buy as little or as much of the protection and security he could afford in the market. Land would need to lose its political meaning as the basis for lordship and become available at its price—rent—to those who would put it to productive use. Wealth, instead of being used for hospitality, ostentation, and worship, would need to be loaned or offered at its price—interest—or employed for profit, and the religious strictures against usury (which in those times meant any interest at all) would need to disappear. The relation of all three of these, labor, land, and capital,[25] to the social and political system would have to be altered in order to fit their new definition as *commodities* in the market.

The change to the market economy was dramatic, although it took several centuries to accomplish. In the process the economic order emerged as a separate focus of endeavor apart from the Church or the State; the concept of working for gain spread from those already engaged in trade to the highest and the lowest orders of society, and the idea of progress became implanted in the minds of whole peoples. It is perhaps best to view this change in three stages, although there was considerable overlap among them and each was far too complicated to be done justice in this brief review. First was the breaking down of the feudal pattern of life in politics, economics, and religion. The second stage was the mercantile period, when the State undertook for itself an explicit economic goal. The third was the great quickening of economic life that is called the Industrial Revolution—a time of sustained and rapid growth that brought home to the meanest citizen the fact that change, and not stability, was the condition of human society.

The Breakdown of the Feudal Pattern.   So many factors entered into the decline of the manorial system that it is perhaps wiser to describe what happened than to attempt to explain why it happened. A political consolidation of

[25] Strictly speaking, *capital* is not money, but is, in its broadest sense, anything that will aid a person in increasing his natural productivity. Because, however, wealth is a form of claim on society's goods and can be used to purchase instruments of production or to pay for education and training, we may use the term, with due reservations, as it is used here.

the nations of Europe occurred, with the growth in the power of kings abetted by the wealthy burgesses of the cities both finding common cause against the lesser nobility. Kings sought to increase their power and wealth, and the cities sought to strengthen their independence from the feudal barons, reducing their exactions and gaining safe conduct for the trade upon which urban life depended. Gradually, and at different rates of speed in different countries, strong monarchies emerged capable of governing their own territories and of giving protection from marauding nobles to a growing flow of merchants' caravans. With the reduction of the feudal nobility came also a cessation of the petty tolls that had vastly increased the cost and impeded the flow of trade across Europe. From the growing trade came a wider use of money that gradually replaced not only the barter of the markets but the feudal rents and dues that heretofore had been payable in the produce of the land. This monetization of feudal obligations changed their nature entirely and had also the effect of introducing the idea of working for pay: A man could pay his due to his lord in money either by selling his produce or by doing cottage work or other labor for piece rates or wages. Although labor thus began to develop a price that would enable it to enter the market, land was slower to become detached from the trappings of political power and hereditary right. It was not until the English barons learned the value of sheep-raising and the enclosure movements occurred (there were two stages, one beginning in the thirteenth century and culminating in the sixteenth, and the other in the late eighteenth and early nineteenth centuries) that land in England came to take on commercial value.[26] The freeing of land in France was achieved as a byproduct of revolution; elsewhere on the continent the process was more gradual. A change in attitude toward wealth occurred as well, partly aided by the Protestant Reformation, which not only weakened the blanketing effect of the Catholic Church's teaching about usury, but actively sponsored in Protestant countries a new attitude toward the material things of this life. Where a religious Catholic might dedicate his wealth to his Church or squander it in a casual disregard for earthly things, the God-fearing Protestant was more likely to prove his predestined sainthood and show his diligence in the productive use of what he had. Whatever the motives of Protestant merchant or Catholic, there was for both an increasing secularization of economic life and a greater emphasis upon it. Religion, meanwhile, moved from the center of attention. After an historically brief flurry in which religious differences produced wars, massacres, and violent persecutions, faith in most countries became a mere matter of toleration—a subject for the conscience, but not for the State to concern itself with.

[26] The actual buying and selling of land and the break up of the old estates did not take on major proportions until approximately the First World War, but land began to be *used* for its commercial value when sheep-raising for profit was instituted. See F. M. L. Thompson, *English Landed Society in the Nineteenth Century* (London: Routledge & Kegan Paul, 1963), pp. 27, 327–333.

Mercantilism. The rising monarchies that developed out of the feudal system were to have an enormous impact on economic life, for under them was established a policy, a goal of national striving that was clearly economic —the mercantile system. Heralded by the great age of exploration, this system was specifically intended to increase the nation's store of gold and silver by trade and colonization, and directed inward, it sponsored industry and widened the scope of commerce. The medieval merchant had welcomed the rise of royal power that had enabled his goods to reach him more surely and more cheaply, but he soon found that it brought difficulties for him as well. Before trade became established on a national basis, the markets in the cities were closely controlled by the merchants' and manufacturers' guilds. Competition was excluded by the guild regulation of production and by the fact that the merchants imported only those goods that were not available locally. Despite the firm opposition and the legal obstacles that the burgesses were able to present, the creation of nationwide markets brought competition into the cities and increased the pressure of economic activity. The development of goods for export, which was a requisite for the bringing in of gold and silver to the country, stimulated manufactures. Tariffs and bounties protected and aided agriculture and local industry, and the building of navies and merchant ships promoted shipyards, ropewalks, and other shipping-related industries. Commercial institutions flourished, and banking and credit assumed major importance. Even the age-old business of farming was affected, as farmers strove to meet the growing demand of the cities for food. However justly Adam Smith may have criticized this system, it did give great impetus to the economic aspect of society by the active intervention of the State, by the opening of new markets around the world, and by emphasis on the accumulation of wealth. The economic order had emerged to become an object worthy of the attention of the State for its own sake and of the citizenry for the possibilities of gain that it presented. And as the commercial classes became more important in the eyes of the State, and their activities essential to its purposes, their members moved nearer to the sources of political power, either through representation in Parliament, as in England, or through influence in the courts of the autocratic monarchies of the Continent. Traditional, rural, landholding-based power was giving way to a new elite that was oriented to economic activity and to progress.

A word must be said about the development of the law through the whole period of change from feudalism to the market economy, for this was of the highest significance to the result that followed. Feudal law was wholly inimical to the organization of society on a market basis. The law of the manor wove together the economic functions of labor and land with political and social obligation, keeping land off the market through elaborate rules of primogeniture and entail and holding serfs bound to the land. The guild law of the cities, by regulating apprenticeship, wages, production, and competition was a bar both to free circulation of labor and to innovation and striving. In addition, various sumptuary laws limited the market for goods, especially those to be bought by the lower classes, who constitute the mass market on which a thriving economy is based. Adam Smith gives a sampling of such laws, which included one enacted in England in 1463 providing that, ". . . no servant in husbandry, nor common labourer, nor servant to any artificer inhabiting out of a city or burgh, shall use or wear in their clothing any cloth above two shillings the broad yard." [27]

The sumptuary laws, in fact, are a part of the story of the awkward and halting adjustment that the law underwent in response to increased and cheaper production. Rather than welcome a growing prosperity in the lower classes, those in power opposed the evidences of it. Only rarely, as in the case of the English patent law, did the law precede and foster the economic change that was occurring. One of the early effects of the partnership of burgesses and King that overthrew the rural nobility was the extension nationwide of the guild laws regulating apprenticeships.[28] Other statutes apportioned production in a noncompetitive way. Heilbroner tells of a *règlement* issued by Colbert, finance minister to Louis XIV in 1666:

> Henceforth the fabrics of Dijon and Selangey are to contain 1,408 threads including selvages, neither more nor less. At Auxerre, Avallon and two other manufacturing towns, the threads are to number 1,376; at Châtillon, 1,216. Any cloth found to be objectionable is to be pilloried. If it is found three times to be objectionable, the merchant is to be pilloried instead.[29]

Even England was not free from the legal stifling of innovation. In 1623, a patent was denied for a stocking frame, and the Privy Council ordered the abolition of the device.[30]

But we should not regard it as at all surprising that the law should have been slow to change, for political leadership had through history held the duty of assuring the orderly performance of society's tasks. It would have been too much to expect the rulers to have looked elsewhere than to past experience to guide them, and far too much to expect that they could envision a self-regulating economy any more than could the leaders of the African nation in Heilbroner's anecdote. As a consequence, much of the legislation that attempted to cope with the changes that were going on simply retarded them. In England the desperate plight of the peasants forced off their land by the enclosures brought forth a succession of laws to aid them, but these laws had the temporary effect of keeping them from becoming a free and mobile labor force. The Elizabethan poor laws provided for a form of "outdoor relief"— payments for the support of the indigent—that required them to remain in

[27] *Op. cit.,* Book I, ch. XI.
[28] Polanyi, *op. cit.,* p. 70.
[29] *Worldly Philosophers,* p. 11.
[30] *Ibid.,* p. 18.

the parish of their origin, or to gain legal settlement by long residence in another parish, and even permitted a laborer to be sent back to the parish of his settlement despite the fact that he had found employment elsewhere.[31] When this law was eased in 1795, it was replaced by one that provided allowances guaranteeing a minimum subsistence, whether working or not, and thus, through a purely humanitarian motive, reduced the incentive of workers to move actively into the market with their labor.[32] Throughout the mercantile period tariffs, trade prohibitions, and bounties attempted to regulate trade and direct production in such a way as to maximize the inflow and retention of gold and silver, but often had the result of stifling and distorting beneficial growth.

Gradually in most countries, in others suddenly, as in the Great Revolution in France, the legal system was reshaped until land, labor, and capital all stood recognized in law as items to be bought, sold, traded, and rented; the latter two were released from impediments to their mobility, and the first was freed of restrictions against its passing from hand to hand in response to economic demand. In the process, however, the ancient protections of individuals against the hardships of economic distress also largely disappeared. The new law was nearly equally impartial in presenting opportunities for failure and opening the way to gain.

The Industrial Revolution. The revision of the law, the reorganization of economic life, the expansion of markets, the increase in agricultural productivity, the decline in prestige and power of the landed nobility, the growing sense of national unity and purpose,[33] and the developing tendency to value a man for the economic contribution he could make, rather than for his birth and traditional status (all of which were set in motion by the mercantile period), were essential conditions for the startling economic growth that followed. Through them society's attention became fixed on economic goals. It was this attention, aided by a quickening interest in science and technological innovation, that prepared the way for the Industrial Revolution.

The first nation to undergo transformation was England, where all of these processes were furthest advanced. She was wealthy, and her wealth was fairly widely distributed among people who were willing to make it available for

---

[31] Smith, *op. cit.,* Book I, ch. X.

[32] Polanyi, *op. cit.,* p. 78 *et seq.*

[33] The significance of this extends well beyond its usefulness during the mercantile period, for governmental leadership played a great, if not always perfectly appreciated role in promoting the Industrial Revolution. Even more importantly today, nationalism is a strong factor in the modernizing of developing nations, although it is not in itself a sufficient cause. National feeling may be directed outward in aggressive wars (as it was after the French Revolution) instead of inward to promoting economic growth. See the penetrating discussion of this factor in W. W. Rostow, *The Stages of Economic Growth: A Non-Communist Manifesto* (Cambridge: Cambridge University Press, 1960), chs. 3, 4, 8.

productive investment in capital goods. She had been unified under one rule for a long time and had developed both a good system of markets and a sense of nationalism that would tend to hold her people together through the strains and agonies of rapid industrialization. Her enclosure movements had clarified the economic value of land and had merged the old peasant holdings into larger units capable of producing more food for the industrial workers who would soon be crowding into the cities. Equally important, but more painful in its effects, the enclosures had turned loose on the land an army of displaced peasants looking for some means of subsistence—a ready supply of workers for the factory and the mill. Finally, there was that remarkable collection of low-born but ingenious men—the barber Richard Arkwright who invented the spinning jenny is the most striking example—who turned the new current of scientific interest into a flood of inventions, and whose discoveries were protected for their use and profit by a farseeing patent law. All of these combined in a movement that changed forever the life of man.

Explosive as industrial growth was, it was not an equal advance on all fronts, but a process in which one industry moved ahead rapidly, stimulating others after it. As manufacturer followed manufacturer in adopting mechanized techniques, the advance became general, reaching down to the fundamental industries—those producing machinery, power, and transportation. In England the leading sector was cotton textiles, and the time schedule is well illustrated by the relation between growth there and that in coal production, which was the basic source of power for all industry. Figure 1 shows the sharp rise in cotton-wool imports that took place after Arkwright's patent was voided and his invention came into general use. (Imports of the raw material are an excellent index of production in a country in which little or none of the raw material is grown.) Coal production followed cotton manufactures upward with a lapse of about thirty years.

Nation after nation soon followed England's example, spreading not only technological advances, but the social and political organization that accompanied them as well. Armed with new tools, and under his new scheme of economic organization, man wrung from nature a wealth that dwarfed all the empires that had gone before. Awakened to the possibilities of acquiring goods he had not dreamed of possessing and to the new-found chance to improve his lot in life, as well as being driven by fear bred of economic insecurity, the ordinary laborer lost the ancient and leisurely habit of working only until his belly was full. The pace of life quickened as the acquisitive drive took hold. An enormous drift of people from the countryside to the city occurred, as, by a cumulative process, the new technology produced machines and fertilizers to permit one farmer to raise more food than three or more had done before, sending the other two to the city to build more machines. Men were for the first time cut free of the soil and a new institution, the factory, dominated the cities that had formerly lived on trade. As if this were not enough, popula-

Figure 1. Cotton-Wool Imports and Coal Production in Great Britain, 1740–1860

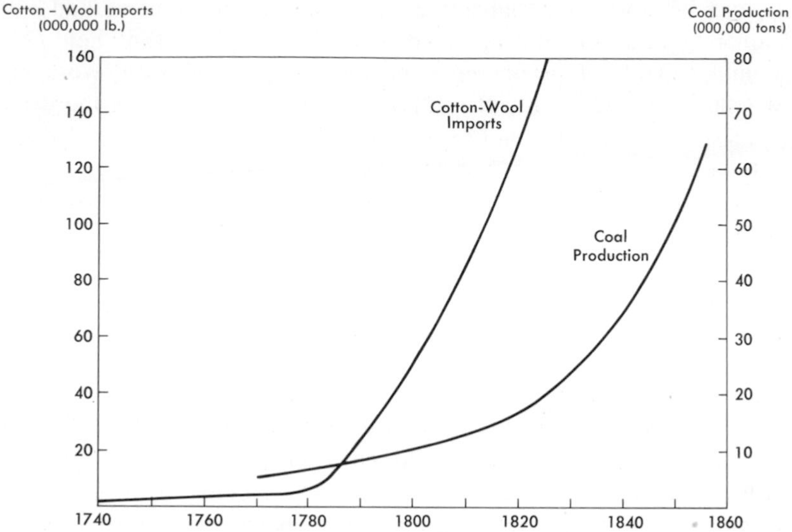

Source: Cotton-Wool Imports: Edward Baines, Jr., *History of the Cotton Manufacture in Great Britain* (London: 1835), pp. 346–347; Coal Production: J. H. Clapham, *An Economic History of Modern Britain: The Early Railway Age, 1820–1850,* 2nd ed. (Cambridge: 1930), p. 431, copyright © 1930 by the Cambridge University Press.

Note: Fluctuations in Cotton-Wool Imports have been evened out to show trend.

tions that had been stable for centuries suddenly began to grow [34] and still the economy produced riches sufficient to raise the standard of living even, ultimately, for those at the bottom of the economic heap. And from this heap there emerged a new ruler of the economic order: the consumer. Guided by the processes of the market in which the consumer made his needs known, the enormous productive forces did his bidding. The overwhelming majority of the production in this remarkable system was brought forth, not in response to royal command or priestly incantation, but to multifarious demands of common people whose wants could be expressed in countless acts of buying and refusing to buy. The energies of society had found a new source of guidance and a new and exciting outlet.

[34] Individual countries developed population growth rates of from 1 per cent to 3 per cent per year as against an estimated average world population increase from the beginning of the Christian era up to the seventeenth century of only .04 per cent per year. For this estimate, see Colin Clark, "Population Growth and Living Standards," *International Labour Review,* LXVIII (August, 1953), p. 110.

The New Economic and Political Orders. The consequences of the Industrial Revolution for all elements of society and for the political and social systems in which they lived were staggering. Surrounded by change, invention, and fermentation of ideas and induced to move from locality to locality in search of employment, even the humblest workmen must become aware that life held possibilities beyond the routine father and son had followed through the ages. Those who had held high station in life through possession of ancestral estates found themselves swamped in a new throng of coarse men become rich, whose industrial empires produced in a day more than their erstwhile betters gained in a year. All society was caught up in a system that, by placing a price of worth on a man in terms of what he could accomplish economically, tended to use the same measure to determine his place in the world of political and social power. At its best, the system held before every man a vision of progress, of a rise in wealth and station utterly unknown before. At its worst, it punished the unfortunate and the inept alike, with a poverty that was felt more keenly when others about them were rich and with the real horrors and indescribable misery of the factory and the slum. Yet even here, the curious dehumanizing of man that was inherent in the treatment of his labor as a commodity led to a regard for each individual as essentially equal to any other, and the new society bred also great movements of social reform, humanitarianism, and democracy.

That democracy should emerge should not occasion wonder, for the system required the destruction of hereditary right, and the social mobility it produced militated against any sort of prescriptive allocation of power.[35] In the new society the poor found themselves no longer bound to their traditional station in life and were content neither to leave politics to a waning and discredited nobility nor to permit it to fall totally into the hands of the new economic elite. Even among the new rising middle classes were found men to whom the logic of political equality was compelling, and some of these gave the workers their support. Others, as we shall see, gave them more: an ideology of protest, the doctrines of socialism.

There were profound differences from country to country in the manner and timing with which the extension of the suffrage took place, and these differences affected the outlook of the laboring classes as they came to power. Most importantly, they influenced both the intensity of economic class feeling and the extent to which the struggle for political rights and material well-being were seen as parts of the same fabric. In England, the first country to industrialize, the franchise was extended gradually, not reaching the workers until the reform acts of 1867 and 1884. They had by then many years of

[35] That it was not entirely successful in doing so, we shall see later. For a forceful argument that industrialization under modern conditions is likely to hinder, rather than to promote democratization, see Karl de Schweinitz, Jr., *Industrialization and Democracy: Economic Necessities and Political Possibilities* (Glencoe, Ill.: The Free Press, 1964).

living in an industrial environment and many years of learning to fight their economic battles with their employers through the economic weapon of the trade union. By the time the British worker gained political power the worst horrors of the period of industrialization were over, and his politics bore only slight traces of the animosities of a class war. There was class feeling, but the habit of dealing separately with economic and political questions had grown up in the then-existing unions—a habit that has been the despair of the radical wing of British labor politics ever since. The worker on the Continent, however, was awakened early to political action, for his aid was required by the rising middle classes in their own revolutionary struggle against medieval privilege. Unlike England, the feudal order.was slow to dissolve, the middle class small, and the landed nobility tenacious of its control.[36] From the start, then, the continental workman's economic and political goals were mixed, with the result that he found himself by turns engaged in promoting economic causes through political action, legislation, and revolution, and political goals by strikes and work stoppages. The delayed emergence of national unification in some European countries also deprived their people of a sense of common nationalism that could knit classes together and soften the fierceness of the struggle that split them apart. In the United States nearly the reverse of the English condition obtained, for in all but the larger original states full manhood suffrage was granted soon after independence, and in those states that lagged the process was substantially complete by the 1850s. The political battle, if such it could be called, was over before the Industrial Revolution was in full swing, for it was not the Industrial Revolution that brought democracy to the United States, but the very special conditions of colonialism and the struggle that brought colonialism to an end. The result was a fitful alternation of workingmen's parties with trade unionism, tempered by the presence of an open frontier to which those who were most severely discontented with conditions could flee. In consequence, no clear-cut opposition of classes occurred.

The attitudes of the working classes were to be of immense importance for the political and economic history of the countries of the West thereafter, for through their votes and actions, as well as those of the middle and upper classes, the new great issue of the relationship of the political to the economic order was to be resolved in a variety of ways, as will be described in the succeeding chapters. The development of universal suffrage did not produce absolute equality of political power; it only broadened the holding of it. The leaders of industry and commerce were closer to the seats of political power than the common workman. They mingled socially with leading politicians. As directors of the important economic functions of society they were consulted when government action affecting those functions was contemplated and they could by their social prestige and their economic power affect votes, assist

---

[36] This interpretation is suggested by Polanyi, *op. cit.,* ch. 14.

favored political candidates, and demand the attention of political leaders even when that attention was not freely given.[37] Where the workers chose to regard the political power of the wealthy as part of a conspiracy against them, their proposals for bringing the two orders together were likely to be more drastic and agreement more difficult to reach than they would be where greater mutual trust and respect obtained. Equally, the attitudes and fears of the economically powerful would affect their reaction to pressures for change.

As the nations emerged from the Industrial Revolution, and increasingly gave their economies over to the regulation of the consumer and the market on what seemed to be the advice of Adam Smith [38] and those who followed him, the separation of the economic and political orders reached its peak. By the latter half of the nineteenth century, especially in England and the United States, governmental intervention in the economy had been reduced to the simple support of the framework of law upon which the market rested and a scattering of other activities, such as postal service, education, tariffs, and a few regulations and subsidies. Yet this was a condition contrary to the whole previous experience of the human race and was destined to be short-lived. Great though its productive miracles were, the market was bound to come under scrutiny by the State if it ever failed to sustain those miracles. Whole peoples brought up to a belief in human progress and economic well-being and endowed with the power of the vote were not likely to refrain from seeking redress in the political order when prosperity seemed ill-spread or economic justice, according to the concepts of their own culture, faulty. The market was serving the purposes of society, and serving them remarkably well. Particular societies, however, had purposes that it could not serve, or could only serve imperfectly without guidance. These would bring the economic and political orders closer together, for only the State had power sufficient to intervene effectively in the market. But the working out of the new relationship between the orders would be quite different from what had existed before, precisely because their separation had shed new light on the nature of each and on their possible contribution to human welfare.

[37] That some also engaged in bribery and vote-buying should not escape mention, although this was not infrequently their side of a coin of which the obverse displayed politicians exacting payments for refraining from harassing businesses with unreasonable assessments, franchise revocations, and other forms of diddling with the law. See the enlightening story *"Boss" Tweed,* told by Denis T. Lynch (New York: Boni & Liveright, 1927), for some examples.

[38] Smith will doubtless never escape the reputation of having advocated absolute *laisser faire,* despite the fact that he recognized clearly the need to hold the economic system to the service of society under institutional arrangements in which the State would play a significant part.

The Problem of the Developing Nations

Before turning to the examination of the particular solutions to this problem, with which the remainder of the book deals, it would be well to look for a moment beyond the limits of Western Europe and North America to consider the situation faced today by nations that are now only beginning to erect modern economies on the remains of traditional societies. In doing so, it will be possible to examine a little more closely the factors that enter into the process of economic modernization and to see the significance of European experience for solving the problems of the late arrivals on the international scene. For they, too, are making choices from among the Western-developed alternatives of capitalism, socialism, and communism.

Despite the great differences that exist between the long-established states of Latin America, the heavily populated and relatively well-prepared new nation of India, and the sparsely settled and nearly tribal condition of some of the states in equatorial Africa, some remarkable similarities between these and Western Europe in various stages prior to the Industrial Revolution can be seen. There is the familiar pattern of a population largely engaged in agriculture as a means of subsistence, a dominance of tradition or of command in the organization of economic life, and social and political institutions comparable to feudalism, if not to more primitive forms.

As in Western Europe, there is a need to break down those social and political relationships that tend to stifle change—to bring into power a new elite whose efforts will direct their people into a flowering of economic activity—and ways must be found to create forms of productive enterprise to raise the efficiency of agriculture and provide that steadily increasing flow of capital development on which long-term growth is based. There is evidence, moreover, that some of the requisites for change are present. The new spirit of nationalism has brought an intense desire to match the prosperity of the West. The technology exists for rapid industrialization. Western nations and the great powers of the Communist bloc are anxious to assist them, in a competitive striving for their allegiance, with infusions of capital and technical expertise. The tools are apparently at hand.

Yet a closer examination reveals disturbing dissimilarities suggesting that the path for these nations may be somewhat different. In the first place, there is a vast difference in the time schedules for the modernization process between Europe's industrialization and that being attempted now. Counting the year 1500 as the end of the medieval period, nearly three hundred years were spent in reshaping the political and social order before the first Industrial Revolution took place in England. The Revolution itself occupied a time span variously calculated from as little as a few decades to approximately a century. During this time it was possible for each of the many subordinate processes to occur gradually, without either demand or supply of a skill, product, service, or factor of production running so far in advance as to upset the balance. As the use of money in the economy spread, demand arose for new products and services. As the demand for factory workers grew, the increase in agricultural productivity made them available. As the legitimacy of the ruling power of the landed nobility declined, a growing and driving middle class stepped forward to take its place. At no time did either the demand or the supply of material goods reach such a peak that saving ceased and capital needed for future growth was squandered in an orgy of conspicuous consumption. Nor did medical science so far outpace the rest of knowledge that the population rose too fast to be absorbed in the growing industrial machine. In contrast, the underdeveloped nations are trying to reshape their political systems and their social structures, train their working scientists and administrators, build their industrial plant, and find their place in the international political scheme, all in a matter of decades.

A second major difference is in the wealth with which Europe entered its stage of rapid growth. Dr. Simon Kuznets has made a comparison between the per capita national incomes of a number of Western countries extrapolated backward to the early stages of the Industrial Revolution and those of certain underdeveloped nations in 1949. He found the European figures to run mostly in the neighborhood of $150–300 per capita (with lows of $110 in Sweden and $90 in Italy). The 1949 levels for nations in the underdeveloped parts of the world ran from one sixth to one third of that, with sample figures offered by Dr. Kuznets of $41 to $60 for India, Pakistan, Afghanistan, Bolivia, and the Philippines; $30 to $40 for Ecuador, Haiti, and several of the Asian countries; and under $30 for Indonesia and China.[39] With such restricted wealth, the difficulties of developing adequate domestic capital and adequate consumer demand to support even the start of industrialization are immense.

A third major difference is the spread of Western knowledge of medicine and public health, which has caused a population upsurge well in advance of industrial growth. A fourth difference, which is not unrelated in its causes, is the fact that these countries are trying to industrialize long after others have done so, and *after,* not *before,* their people have gained an acquaintance with the shiny new devices and the expensive but prestige-bearing consumer goods that in the early stages their own economies cannot produce, or can only produce at the cost of more durable and productive investment in capital equipment and machinery. The demand for freedom from disease and the temptations to buy rather than to build work hand in hand to impose unwonted burdens on an economy newly struggling to put itself in motion.

In short, the process that these nations are trying to undergo is a *derived* development: It does not stem from a working out of productive forces that originate in the societies themselves; it tries to create those forces so that a

[39] "Underdeveloped Countries and the Pre-Industrial Phase in the Advanced Countries: An Attempt at Comparison," *Proceedings of the World Population Conference,* 1954, Papers, Vol. V, pp. 956–958.

highly visible model, that of the Western nations, can be copied. To some degree, all industrializations since England's have been derived developments, but none has faced quite the temptations to imbalance and excess that these face, and none has had to endure the premature surge of population.[40] The significance of derived development lies in the fact that, as the author of the term, Henry C. Wallich, has pointed out, the economy is consumption-oriented. The driving force behind it is not the desire of the entrepreneur to make profits, but of the people, often as expressed through their government, to better their standard of living and to obtain what others have.[41] The fact that the governments of these countries are often either popularly chosen or appeal strenuously to their people for support is not without significance here, for not only must the government seek to modernize the economy, but it must also try to deal with the harsh necessity of suppressing the desire of its people to buy with whatever funds they have, in order to ensure the necessary saving that will build capital to keep the development going.[42] This has produced a strain that has further retarded development, for as was related in a footnote earlier, leaders of a newly unified and strongly nationalistic country have always been tempted to use their strength in territorial aggrandisement rather than internal developments, and the urge to escape the dilemmas of modernization only increases the attractiveness of the militaristic alternative. Seen in this light, the aggressiveness of Mao Tse-Tung in China and Sukarno in Indonesia, and the enthusiasm with which India and Pakistan rushed into conflict over Kashmir in 1965 become comprehensible, however unwise.

The new State that rules the emerging society is neither the trade-oriented State of the Western mercantile period, nor the production-oriented one of the Industrial Revolution. Its problems, despite the knowledge that is available on the techniques of industrialization, are infinitely more complex and intractable. Its leaders, if they are to succeed in bringing their people fully into the modern economic world, must exercise a type of command over the economy that is far more distasteful than ever the holders of political power in the West were called upon to use.

With these considerations in mind, it is now possible to trace the general process through which a backward society today must pass to moderniza-

[40] The population growth that did occur in Europe and in North America after the Industrial Revolution began was partly siphoned off by emigration and the frontier, respectively, so that this growth posed less of a problem than the more densely populated parts of Asia face today.

[41] "Some Notes Towards a Theory of Derived Development," a paper presented at the Third Meeting of Central Bank Technicians of the American Continent, Havana, 1952, published in A. N. Agarwala and S. P. Singh, eds., The Economics of Underdevelopment (New York: Oxford University Press, 1963), pp. 189–204, at pp. 194–195.

[42] It is worth noting, in this connection, that Canada and Australia, which were two of the last "Western" countries to industrialize and whose development could be regarded as more derived than the others, developed a mass-consumption economy even before the process of industrialization was complete. See Rostow, op. cit., p. 69 and chart facing p. 1.

tion. There must first be an alteration in the structure of society and government in order to break up primitive or feudal traditions that limit the spread of economic benefits, deny the possibility of progress, and keep political power in the hands of those whose interest lies in maintaining the existing economic and social order. This is usually accomplished by nations coming out of colonial rule but may be quite difficult to achieve in already-independent countries, such as those in Latin America or the kingdoms of the Middle East. In any case, a new economically oriented elite must come forward. Secondly, agricultural productivity must be increased not only to provide sustenance for those who must be taken off the land to work in industry, but to provide exports, which will enlarge the funds available both for investment and for the creation of a domestic market for whatever goods are manufactured locally.[43] A domestic market is essential, for foreign nations may well erect tariff barriers against a flow of cheap manufactured goods (as the West did against Japan in the 1930s, which helped turn her to a partly retaliatory aggression). Moreover, the greatest potential market is at home among those who do not have, but will soon learn to want, consumer goods. Where national income is low, and barely above subsistence at best, this infusion of money is essential to start the buying process, and agriculture is the quickest to respond to a very small application of capital. It should be added that, where the pattern of landholding is such that mechanized agriculture is not possible or will not be undertaken by the owners, a land reorganization program must be instituted. In the West the English enclosures and the French revolutionary confiscations were the processes comparable to this.

Thirdly, and it must be admitted at this point that the listing of measures as if they were to be taken chronologically becomes increasingly indefensible as it proceeds, capital must be brought into productive investment. This means that either those who hold wealth must be induced to invest it usefully, instead of spending it on their own personal well-being (we noted the change in outlook toward wealth that took place between the Middle Ages and the Industrial Revolution), or their wealth must be taxed or confiscated and put to work in the command of the State. Because the per capita national incomes of the underdeveloped countries are so close to the subsistence level, it is doubtful that sufficient capital will be provided unless additional funds come from foreign investment and aid programs.[44] Both of these will generally require the local government to give some assurances of a reasonable reception. The kinds of investment made at this time are extremely important. There is, first of all, that type known as *social overhead capital*.[45] This con-

[43] Indeed, in many underdeveloped nations agricultural methods in use do not even supply present needs, and precious foreign exchange is spent on foodstuffs that could be raised locally.

[44] Capital needs are accentuated if the population rises, for capital must grow at a rate sufficient to outstrip the population increase and thus provide improvement in the standard of living.

[45] Rostow, *op. cit.*, pp. 24–26 gives an excellent succinct discussion of this.

sists partly of highly expensive projects that have a long period of "gestation" before they begin to earn a return, such as railroad systems, water supply systems, and hydroelectric plants, but that provide a foundation for other developments. It also includes investments in education, technical training, roads, and sanitation that may, at a given stage of economic development, give no return at all in a direct financial sense but are of equal basic importance. Considerable outlays of public funds may be needed for these, and the market is likely to supply very little. Secondly, there is investment in capital goods-producing industries. These are the heart of economic growth, for they are the industries that supply the tools other industries use to expand production. Of course, it may be possible for a country to import its machinery for a considerable period of time, but a self-sustaining growth ultimately requires one segment of industry to be turning out machines to supply the needs of the rest of the industrial complex for the instruments of rapid and cheap production. Finally, there is investment in those sectors of the local economy that are most likely to give an immediate return and further build the wealth of the country. Growth does not occur across the whole economic front at once, but in sectors that advance in turn. Both of these last two forms of investment may be called forth by market forces because they are profitable, but we may recall what was indicated earlier about the nature of derived development. The market, after all, responds to the wants of consumers, and if the chief wants expressed in it are for Western-made goods and gadgetry, or for local facsimiles, the capital goods-producing industries may be shunned by investors in favor not only of consumer goods production, but even of lending opportunities—lending money not for productive investment, but for the use of those who will spend it immediately outside the country. Clearly, some direction of the market by the State may be required, if only in discouraging imports and favoring one kind of investment over another by tax concessions, and so forth. The subject of capital-formation occupies a large place in the literature of underdevelopment, and well it might, considering its complexity.

The fourth major element in our generalized process of modernization is the replacement or breaking down of the monopolistic market structure that normally exists in a tradition-dominated economy, as it did in medieval Europe. If market forces are to be used to direct economic effort, competition must be introduced. Alternatively, the State must take over the market function itself, or regulate prices and production, in order that the general spread of prosperity (on which a mass-production economy depends) not be retarded by the overpricing of goods and the deliberate restriction of their supply. Very often a good part of the market is dominated by foreign traders, while local people lack the skills to compete effectively with them. The introduction of competition, then, may not be a simple matter of changing the legal structure, particularly if time is an important factor, as it generally is.

A fifth requirement is the development of that special set of skills and drives that will bring together the productive forces of society in effective combination to realize the potentialities for growth in the economy: the qualities of the entrepreneur. In the market economy of the West we noted these as being released by the change in outlook toward gain and by the increasing social mobility of the population. The entrepreneur became the motivating power behind industrialization. In derived development, however, the motivation springs from the desire to emulate the consumption pattern of more advanced countries. The possibilities, moreover, of great reward coming to an innovator are less, for technological processes do not need to be invented, but merely borrowed. Entrepreneurship under such conditions is a more prosaic business of organizing and calculating.[46] It is also more difficult and requires a different and higher order of skills. It deals with processes more complex than the application of a new and relatively simple improvement to an existing productive operation, because the borrowed technology is advanced and must ordinarily be introduced in a form that will bring a startling increase in productivity if successful. It must be accompanied by the immediate creation of systems of distribution and the preparation of a market to absorb the product. However willing the people at large may be to obtain and consume each new good, a market cannot exist unless they have money to spend on it. This, in turn, requires a simultaneous growth of other industries employing other people who will have wages to spend, and so on. The entrepreneurial function, then, requires conscious development and planning to the point that the State is often the only organization capable of undertaking it.

Finally, the labor force must be trained in the use of modern tools, taught to care for them, and induced to sacrifice leisure under either the whip of command or the lure of money and goods. Men must learn to work steadily at their jobs and not quit them as soon as they have earned enough to fill their traditional wants. Like the feudal peasant or the slave of antiquity they must either be driven to their labor or taught to expect and strive for personal betterment.

Surely the points of similarity are many between the economic rise of Europe and the modernizing of present-day Africa, Asia, and Latin America. The forced-draft nature of the latter, however, suggests that the political order will play a far larger role in it, and that the separation of economics and politics will not come soon, if indeed it comes at all, to those portions of the world. The countries there face decisions on the relation between the two on far different ground than do the older and more mature societies of the West. It would be surprising if, in consequence, the choices that they make are not new ones; ones that do not wholly conform to any of the great alternatives to which we now proceed.

---

[46] Like the earlier discussion of derived development, this point follows the insight of Henry C. Wallich, *loc. cit.*

2 / Capitalism

The form of organization of the economic order that had swept over most of the Western world by the middle of the nineteenth century, and the structure of the law that supported it, has been given the name capitalism. In a sense this is a misnomer, for it identifies only one of the three basic elements —land, labor, and capital—whose free interplay in the market is its distinctive attribute. Yet there is a logic in it that singles out the private possessors and utilizers of capital as the moving spirits behind its productive miracles. Not even its fiercest enemies would deny to capitalism the credit for the growth that Europe and the United States experienced in the decades following the Industrial Revolution, and only a thoroughgoing iconoclast like Thorstein Veblen could deny to the capitalist his role in leading it.[1] Karl Marx and Friedrich Engels, in fact, in a much-quoted passage from the *Communist Manifesto* delivered as glowing an encomium as the most ardent defender of capitalism could desire to hear:

> [The capitalist class] during its rule of scarce one hundred years, has created more massive and more colossal productive forces than have all preceding generations together. Subjection of nature's forces to man, machinery, application of chemistry to industry and agriculture, steam-navigation, railways, electric telegraphs, clearing of whole continents for cultivation, canalization of rivers, whole populations conjured out of the ground—what earlier century had even a presentiment that such productive forces slumbered in the lap of social labor?

[1] Veblen, whose two important works, *The Theory of the Leisure Class* and *The Theory of Business Enterprise* portrayed the capitalist in a parasitic role, simply milking the economic system for its profits, wrote in the United States at the turn of the nineteenth century when the ruthless financial manipulations of the "robber barons" often appeared to justify this characterization.

The Development of Theories of Capitalism

Capitalism was not invented, but evolved in the process by which mankind emerged from its historic dependence upon an agriculturally-based economy. It is not somebody's theory put into practice, but practice that many have tried to explain in theory. As a consequence, it has proved to be one of the most difficult economic systems to describe, and even as the process of describing it was going on, it changed and showed new aspects of itself. Its complexities have been underestimated time and time again, and even today, there is vast disagreement over what it actually is, and what its necessary conditions are. A brief scanning of the United States President's *Economic Report,* the annual reports of the Council of Economic Advisers, and the responding reports and minority reports of the Congressional Joint Economic Committee will suffice to show how wide the divergences of view may be concerning what is needed to keep a capitalist economy healthy. To descend a step in terms of economic sophistication, a moment's attention to the tumult and the shouting of American political debate will disclose what remarkably different opinions are held about the very nature of the system.

It would be beyond the scope of this book to trace the full history of the development of capitalist theory, but some points need to be touched in order to show the strains of thought that entered into it. Each of these rested in part on particular intellectual currents generated at various stages of capitalist evolution. It is this blending of ideas from different points in time that helps create the atmosphere of confusion that surrounds much of the present discussion about the relation of the political and economic orders in a capitalist society.

The strain of thought that has been at the same time the most productive and the most serious obstacle to a full working out of the relationship between the two orders was that established at the start. This was the effort to describe the economy in terms of the operation of natural laws of human behavior. The men who laid the foundations of classical economic theory—Adam Smith, Thomas Malthus, and David Ricardo—were strongly affected by the developments in the natural sciences that had followed the discovery of physical laws controlling the behavior of objects in nature. These discoveries, in fact, had led to the remarkable technological improvements upon which the Industrial Revolution depended.[2] In their search for similar laws in the economic sphere, they gave an imprint of inevitability to the economic processes that was visible not only in the later writings of proponents of capitalism, but even more

[2] The enthusiasm for applying natural laws to human behavior had already affected the study of politics, as witnessed by Thomas Hobbes' reduction of human drives to three—competition, diffidence, and glory-seeking—in explaining the origins of the state. Contemporaneously with Smith, Malthus, and Ricardo, Jeremy Bentham was developing his pleasure-pain utilitarianism, applicable equally to politics and economics.

noticeably in the work of Karl Marx, who saw the inanimate forces that governed capitalism leading to its ultimate destruction. With the exception of Adam Smith, to whom we shall have occasion to return, the classical writers gave a curiously inhuman touch to economics generally, and to capitalism particularly. The gloomy parson, Malthus, saw the fruits of economic development inevitably eaten up by an expanding population. The poor were condemned to a wretched subsistence from which higher wages would only lift them briefly before they would destroy their own well-being by producing more children who, competing with them for wages and food, would drive them back into their misery. Wars, disease, and ultimately if these failed, famine would hold the population at levels that the world could support, but only moral restraint—late marriage, fewer children—could bring any betterment to the condition of the poor. Ricardo, in his turn, saw the capitalist entrepreneur struggling in vain against a rising tide of wages and rents, his profits squeezed out by a complicated process in which population growth required the cultivation of more and more (and poorer and poorer) land at increasing costs, thus raising food prices and the wages needed to give minimum subsistence to the workers. In this depressing theory the only beneficiaries were the fortunate owners of good agricultural land who could grow food at low cost, but could sell it on a market whose price was dictated by the cost of producing food on the most marginal land then in use. The tendency of these theories was to suggest that the poverty and misery visible everywhere in the early stages of industrialization were neither preventable, nor the fault of those in command of the economic order. At a later date when a greater optimism was entertained for the welfare-producing possibilities of the economy, and more emphasis was placed on the bounteous world foreseen by Adam Smith, the fatalism of these early theories still forestalled serious consideration in capitalist economic theory of alleviating the condition of the poor. What society did for them was useless, if not actually harmful, in the minds of at least some who came later.

John Stuart Mill's monumental study, *Principles of Political Economy* (1848), stands as a landmark in economic theory, for this great and many-sided philosopher turned to economics the same reasonableness, quiet optimism, and clarity of thought that marked his political and other writings. In the course of ranging through the entire subject matter of economic knowledge of his time, he denied the pessimism of Malthus and Ricardo and saw the possibility of progress as men gained greater understanding of their economic and social life. He also foresaw the day that men might choose to alter the way in which the output of society was distributed. He saw no fixed law here, but only social institution. Enormously widely read in his time, by rich and poor alike, his writing opened the door to an optimistic capitalism and an optimistic socialism as well, but his reasonableness was drowned out on both sides by writings and events that were to have a far more lasting impact. From the far Left came the strident call of the *Communist Manifesto,* published the same year, and from the Right, Herbert Spencer's *Social Statics.*

At this point our understanding of the development of capitalist economic theory must proceed on two levels. On the one hand was popular understanding, which was not theory at all, but was enormously important insofar as public discussion leading to governmental action was concerned. On the other was the emergence of trained professional economists—such men as Alfred Marshall and W. Stanley Jevons in England, and F. W. Taussig and John Bates Clark in the United States—who wrote toward the end of the nineteenth century and into the beginning of the twentieth. These scholars developed the science of economics, bringing mathematical tools to bear upon it and working out theories by which the equilibrium of supply and demand in the market could be explained. They wrote, however, just at the time that the separation of the economic and political orders was greatest, and their theories reflected this in their preoccupation with strictly economic phenomena refined and abstracted into mathematical equations, curves, and graphs. It was one of them, Stanley Jevons, who remarked, "About politics, I confess myself in a fog." [3] By their omission of the State, they could be taken to deny both its relevance to economics and the propriety of its intervention, and this is precisely what happened.

These men's works were read by businessmen and by aspiring businessmen who received them as textbooks in college. They were read, however, in an atmosphere colored by a school of social philosophy that had grown up following the biological discoveries of Charles Darwin and the partial appropriation of the theoretical idea of evolution by Herbert Spencer. Spencer saw evolution in the whole process of social change, and his ideas were caught up by a flood of popular imitators whose new philosophy, *Social Darwinism,* proclaimed the harsh doctrine of "Survival of the Fittest." [4] It was easy to see how this could be applied to the clean, mechanical world of economics, and how readily the fatalism of Malthus and Ricardo could become mixed with the optimism of Mill to produce a popular economics that saw an infinite vista of progress made possible only by the merciless struggle of unrestrained economic beings destroying their weaker kin to make the world a richer, finer, purer place.

The theory of Social Darwinism was short-lived in its hold on legitimate students of society, but its imprint remains on popular economics, especially that espoused by those most vociferously opposed to government action to help the weak or to regulate the excesses of the economy. For by it the drab

[3] Robert L. Heilbroner, *The Worldly Philosophers,* rev. ed. (New York: Simon & Schuster, 1961), p. 155.

[4] For an account of these doctrines and their impact in America, see Richard Hofstadter, *Social Darwinism in American Thought,* rev. ed. (New York: George Braziller, Inc., 1959).

laws of supply and demand were elevated to become God's mysterious plan for the betterment of mankind, in which man and the State could interfere only at their peril. A new Eleventh Commandment read: *Laisser faire!*

Neither in popular nor in professional economics does *laisser faire* stand unchallenged. Even while the major economists of the Victorian Age and after were burrowing in their mathematical abstractions, popular outcry, especially in the United States, was leading government to take action, first slowly and ineffectually, but later with more firmness, to counter the effect of a new wave of monopolies [5] that had grown up and threatened to dominate the business world. Even a popular economics that visualized an ideal system of free competition unhampered by government controls could see that monopoly was not competition, and could grudgingly admit that some sort of intervention might be helpful. Antitrust laws and commissions to regulate public utilities and railroads were justified on the grounds that these were fields where the normal economic "laws" did not work, and the government's role was seen as that of setting up conditions so that they would. Other legislation designed to protect the health and safety of workers was passed, not on the basis of any particular economic justification, but simply because society demanded it. Factory legislation, wages and hours laws, mine safety laws, and the like were not expressions of economic theory, but expressions of the purposes and aspirations of the various nations in which they were enacted. They were reminders that society has never let any aspect or part of human social organization become so walled off from the rest that it has become permanently exempt from the application of the more deeply felt moral standards of the community. General opinion, then, became adjusted to a certain amount of political tinkering with the economic machinery.

It was among the professional economists, however, that an insight was developed into a way in which government might play a very large and useful role in the economic order and still preserve the freedom of individual decisions on investment, production, and consumption that a capitalistic order requires. The discovery came from an increasing attention given by economists to a rather awkward aspect of the economic system: its tendency to operate in fits and starts, booms and depressions. At first these *cycles,* as they were called, were ignored in pure economic theory; later, they were studied, but viewed as self-correcting, if painful, stages in a growing economy. With the Great Depression of the 1930s, however, the happy confidence in self-correction gave way to an embarrassing, then frightening realization that the self-regulating market—an article of faith since the idea was first propounded

---

[5] Unlike the legally established monopolies of the guild merchants and manufacturers, these were the outgrowth of competition carried to the point of elimination of the weak, and agreement or merger among the strong. Only a few, if any, were monopolies in the strict sense of being the *sole* supplier of the class of good in question, but their vast size and power to control prices and production had a great impact on public opinion.

by Adam Smith—had a flaw. The analysis of that flaw was contributed to by economists from a number of countries, often hampered by the difficulty that translations of one man's work were not available to others.[6] It fell, finally, to a student of Alfred Marshall, John Maynard Keynes, to present a statement of both the problem and the solution in his *General Theory of Employment, Interest, and Money,* published in 1936. An exposition of the general content of Keynes' theory will have to await a fuller discussion of the economics of capitalism later in this chapter. For our purpose at this point it is only necessary to show his effect on economic thought. What Keynes said, in essence, was that in a *modern, industrialized nation,*[7] it was perfectly possible for the market to operate without using all of the available resources, that the balancing and regulating mechanisms of the market were perfectly capable of achieving equilibrium at a level that would leave a large portion of the labor force unemployed permanently. Worse yet, these same mechanisms, if uncorrected, tended to bring to a halt any economic boom and to turn the economy downward again. The self-regulating market could, in short, regulate itself into stagnation, and this is precisely what it had done in the 1930s.

The understanding of these mechanisms, however, also provided a possible key to the problem. Keynes showed that the regulators themselves might be adjusted or counteracted by government, provided only that the economic impact of government was large enough, and that it was consciously directed according to the principles that he explained to keep the economy at a high level of employment. Here, indeed, was a proposal for an enormous involvement of the political order in the economic order! We shall see later how this could occur while still leaving the market economy functioning. Keynes' work was not accepted immediately by his colleagues, and still occasions sharp debate; yet many of the measures he proposed are today a part of the policy of most modern nations in which the market plays an important part in the regulation of economic life.[8]

The ideas, beliefs, and theories that have become a part of the intellectual heritage of capitalism are, as we have seen, partly conflicting and have changed with time even as the system itself has changed. Yet a common pattern underlies most of the theoretical writing and displays itself both in the attitudes of

[6] The point is discussed by Alvin H. Hansen in *The American Economy* (New York: McGraw-Hill, 1957), p. 161.

[7] As indicated at the beginning of this chapter, the capitalist economy changed markedly over the one hundred and sixty years that separate the *Wealth of Nations* from the *General Theory of Employment, Interest, and Money.* Keynes' theory dealt with one of the most significant of those changes: The men who decide to invest capital in new productive facilities are no longer the same men as those who save the money that is to be invested. A new problem is thus presented, that of ensuring that the savers save enough, and the investors invest enough, to keep the two in balance.

[8] A very readable account of the grudging acceptance of Keynesian views in the United States is contained in John Kenneth Galbraith, *Economics and the Art of Controversy* (New York: Random House Vintage Books, 1955), chs. IV, V.

the people in countries where capitalism has flourished most strongly, and in the broad outlines of the practice of capitalism, however much the particular aspects have altered from time to time. Capitalism is not a rigid, clearly specified form of economic organization any more than, as we shall see, is socialism. It is a genus or class. It is also a politico-economic system; its basis lies not only in the economy, but in the structure of law that defines economic relationships. It does not exist apart from the rest of the organization of society: A public that chooses or suffers capitalism to continue as its method of performing the economic function is expressing thereby certain values, certain objectives, that it hopes or expects to attain by its continuance, and that it feels are morally good or right. Too much history has gone by and too many countries have partly or largely abandoned the capitalistic method by their own choice exercised through a free ballot for us to accept the communist assertion that capitalism is imposed and maintained by force in those countries, particularly the United States, Switzerland, and Canada,[9] free countries all, which still maintain it at the core of their economic organization. To explain what capitalism is, therefore, we must look first at the values or objectives that lead people to choose it in preference to its alternatives. We shall examine then the broad outlines or principles on which the system operates and by which its followers seek to realize those values. Finally we shall look at the actual working of the system to analyze it: To see to what extent the principles do serve to promote the objectives sought, and to see to what extent they have changed or been modified to conform to other values that the society as a whole might have and that it might also seek to conserve.

The Objectives of Capitalism

Values or objectives are often best expressed when most simply stated, without the qualifying comments, the grudging obeisances to the real world in which they can never be fully realized, and the thoughtful adjustments where it seems that one value, if not most carefully defined, might be presumed to detract from another equally desirable. To begin, then, let us look briefly into a capitalist utopia—the glittering picture that might lie before the mind's eye when the virtues of capitalism are discussed without regard to its faults.

The striking thing about the idealized portrait of capitalism is that it is not a system that has reached a happy state in which everything has been perfected. It is not a utopia in the usual sense at all. If we are to describe it, we must use words that connote motion: It is growing, exciting, and free. It is a place where no limit is seen to what the future may provide. Inventions yet

[9] In Canada there has been a larger socialist movement than in the United States, which managed to direct the government of two of the provinces (states) in the Canadian federal system, but the two largest parties in the Dominion (national) Government are capitalist in outlook, with the socialist-leaning New Democratic party placing a poor third or fourth, depending on the election year.

undreamed of lie ahead; recognition, reward, and honor await the men who make them and those who put them to productive use, however humble may have been their start in life. No vested right or hereditary privilege, nor any decree of central authority can deny a man his choice of calling, or prescribe the goods he is allowed to buy, or refuse him his chance to try a new idea and reap the gain if he is successful in it. It is not a quiet place; it challenges each individual to make the most of what he has, and rewards him if he does so. It looks upon striving as moral. In sum, it is a picture that draws from the experience of Europe and North America in emerging from an ancient and limiting way of life and projects it on indefinitely into the future.

The goals, then, of capitalism are a continuation and perfecting of the processes that were set in motion by the Industrial Revolution, just as capitalism itself is a continuation of the form of economic organization that emerged from it. Briefly stated, the most widely shared objectives toward which a capitalist system is oriented are: *An economy of ever-increasing abundance, personal freedom of choice* in matters relating to decisions made in the economic realm, and *recognition and reward of persons on the basis of merit.* But, as suggested before, these objectives and the values they imply are not confined to the economic order alone. They are affected by, and they extend their influence into other aspects of the society within which the system operates, as we may see if we examine them more closely.

An Economy of Ever-Increasing Abundance. Because in capitalism the economic order is more nearly separated from the political order, and thus more clearly oriented to its productive task than any of the alternatives with which this book deals, it is appropriate that we consider first the most distinctively economic of the three: the goal of increasing abundance. This, after all, is what one would expect the purpose of an economy to be, if not directed by political or religious considerations as the economies of antiquity were. The objective of abundance was set for capitalism in the very title of Adam Smith's book, *The Wealth of Nations,* and with the exception of Malthus and Ricardo, the promise of increasing production and wider and wider spreading of the benefits of that production has stood out through the work of all of the writers in the capitalist tradition, even of those who felt that there would be many who, through "unfitness" or other failing, would be losers in the economic struggle. Even more emphatically today the United States, as the major national exponent of the capitalist form of economic organization, stresses the wealth that a privately run economy can produce, and the well-being of her citizens under it. No United States pavilion at an international exposition is complete without some showing of the country's economic might.[10]

But the belief in abundance is more than a simple assertion of what has

[10] And this, one might add, despite the fact that the appropriations for the United States exhibit are likely to have bordered on the niggardly!

been done. It is a promise founded upon a thoroughgoing optimism. The widespread faith in capitalism or "Free Enterprise," as it is currently called, that one encounters in the United States, and the hard sledding that socialist and communist doctrines have suffered there, is not due merely to a gratitude for past successes, but to a belief that the future under capitalism holds even more benefits than have been offered before.[11] The sense of progress is pervasive, and both the individual and the society tend to look hopefully, if not always confidently, to the future. It affects politics, and probably adversely so when the problems of international affairs and human relationships prove so much more intractable, so less prone to solution through innovation, and so very frustrating in comparison with the orderly intricacies of productive technology. It is imbedded in popular myth, and in the well-known slogan of the manu-facturer who proclaims, "Progress Is Our Most Important Product." The objective of increasing abundance looms large in capitalism, then, not merely because people in capitalist nations desire abundance and others do not. Such a contention would be absurd. It is important because it is combined with a faith that past experience has not tended to refute, that further growth is possible and will come.[12]

Personal Freedom of Choice.   Personal freedom of choice in the economic realm, with all that it implies in terms of the limitation of the power of any central authority to allocate economic values or to grant or withhold its approval for an undertaking that some individual may wish to try, is the second objective of capitalism. It is also the one that most nearly touches on a widely shared ideal in modern society, the love of individual liberty. It is this ideal that current defenders of capitalism have tried to emphasize by renaming the system Free Enterprise. And the history of capitalism partly justifies a tendency to connect economic freedom with political freedom, as the rise of democracy after the Industrial Revolution showed, and as is evident in the way that capitalist countries have tolerated and even supported dissenters and critics whose speech and writings have been hostile to the system itself.[13] The freedom that capitalism promotes is highly individualistic. It reflects the values of a society where rich and poor alike tend to wariness or suspicion of political or other central authority, where virtues of self-sufficiency are preached more

---

[11] It is worth remarking that current American writing on economic subjects so clearly assumes a continuation of economic growth that the questions raised include "What shall we do with it all?" See John Kenneth Galbraith, *The Affluent Society* (Boston: Houghton Mifflin Company, 1958).

[12] A rather striking indication of the degree of optimism in the United States, which seems to suggest that it is, if anything, increasing, is contained in Robert E. Lane, "The Politics of Consensus in an Age of Affluence," *American Political Science Review,* LIX (December, 1965), pp. 877–880.

[13] Joseph A. Schumpeter, in a wry and witty chapter of his extraordinary book, *Capitalism, Socialism and Democracy,* 3rd ed. (New York: Harper & Brothers, 1950), ch. 13, displays this unexpected side of capitalism with devastating effect.

than those of community feeling whether that community is one of the whole people or one of class or caste. In the economic realm the theory holds that capitalism offers maximum opportunity for a customer to choose the goods he wishes, a worker to select his occupation, a holder of wealth to invest or to consume it, an owner of land to put it to productive use or enjoy its beauty, and for an innovator to experiment with ideas. These are fundamental to the idea of abundance as well, for it is through invention that the progress toward greater production is assured. It is the free movement of capital and labor, the ready transfer of land ownership, and the willingness of consumers to try new things that draws maximum advantage from invention. It should be noted that the freedom promised by capitalism is but one kind of freedom, for it does not include freedom from care, from hardship, or anxiety. It demands freedom from rigid control by a centralized State and a dispersion of the powers of economic decision-making, but makes no direct promise that the economically successful will not be able to exercise considerable power of their own. There *have* been restraints placed on the freewheeling use of economic power, but they have come in part at least in response to demands made in the society itself; they do not stem from the logic of the economic system. Capitalism, however, operates within the framework of a total social and political structure, and this listing of objectives does not include the other objectives that a society might entertain and that may be sought concurrently, as we shall see.

Recognition and Reward on the Basis of Merit. If the first objective of capitalism contemplates the future, and the second is broad in outlook, the third, recognition and reward on the basis of individual merit, would appear to be narrow and more heavily oriented toward the past. It was an outgrowth, initially, of the struggle against hereditary privilege and hereditary abasement, when the economic order first opened up the route to an improved status to those in the lower orders of society. Recognition of merit was the opposite to social gradations based on class. In the New World, perhaps, the influence of this sort of feeling was not as great, and the idea of personal striving for personal reward may have been derived more from the individual self-sufficiency of the Frontier. In both the old and the new the tendency has been for both merit and reward to be defined in narrowly economic terms, so that the greater rewards were promised to those whose efforts were visibly productive (at least until the days of movie stars and baseball players), and fewer were given teachers, political leaders, musicians, artists, writers, and clergy. Nevertheless, capitalism strikes a responsive chord in those who favor rewarding the industrious over those who merely meet their due, the adventuresome over the timid, and the able over the dull. It seeks to encourage emulation and striving, and it is hostile to prescriptive right. Its call is for *equality of opportunity,* but not equality of reward. A social atmosphere in which the successful man is respected rather than resented, where competitiveness takes precedence over both deference and jealousy, is compatible with this objective of capitalism. Like the objective of increasing abundance, this one implies a society geared to action. Its moral prescription, however, is more specific: "As ye sow, so also shall ye reap." But perhaps this is putting it too strongly and in too puritanical a fashion. The capitalist belief in abundance allows the reward to be generous, and not exact. There is an element in it that appeals to the gambler as well and looks amiably upon the success of the man who, by the luck of timing or his shrewd judgment of the market, "strikes it rich" beyond what he might have expected as the reasonable reward for what he has done. One could not say that capitalism aims to do this, but, as will become apparent later, the fact that the moral outlook supporting the system permits it, has important effects in making it work.

Beyond these central objectives of capitalism are many others that could be stated, and a list of considerable length could be compiled. The purposes of this investigation, however, are to distinguish the most important and widely held values that give the system its form and set it apart from other economic societies and to sketch the type of culture most congenial to it. It is important to remember also that a society that adopts capitalism will have other aims as well; that the economic order is only a part, and not always the dominant part of social organization. Religious attitudes may sometimes support unstinting economic activity, and at other times call for forbearance, charity, and concern. The demands of patriotism may sweep the economy into preparation for war and supplant the ideal of free choice with a call for loyal obedience. These and other things have modified and tempered the values that capitalism serves in one country or another, and too great a detailing would only obscure, rather than illuminate, the essential nature of the system.

The Operating Principles of Capitalism

On what basis and by what methods does the capitalistic economy operate to fulfill its stated purposes? In outlining these we shall follow the same rule of listing only essentials that may be the more readily compared when we come to discuss the other alternatives. Like the objectives, these can be reduced to three: a *market economy, private ownership,* and *competition based on expectation of gain.*

The Market Economy.   The market economy has already been discussed in the course of our history of the economic order,[14] but it is well to enlarge upon its working here. It is, after all, the heart of the economic mechanism of capitalism and, as was suggested in Heilbroner's little anecdote about the advisers to the new African nation, it is in many respects a most unlikely and

---

[14] See pp. 19–20.

unpromising device. The task of an economy is to bring together at the right times and the right places the various productive elements needed to supply the goods and services desired by society, and then to see to it that they are distributed in accordance with the standards of justice that are accepted there. In a highly industrialized and interdependent society where materials must be brought from the far places of the earth and enormous aggregations of capital must be brought to bear on their manufacture and reworking, the utterly astounding characteristic of the market economy is that it decentralizes economic decision-making. It lets the whole process be guided by a multitude of individual choices made by people who never meet, and who do not even have a central clearing-house in which their various offerings and demands are totted up and the necessary orders given. What it does, essentially, is to cause the productive forces of the economy to respond closely to the choices or demands made by consumers. Its regulating mechanism is not an authoritative command that, through democratic processes or otherwise, establishes what is held to be desirable or socially valuable and directs that this be produced. The assumption underlying the market economy is that the purpose of economic activity is to serve individual wants, however capricious, and that no better way of finding out or fulfilling those wants exists than by letting them be expressed in the prices people are willing to pay. A balance or relative evaluation of the various possible uses of the resources of society in producing different goods and services and various qualities and quantities of each good will be struck in terms of those prices. How? because the *market* is really two markets, the first of which is the one just described. If a producer, or potential producer, finds that the price in that market for a particular good is much higher than the cost of making it, he will enter a second market, the market for land, labor, and capital—the factors of production—and attempt to buy, through rents, wages, and interest, sufficient quantities of the factors needed to produce the good, attracting or luring those factors from other productive or nonproductive uses. This he will continue to do until any one of three things happens: First, the cost of attracting the resources rises so high that it meets the price of the good, and thus wipes out his potential profit; secondly, the price of the good falls because people have lost interest in it or are satisfied; and thirdly, his success in luring resources away from the production of other goods causes *them* to become so scarce that their prices rise, and the pull on the productive resources begins in another direction. A coordinated process is carried out despite the fact that nobody is granted the overwhelming power to direct it.

And the process is the same for all of the subordinate parts of the market. It entices people to enter one occupation or another and induces them to develop the most urgently demanded skills that their abilities will permit. The prices or rewards that the market provides—the distributive part of the economic function—are highest for those whose individual talents and services are most needed and, by the terms on which the market operates,[15] most valuable to society.

Of very great importance for the operation of capitalism is the manner in which innovation is handled in the market economy. Because there is no central authority that must give its approval to the allocation of resources to an untried enterprise, the entrepreneur need only raise sufficient capital to command the resources needed for production and to sustain the business until it is known whether the market will accept the product or not. The entrepreneur and his backers must run a risk, but they are not barred from entry on any other account. In fact, this leads us to a most important and fundamental quality of the market system: *There are no arbitrary exclusions* of individuals, either from managing, owning, or working in it. Its standards for entry are wholly economic and perfectly consistent with its purposes. Humans operating a market economy may engage in racial discrimination, nepotism, and other irrational practices and the law may support them, but the long-run tendency of the market, barring problems of mobility that have been evident in the case of the Southern Negro in the United States, is toward a most impersonal and impartial favor for those with ability in the particular skills it needs.

One other aspect of the market economy should be noted: *It is more efficient in serving widely shared demands than it is in providing for the wants of the wealthy few.* It is true that the very wealthy can buy substantially any luxury good they wish in a market economy, but the rarer and more precious the good, the less likely is the process of obtaining it to resemble a market transaction. Ultimately, it will become akin to the mission of some merchant of antiquity commissioned to bring back a rare spice that he alone can obtain to the one person or buyer who can afford it. The fewer the potential buyers and sellers, the more likely the price will be set either on monopoly terms, or by a negotiation between the buyer and seller. This type of business is of interest to and offers reward to very few; it is not of sufficient importance to warrant the attention of the market. The economies of large-scale production and intensive division of labor can only be evoked by a mass market, and it is, therefore, to the many of modest means, rather than to the few who might be able to pay a great deal for each item, that the market directs its best efforts. A simple illustration of this can be shown in the early history of the Ford

---

[15] There are some skills, such as those of the politician, priest, teacher, writer, artist, and musician, for which the market as it is presently structured does not seem to provide a reliable measure of social value. For some of these, the political order either fixes or supplements wages—making its own judgment on social value—but it almost never equates with the evaluation given by specialized markets in which these skills and services are traded at very high premiums. For example, the markets for lobbyists and for management consultants provide extremely generous remuneration for skills that are essentially those of politician and teacher, respectively. For an interesting proposal to restructure the market in education, see Milton Friedman, *Capitalism and Freedom* (Chicago: University of Chicago Press, 1962), ch. VI.

Motor Company. As Table 1 shows, the price was able to fall as production economies took hold, and as it fell, the car came within reach of increasing numbers of people. The company, moreover, was rewarded handsomely for making its product thus widely available. The natural tendency of the market militates against restriction of its benefits to the elite.

Table 1 Prices of Typical Model Cars, Total Unit Sales, and Net Income, Ford Motor Company, 1903–1917

Date	Typical Model & Price		Sales, all Models	Net Income*
1903–4	Model A Runabout	$ 850	1,700	$ 246,000
1904–5	" B Touring	2,000	1,745	289,000
1905–6	" B "	2,000	1,599	116,000
1906–7	" S Runabout	700	8,423	1,163,000
1907–8	" K Touring	2,800	6,398	1,145,000 (15 mos.)
1908–9	" T "	850	10,607	3,062,000
1909–10	" " "	950	18,664	4,163,000
1910–11	" " "	780	34,528	7,339,000
1911–12	" " "	690	78,440	13,543,000
1912–13	" " "	600	168,304	27,087,000
1913–14	" " "	550	248,307	24,698,000 (9 mos.)
1914–15	" " "	490	221,805†	23,532,000 (10 mos.)
1915–16	" " "	440	472,350	57,157,000
1916–17	" " "	360	730,041	27,288,000

* Figures rounded to thousands. Figures for 1903–1908 are fiscal years ending September 30; for 1909–1913, calendar years, and for 1915–1917, fiscal years ending July 31. Other periods as marked.
† Ten-month period.
Source: Allan Nevins, *Ford: The Times, the Man, the Company* (New York: Charles Scribner's Sons, 1954), pp. 644, 646–647. Copyright, 1954, by Columbia University. Used by permission of Charles Scribner's Sons, Publishers.

Private Ownership. Private ownership of property is usually regarded as the distinctive characteristic of capitalism and so, in a sense, it is. Yet this phrase is hardly adequate to convey the very important concept that is embedded in it, nor does it suggest the true function that private ownership serves in a capitalist political and economic system. Just as the market treats all of the factors of production—land, labor, and capital—as if they were commodities, so also is the meaning of property rather broadly expanded to include a man's "property" in his own labor as well as that represented by land, money, and goods. This is inherent in the much-abused concept of *freedom of contract,* by which, among other things, a worker is deemed to have the right to sell his services to whomsoever he chooses, and for whatever price he is willing and able to take for it. Private property is the basis on which rests the right of each individual or group to experiment with solutions to the economic problem. Its *function* is to guarantee the decentralization of economic power through which the market operates. As such, it need only convey so much right as is required to keep that function from being impaired. Limitations can be, and are, imposed upon it when it does tend to destroy, rather than serve, the purpose of the market, as when the law forbids the creation of a monopoly under private ownership.

But the right embedded in private property is a right to engage in experimentation and bargaining. For this reason it permits individuals to join in common cause, as well as to act separately, so long as they do not create a monopoly by joining. It permits workers to organize into unions in order to improve their bargaining position and permits the existence of cooperative societies within a capitalist economy, so long as no law requires all economic activity to be cooperatively organized. By the same token, no system that can direct the worker into his employment by command or that places the control of capital investment in the hands of the State can be called capitalism. The fascist systems of Germany and Italy did not assume ownership of the means of production, but they directed their employment by State command, and thus destroyed the true meaning and function of ownership and the capitalist system as well.[16]

From this it can be seen that private property is related to freedom, if by freedom is meant the absence of absolute power. It is not a perfect or universally shared freedom, for the greatest latitude of choice lies with those who have substantial wealth, and they, in turn, may exercise some rather impressive power over their fellows. A central problem in capitalism is to achieve the benefits of decentralized power without having the individual holders of it become petty tyrants accountable to none. The market and the principle of competition tend to erode some centers of power, but these same forces can lead to a steady elimination of less able competitors until a single monopoly is achieved, at which point the system breaks down and freedom, competition, and the powers of the market to regulate all disappear.

Competition Based on Expectation of Gain. The third operating principle of capitalism, competition based on expectation of gain, is probably the most seriously misunderstood of all. The analysis of it has been greatly hampered by the divided intellectual heritage of capitalist theory. As a result theoretical statements have run the gamut from the assertion that unlimited accumulation is a requirement of capitalism, to the idea that competition must be perfect or "pure" in the sense of a market in which both buyers and sellers are so numerous and so weak that none of them can affect the price individually, and nobody makes any important profit at all. Neither of these extreme conditions is in fact required. The heart of competition lies in that impartiality with which the market permits people to enter and move about in the productive process at their own risk. Competition may be *in esse* or *in posse,* in being or merely threatened in the future. It may exist between firms offering the same product or between those offering different ones, like steel and aluminum, which are subject to substitution. Finally, it may be between buyers to buy,

---

[16] Some writers have equated fascism with so-called State capitalism, but this ignores the vital distinction between the State as one entrepreneur among many, and the State as ruler of the economy whether or not it bothers to take actual possession.

sellers to sell, workers for jobs, landowners for rents, and investors for opportunities. In every case one function of competition is to compel existing firms, workers, landowners, and so forth to perform at their highest level of efficiency or quality, or face displacement or reduction of reward in favor of others who are either already in the field or might be drawn into it by the prospect of gain. Competition is supposed to dispose of firms with inefficient and wasteful practices or obsolete products, thus replacing less productive uses of resources with more productive uses.[17] But this is not its most important function. The real usefulness of competition lies not in its giving the economic system the maximum possible efficiency at any one point in time. If it ever did, it would halt progress on the spot, for with every single resource fully employed in production, there would be nothing left over for research and innovation. Research, after all, only helps future efficiency; it is a diversion of resources from present use in production, and requires that firms charge a little more for present goods to support it than they would if they were carrying on no research at all.

The significant part of competition is the part *in posse*. It is so likely under capitalism that sometime in the future someone will produce a better technique or a better product or a cheaper process, that firms devote considerable expense and effort to research designed to replace what they are doing now with something better. It is this effect of competition that Joseph A. Schumpeter called "Creative Destruction." [18] Viewed this way, the phenomena that puzzled economists steeped in the old equilibrium theory of market competition become explicable. It has been noticeable for some time that the most advanced firms, those that devote the greatest funds to research and product improvements and that *do* introduce innovations, are often ones whose *present* competition is the least demanding. In 1964, nearly half of all private industry funds for industrial research and development were spent in the chemical, petroleum, motor vehicle and transport equipment, and aircraft and missile industries,[19] all of which are characterized by their domination by relatively few large firms whose control over prices is sufficient to limit present competition severely. The motor vehicle and transport equipment industry spent $865 million for the purpose in contrast to the $30 million spent in the highly competitive textile and apparel industry. The apparent inefficiency of rigid or monopolistic prices provides the margin of safety behind which research and innovation can take place.

[17] In some of the more fetching versions of "Social Darwinism" inefficient people were disposed of too. In practice this has not seemed necessary for the success of capitalism, although the ruthless discharge of workers has often been justified on these grounds.

[18] *Op. cit.,* ch. 7.

[19] *Statistical Abstract of the United States,* 1966, Table 778, p. 545. These figures are for private industry funds alone, not government-supported research, and omit expenditures for geological and geophysical exploration by petroleum companies which would increase the proportions even more.

Competitive or not, if an industry fails to produce innovation on its own accord, the lure of profit may bring others in. In the early part of the present century railroads used principally steam locomotives whose production was dominated by three large firms. The invention of the diesel engine provided an opportunity for innovation that they failed to seize. General Electric entered the field in the 1920s, producing diesel electric switching engines, and was followed in the early 1930s by General Motors. Less than ten years after its entry the latter was outselling all other locomotive manufacturers combined.[20] A similar invasion of a stagnant field may be seen in the construction of whole houses by manufacturers who formerly only dealt in building products. The housing industry, which is competitive and had been stagnant before the Second World War, has recently been jogged into innovation by newcomers. In the decade 1952 to 1962 the proportion of factory-made houses rose from one sixteenth to one sixth of the total.[21]

In addition to its economic function of fostering innovation and efficiency, competition has a political function: It is one of the principal means for limiting economic power. The dispersal of decision-making brought about by private ownership is only part of the system of power limitation. Through competition the various holders of economic power tend to check one another and to limit exploitative abuses. This is most obvious when pure competition is compared with absolute monopoly, but it occurs in less extreme situations where the threat of the entry of a new firm into a field that is dominated by only a few producers inhibits the present occupants of that field from taking maximum advantage of their control over prices. It protects employees to some degree, as well as consumers, because the presence of alternative places of employment provides a means of escape from an employer who misuses his authority or attempts to undercut prevailing wage levels. As will be shown later, competition has proved to be insufficient and has had to be supplemented by employee organization and government action to restrain the economic power of management. It has not, however, lost its significance in this respect.[22]

The idea of gain also requires a little elaboration, for the amount of profit that is necessary to keep a capitalist system growing is less than has often been supposed. Striking figures can be assembled easily enough to show the

[20] Alfred P. Sloan, Jr., *My Years With General Motors,* John McDonald and Catharine Stevens, eds. (Garden City, N.Y.: Doubleday, 1964), p. 341. It is interesting to note that today gas turbines are being developed by General Electric, Westinghouse, General Motors, and others, and a new innovative race is on.

[21] *House and Home Magazine,* Vol. XXIII, No. 1 (January, 1963), pp. 63, 67.

[22] A good exposition of the power-restraining function of competition is contained in John Kenneth Galbraith, *American Capitalism: The Concept of Countervailing Power,* rev. ed. (Boston: Houghton Mifflin Company, 1956), ch. III. Galbraith's book is, in fact, a theory of the means by which this function has been supplemented in the United States.

high earnings of, say, United States Steel during some year in which it was operating at 70 per cent of capacity, and even average figures for corporate profits look at least comfortable. In 1965, the rate of return on stockholder's equity (after taxes) for manufacturing corporations was 13 per cent. What this average conceals, however, is the presence of wide variations between the successful and the unsuccessful. In the last year for which detailed figures are available, 1962, more than 37 per cent of all corporations suffered net losses, and comparable figures for partnerships and proprietorships show losses to 21 per cent of these.[23] As Joseph Schumpeter observed, the struggle for profits has something in common with the game of poker. It requires "ability, energy and supernormal capacity for work," but has an "enticing admixture of chance."

> Spectacular prizes much greater than would have been necessary to call forth the particular effort are thrown to a small minority of winners, thus propelling much more efficaciously than a more equal and "just" distribution would, the activity of that large majority of businessmen who receive in return very modest compensation or nothing or less than nothing, and yet do their utmost because they have the big prizes before their eyes and overrate their chances of doing equally well.[24]

Actual gain is only part of the incentive that induces effort and daring on the part of the entrepreneur, and such gain as there is is probably no more expensive to society than alternative ways of calling them forth.[25] Motivation of entrepreneurs is a combination of the lure of profits and the adventure of trying out a new idea or doing a job well, both of which are appealing in themselves. The three tend to support one another. For a time a problem was posed by the separation of ownership and management that characterizes the modern private corporation in capitalism, for the entrepreneurs—the managers —were salaried and did not automatically share in profits. Since the late 1940s, however, the practice has grown of giving stock options as well as salaries to higher management, thus restoring the profit motive to them.

The incentive of gain is not, of course, limited to entrepreneurs in capitalism. It is used in attracting workers from one industry to another in pursuit of higher wages (a practice that is followed in all socialist and most communist countries as well), and in inducing the holders of the other factors of production to contribute them to the productive process. In most of these areas the potential gains are not so striking, are relatively easily calculated in advance, and are more related to the scarcity of the factor concerned and the need for

[23] In that year corporate profits were lower than in 1965, but still averaged a comfortable 9.8 per cent. Overall rate of return (profit) figures from *Statistical Abstract of the United States,* 1966, Table 698, p. 497. Others from U.S. Internal Revenue Service, *Statistics of Income, 1962: U.S. Business Tax Returns,* Tables 4, 17, and 31.

[24] *Op. cit.,* 3rd ed., pp. 73–74.

[25] See p. 78, for some statistical support of this claim.

it in production than to the effort required to furnish it.[26] Gain to these serves the purpose of drawing them into production and is expressed, not in profits, but in wages, interest, and rent.

In sum, gain is a part of the spur that drives competition and invites risk-taking innovation, and plays a larger but more sober part in drawing the factors of production into the fields in which they are most needed. It is also the vehicle for distributing the fruits of production, however, and this has caused difficulties for the smooth running of the system and has led to what society has judged to be inequities sufficiently serious to require correction by the political order. This we shall see as we proceed to review the extent to which the practice of capitalism has borne out the expectations held for it and to describe the modifications that have been made to suit society's purposes.

The Practice of Capitalism

The United States is, by agreement of friend and foe alike, the leading exponent of capitalism and example of a capitalist nation. To the extent that any deny this, they generally deny that any nation still practices a predominantly capitalistic method of economic organization. And it is true that only a few nations do practice something approaching pure capitalism, principally because the cultural traits that were described as providing a favorable environment for it and the economic, social, and political conditions conducive to its operation have not been characteristic of most of the countries of the world. Because substantially all of our examples of capitalism in action will be drawn from the United States, it is well to deal briefly with these background conditions, bearing in mind that not all countries that enjoy capitalism have reached it by the same route.

[26] Two types of extraordinary gain that appear in capitalist systems are windfalls and speculative gain. Windfalls occur when property, usually land, is found to have hitherto unsuspected value, as when mineral wealth is discovered under it. There is no incentive value in windfall gains, except in the marginal sense that a landowner might be willing to allow prospectors on his property in the hope that something will be found. The legal structure that developed under capitalism to support property rights happens to protect windfalls, but it is not at all clear that they are needed to make the system work. Pure speculative gain is derived from the purchase of property, including not only land, but rights in land, corporate shares, and other intangible property that is expected to increase in value. Speculation is generally regarded as serving to keep the market in these properties flexible and open to potential buyers and sellers at all times. It may, therefore, have a somewhat greater usefulness to the system. Both of these types of gain tend to be confused with entrepreneurial profits, and indeed, they may appear as part of the returns (income or additions to net worth) of a business or an individual. As such, they may be pointed to as showing the "gross injustice" of the capitalist profit system when in fact they are peripheral to it. It is entirely conceivable that the structure of law that protects windfall gains could be changed to eliminate them without affecting the capitalist system at all. Arguments against capitalism based on them are trivial and do not touch the fundamentals of the system.

The United States was the third major country in the world to undergo industrialization, and although the process was interrupted by a tearing civil war, there were many factors that rendered it the least painful of all of the early industrial revolutions. There was less of a social upheaval because there had existed no feudal class structure to be torn down to make way for it. It occurred in a society already oriented in large measure to economic goals, an orientation that is often obscured by the historical attention given the Pilgrim Fathers in New England as against the adventurers who colonized Virginia, the trading Dutch in New York, and the mercantile purposes that underlay the majority of the companies that organized and supported colonization. There were all of the usual horrors of early factory life, but escape from them was possible and wages were higher, because unclaimed land at the frontier was available to which the unemployed and the disenchanted could repair. There were not, as there were in England, wandering armies of dispossessed peasants whose search for work drove wages down and bred insecurity and fear. Because they were among the first peoples to industrialize, Americans did not suffer the stresses of forced-draft development that characterize many parts of the world today. England and France were far enough away, and their goods sufficiently difficult to bring across the ocean, that America's growth was not distorted by a too early appearance of an intense desire for goods the economy was not ready to produce itself. When growth did occur, however, a vast and seemingly limitless market, unbroken by tariff walls, gave opportunity and reward to those who dared to offer it new things.

It should not be thought that the process was painless. It was not. No perusal of American history from the 1840s onward would fail to reveal misery, dirt, slums, sweatshops, depressions, and all of the other plagues that attended industrialization in England and elsewhere. They were less horrible, however, and more strongly overbalanced by buoyant growth, the excitement of sudden wealth, and the other bearers of an aggressive optimism. Straight up through modern times no other country so frequently portrayed examples of the rags-to-riches story, and in no other was a competitive individualism so strongly nurtured, not only on the frontier, but in the cities and factories where fortunes were built. It is a very trite story, this, but a conscientious comparison of the United States in the nineteenth century, and even as far as the 1920s, with other nations cannot but reveal a difference that could only bring a different outlook and a different set of values to dominate popular thinking.

Two expressly political factors need to be mentioned as well before we can summarize the effects of these developments. As was mentioned in Chapter 1, the franchise had been extended without serious opposition (except in a few of the original states) to all white male adults before the Industrial Revolution started, thus removing a possible cause for the growth of intense class feeling during the process. Secondly, the United States enjoyed a happy immunity from armed invasion. A threat of invasion tends to emphasize the State as protector of the people and draws energies away from the productive task in hand. The Civil War did the latter, but neither its slogans nor its results operated to endear governmental power to the people. This, and perhaps the confusion of loyalties brought about by the existence of a federal system, tended to weaken the already low prestige of governmental power in general—power that had once belonged to the colonial ruler across the sea, and power of which the framers of the Constitution had shown their fear and dislike by dividing and scattering it about in a way designed to make it largely unusable.

In no other country has the ground been prepared so well for capitalism. Not only its economic success, which a great many other nations have shared, if less impressively, but every facet of its political and social experience tended to produce a people lacking in affection for government, optimistic about their own possibilities of self-betterment, free of class antagonisms,[27] and aggressively individualistic.[28] With all of these were combined certain attitudes of a milder, kinder sort: The cooperation on a community scale that was necessary in frontier life, religious attitudes that bespoke charity and concern for the weak, tolerance of differences (except in the scarifying matter of race), and generosity bred of confident self-sufficiency. These were to have their effect in modifying the application of the principles of capitalism, and were, in fact, the ones that were transferred to and expressed in the political order.

The Political and Economic Orders Under Capitalism. The principles of capitalism require a limitation of the impact of the political order on the economic order, but actual practice has shown that that limitation is far from absolute. Political intervention has never been absent and has often been rather massive. At least five major (but overlapping) forms can be distinguished. First, government has been called upon by the various competitors in economic struggles to give them an advantage or to counter an advantage held by their opponents. Secondly, government is responsible for the framework of law within which the capitalist system operates. In that capacity it has had to make adjustments of that framework from time to time as the system evolved in order to help it continue under new conditions or to improve its operation where defects were discovered. Thirdly, the political order has intervened to correct and supplement the effects of the market in meting out rewards and allocating power. It has registered society's refusal to abide by the results of the play of market forces within the particular market structure

[27] Even today sample surveys indicate that Americans find great difficulty in identifying the social class to which they belong, and when they do, the great majority choose "middle class."

[28] If any have been misled by recent writings about suburban conformity to believe that aggressive individualism has died out, consider what lies behind the deadening monotony of urban sprawl: Each individual wants *his* own house on *his* patch of ground despite the hardships and burdens of commuting, home maintenance, lack of service, and above all, cost.

that existed. Fourthly, efforts have been made to correct the so-called business cycle—the great alternation of prosperity and depression that came to attend the unregulated market. Finally there are the occasions and conditions in which the government has stepped in to control and even supplant the market in the performance of the economic function, suspending, limiting, or replacing the capitalist system entirely. The first two of these five forms of intervention arise from the necessary connection that exists between the political and economic orders in any society. The last three grow out of the government's function as custodian for what is often called the general interest—those values so widely shared that it is not felt amiss to express them authoritatively if need be, and to which every order of society must, in the last estimate, conform if it is to be allowed to function otherwise undisturbed.

Government Intervention in Economic Struggles. The political order never was totally separated from the economic order—and never could be because laws established in the former were essential to the functioning of the latter. And despite the best intentions of men, the law is never quite neutral. This fact was discovered early, before industrialization was well under way in America, when the Common Law of conspiracy which did not prevent employers from joining together to keep wages down,[29] was found to apply to a union of employees seeking to raise them. The temporary success of the employers in using governmental power to aid them (this particular application of the conspiracy doctrine was overturned in 1842, although vestiges lingered well into the twentieth century [30]) was merely one event in history of the use of governmental power by economic contestants that runs back before the days when medieval merchants and guildsmen used the force of law against competitors and apprentices and continues forward to the present and undoubtedly beyond. A major part of the story of capitalism is told in efforts by various parties to gain the helping hand of government, often abetted or opposed by altruistic groups and others whose prime interest was in curbing abuses of economic power. Thus it is that tariffs, labor legislation, patent laws, land grants, bounties, subsidies, sumptuary taxes and special tax advantages, exclusive franchises, favorable postal rates, price supports, resale price maintenance laws,[31] and rate regulations have been a regular part of the business of legislative bodies in capitalist societies.

The regulatory and promotional activities called forth from government in this fashion are many and varied and it would be beyond the purpose of this

[29] It was later held that it did.

[30] See the discussion of its apparent use in a 1917 case, *Hitchman Coal & Coke Co.* v. *Mitchell* in John ҟ. Commons, *Legal Foundations of Capitalism* (Madison, Wis.: University of Wisconsin Press, 1959), p. 296.

[31] Resale price maintenance is the general category of laws that have been dubbed "fair trade" or "quality stabilization" by their proponents. They are laws requiring all retailers to sell goods at a price fixed by the manufacturer, thus protecting both against price competition.

analysis to attempt to describe them. It is important, however, to note that they fall into three rather broad categories having different results in terms of the operation of the market. In the first and largest category are those that leave the market functioning, but change either the costs of marshaling the factors of production or the prices of goods on which market choices are based. These include tariffs and sumptuary taxes,[32] which raise the price of some goods in comparison to others; bounties and subsidies, which may lower the prices of the affected goods and services; and favorable postal rates, tax advantages, and land grants, which reduce the costs of doing certain types of business. A second group also leaves the market standing but alters the bargaining power of the participants, the prime example being labor legislation, which will be discussed more fully subsequently.[33] A third category affects the market more directly by setting prices or restricting access to the market. This includes rate regulations, resale price maintenance, price supports, exclusive franchises, and patents. This confusing welter of governmental actions does not serve private purposes only, but often helps to achieve goals that society hopes to achieve either through or concurrently with those served by capitalism. In many of these struggles for legislative assistance private interests and disinterested reformers have stood side by side and a considerable number of the resulting governmental actions have directly assisted the working of capitalism and the spreading of its material benefits among the population.[34]

Labor legislation affords an excellent example of constant blending and readjusting private advantage and social benefit. Labor was at a disadvantage before the law at the start, and its cause found many champions. The poet-editor, William Cullen Bryant, bitterly criticized the conspiracy doctrine in his paper, and Horace Greeley supported numerous labor causes in his. The New England transcendentalists attempted utopian schemes at Brook Farm and elsewhere. Serious efforts to write changes into the law began with the Ten-Hour Movement in the period from the late 1830s to the late 1850s, to be followed by laws controlling wages and hours for women and by child labor legislation. This last is a compelling example of a mixture of public and private purposes, for adult workers were glad to be rid of the cheap labor competition of children and society at large had become appalled at the conditions under which very young children had been forced to do factory work.

---

[32] A sumptuary tax is a tax on a particular good destined for the consumer market that raises its price in comparison with a substitutable commodity. An example is the tax on artificially colored oleomargarine, which was enacted in response to dairy interests that wanted to make the product comparable in price to butter. The tax was repealed when the oleomargarine makers and corn growers gathered enough strength and consumer support to turn the tide the other way.

[33] All of the measures have some effect on prices also, because prices are the market's indicator of all of the relationships that go into production and distribution. Similarly, the measures in the third category affect both bargaining power and prices.

[34] The most obvious example of a direct assist is patent legislation, the effect of which in helping the English Industrial Revolution was discussed in Chapter 1.

Employers sought refuge in the courts against the legislative onslaught and won some notable, if temporary, victories. In one of these, the famous *Danbury Hatters* case,[35] they even managed to turn against labor a law that had originally been passed (partly with labor support) to attack business combinations: the Sherman Antitrust Act. By a combination of changing attitudes in the courts and new legislative protection, the tide turned again in labor's favor with the Clayton Act (1914—an illusory gain, because the courts had not yet changed and they quickly emasculated the relevant provisions), the Norris-Laguardia Act (1932), and the Wagner Act (1935). The last of these marked labor's high point, and not only established firmly labor's right to bargain collectively, but created a governmental body, the National Labor Relations Board (NLRB), to oversee the process. More recently, the Taft-Hartley Act (1947) and the Landrum-Griffin Act (1959) have operated to reduce somewhat labor's power and to declare some of its tactics illegal.

The battle has been a seesaw one, and there is no likelihood that the political order will abandon its role in this aspect of the economic order, or that the law will remain unchanged in the future.[36] The net effect in part, however, has been to approach a near-equality in bargaining power between what have become two giants in the economic realm and, by raising the power of labor, to permit workers to share more widely in the growing prosperity of the nation through higher wages. Thus the capitalist objective of an ever-increasing abundance has been brought within reach of a larger and larger proportion of the population. Impressive throughout the struggle has been the failure of a sharp class cleavage to emerge, although it has threatened from time to time as the economically (and politically) more powerful employers used their power to slow down or defeat changes in the law. That the threat has not materialized is probably due at least partly to the attitudes and events that were earlier described as militating against class feeling, and partly to the success that labor has had, aided by reformers whose impulse to help came as an expression of concern for the disadvantaged.

Adapting the Legal Framework of Capitalism. The changing nature of capitalism over time, and the gradually deepening understanding of its workings has been a major source of political action and legislation in the economic order. As was stated before, an economic system cannot function without a structure of law to support it. The law establishes the rights of ownership, the enforceability of contracts, and the standing of parties to deal with one another. In addition, government not only preserves the peace and

---

[35] *Loewe* v. *Lawlor,* 208 U.S. 274 (1908). This case applied the Sherman Act to secondary boycotts—efforts by workers to pressure an employer by picketing or otherwise interfering with the business of those who deal with him. The hatters were assessed triple damages.

[36] At the time of this writing, labor is mounting a campaign to eliminate one of the sections of the Taft-Hartley Act that it finds objectionable and too disadvantageous to it.

order essential to the transaction of business and maintains relations with other nations on the basis of which international trade can take place, but has assumed or been given the function of regulating the value of legal tender or money used as tokens of exchange in buying and selling. Changes in the functioning of the system, therefore, were bound to require adjustment of the underlying law.

Perhaps the best way to approach this part of the analysis is to look at the changes wrought in and by the entrepreneur, the driving spirit of capitalism. The original entrepreneurs were those who invented, or who provided the means for the application of, new devices and ideas in the early days of the Industrial Revolution. These men operated on a relatively small scale, obtained their capital backing from a few wealthy individuals, and built their fortunes on the basis of their personal involvement with the productive process. As they improved on the existing technology, however, they paved the way for larger and larger industrial enterprises that utilized capital resources too great for single individuals to accumulate, with the exception of an extraordinarily favored few. There existed in the law, however, a device called the *corporation,* which permitted many persons to contribute their money to a venture. In return they received shares in the profits, but the direction of the business was allowed to lie in the hands of a small group elected by the shareholders. This facilitated the gathering together of large amounts of capital without the nuisance of daily business consultations among a multitude of partners. There were other advantages to the corporation, too. The shareholders could be promised a limited liability for possible losses incurred; their risks could be reduced to the amount that they had put into the corporation, and no more, in contrast to a partnership in which every member was liable for his share of the debts. Shares could be sold more readily than partnership shares, and without consulting the rest of the owners of the corporation. The corporation itself had the standing in law of a single legal person, and could own, borrow, buy and sell property, sue in the courts, and continue in business even though the original members died or sold out their interests. Originally, the corporate form had been used only for special purposes in which the State had an interest and that it wished to promote, such as colonial ventures in the mercantile period. Incorporation was a privilege granted only because some clear public purpose was to be served by it. Toward the end of the nineteenth century, however, governments began to make the corporate device freely available as an aid to assembling capital and running an enterprise. New general laws were enacted that permitted any group of individuals, so long as they met certain requirements, to file a petition for incorporation with some public official who had no discretion to deny it if the conditions were met. Soon the corporation became the predominant form of business organization.

The corporation was to have many effects, the first of which was to allow the growth of enterprises so large that those who directed them could no longer have time to deal with the details of innovation and production. To command these giants, a new type of entrepreneur arose, no less driving in his ambition than his predecessor, but oriented to the problems of organization and to the possibilities of financial empire-building, rather than to invention and development. These business leaders, "robber barons" as they came to be called, at first proceeded to treat the country to a display of unbridled and murderous competition accompanied by ruthless and often quite unprincipled financial manipulation. Then, when their ranks had been somewhat thinned and the costs of the competition had been assessed and found to be too high for reasonable men to permit, they turned to the construction of voluntary [37] agreements to split the market and, when these broke down, to the building of an extraordinary structure of trusts, holding companies, and mergers to which the corporate device lent itself admirably. It could not be said that government stood idly by during these happenings, for it was the kindly complaisance of the New Jersey legislature, for example, that provided the legal authority on which the great Standard Oil trust was built. Nevertheless, it was the businessmen themselves who undertook to tame the market, and only when they had done so in a manner that seemed to be opposed to the general interest [38] did popular revulsion find expression in legislation to break up the trusts in an effort to return to an earlier form of competition. The Sherman Antitrust Act in 1890 and the Clayton Act and the Federal Trade Commission Act in 1914 not only attempted to break up the enormous aggregations of capital into small competing units, but outlawed some of the forms of competitive practice that had been found so destructive in the preceding years.[39] In the former effort they enjoyed only a limited success, but in the latter, they provided a climate for competition that was considerably healthier than had existed before. Various types of deceptive practices, price-fixing agreements, and financial manipulations were outlawed or subjected to governmental scrutiny.

The breaking up of the trusts was a limited success in that it only succeeded in producing a situation where, instead of a single dominant producer being able to control the market for a particular product at will (the condition described as monopoly), a number of very large firms opposed each other in competition over that product.[40] With few and very large firms facing each

[37] Binding agreements were found to be illegal under the same Common Law rule of conspiracy that had proved so damaging to labor at an earlier date.

[38] A sidelight to this story is the fact that during the Great Depression of the 1930s the government did an about-face and tried to promote voluntary agreements under the short-lived National Industrial Recovery Act.

[39] The Securities Act of 1933, the Securities Exchange Commission Act of 1934, and the Public Utilities Holding Company Act of 1935 were also at least partly directed at the limitation or dissolution of certain types of combination.

[40] Actually, it was some time before even this was achieved. Early court decisions substantially emasculated the Sherman Act (except in its application to the unfortunate Danbury Hatters), and the intensity and effectiveness of antitrust enforcement has varied over time.

other, and none of them very anxious to engage in a price war that would eliminate both their profits and their funds for further expansion and innovation, it became relatively easy for them to watch one another's pricing schedules and adopt uniform prices without overt or even actual collusion.[41] In the industries in which this situation exists, including automobiles, steel, aluminum, electrical equipment, oil, chemicals, paper, cigarettes, and others, one or two "leaders" may set their prices based on the returns they feel they can and would like to gain; the rest follow suit. Competition is carried out not through prices, but through service, product differentiation, and advertising. This new arrangement is called *oligopolistic competition,* in distinction to the *pure competition* that was described in connection with the market system. It is still a market,[42] but it requires rather different rules to hold it to the effective supplying of consumer wants.

It will be recognized that this form of competition is precisely that discussed earlier in connection with the effect of competition in keeping the innovative process going. It is not efficient in producing the lowest price for consumer goods at any moment in time. However, the pressure of competition is directed forcefully into the development of new products, because the offering of a better product at the old price (or a different price, for that matter, whether higher or lower) is a means of attracting customers away from competitors without engaging in a "price war." In such a market the ability of the buyer to distinguish higher quality goods from lower, and real improvements from advertising gimmicks, becomes of the highest importance, for these, rather than price choices, become the controlling ones. It is with this particular problem that the political order is presently trying to deal through marketing and labeling laws, penalties for false advertising, and what are called truth-in-packaging and truth-in-lending bills.[43] Modern consumer products are so complicated and contain such a variety of substances that very few consumers are in a position to judge quality. In fact, a special type of business has grown up that consists of testing products and reporting to consumers on their relative qualities and values. Government's efforts to provide accurate labeling and honest advertising are hampered in part by the value society sets on free-

---

[41] Examples of actual collusion do still crop up, as happened in the electrical industry in several years prior to 1959. Upon the discovery of this, several top executives of the affected concerns went to jail.

[42] And the over-all production-directing function of the market is not destroyed by it because that function applies to consumer choices of the product of one industry against that of another, as well as choices within an industry.

[43] Deceptive packaging is a direct substitute for price competition, for if the customer can be made to feel that he is getting more in one package than in another of equal price, he will choose the apparently larger package. Consumer credit plans are another alternative to price competition that truth-in-lending bills are designed to control. Consumer credit is a convenience, or service, for which a rather large hidden price can be charged without being directly registered in the prices of the goods sold.

dom of speech and its associated rights. Therefore, a sound legal framework for this new type of market has not yet fully evolved.

The problem of oligopolistic competition presents itself in another form not in the consumer market, but in the market for products that are sold by one business or industry to another, either in the form of materials used in later stages of production or in the purchase of goods by wholesalers and retailers for ultimate sale to the public. Here it is possible for one corporate giant to face another *across* the market, so that each can use its own leverage to induce the other to accept a price nearer to the one that would be found in "pure competition" than is the case when a few large sellers face a multitude of unorganized buyers, or vice versa. It is notable that this situation obtains, for example, in the purchase of steel, aluminum, chemicals, and other materials by the automobile industry. Where the market consists only of large units of this sort, the market is regulated by what Professor John Kenneth Galbraith has called *countervailing power*.[44] The power of the buyer serves to counteract the power of the seller. There are two consequences of this of interest to government: The first is the tendency for corporations to try to acquire their own sources of supply and distribution, either by entering new fields or by buying up and merging with their suppliers and distributors. This is known as *vertical combination,* as opposed to the *horizontal combination* when a firm acquires ownership of a competitor on the same side of the market. Vertical combinations made an appearance in the wave of corporate mergers that occurred between 1925 and 1931 and have been an important contributor to the new wave since the Second World War. It was not long before the antitrust laws were applied to this device also. Why? Because a vertical combination is capable of developing such an advantage in a market that its position and power become substantially unassailable unless one of the other giants decides to move in from another field. It may well be that there are efficiencies to be gained by vertical combination, but public and governmental uneasiness about concentrated economic power has produced efforts to discourage this type of growth.

The other consequence that concerns government is the presence in the market of small firms that do not possess the countervailing power of their larger brethren. This has led to legislation and regulatory and court decisions outlawing various exercises of buying and selling power that seem to produce unfair effects in competition. Thus, "tie-in" sales—where a powerful seller

[44] *American Capitalism: The Concept of Countervailing Power,* rev. ed. (Boston: Houghton Mifflin Company, 1956). Galbraith notes the same phenomenon in the dealings between powerful unions and management. A warning that neither countervailing power nor the "creative destruction" carried on by oligopolistic competition can be safely relied on to curb power and ensure efficiency and innovation without government monitoring is contained in Walter Adams, "Competition, Monopoly, and Countervailing Power," *Quarterly Journal of Economics,* LXVII (November, 1953), pp. 469–492.

compels a weak buyer to buy things he does not want if he is to get what he does want—and unreasonable discounts to large buyers are both forbidden. In this piecemeal fashion the framework of law undergoes continuous revision.

Correcting and Supplementing the Market. The concept of countervailing power has been offered by Galbraith also as explaining the operation of government price supports and acreage control in agriculture, a subject that brings us to the third of our major categories of political involvement in the economic order, the corrective and supplementary function of government. It was a curious happening that agriculture, the chief economic support of society throughout most of human existence, proved to be the one branch of productive activity that did not and, in a sense, could not share fully in the increasing abundance of capitalism. The reason was simple enough: The demand for agricultural products does not rise at a rate nearly as great as that for industrial goods. Insofar as the products concerned are foods, there is in any society (even among the Romans with their repulsive method of maximizing food consumption) a limit to the amount of them that can be consumed at a given population level. Furthermore, they are *consumed* and cannot grow obsolete or be replaced with new models. New foods cannot continue to be absorbed without driving the old ones off the market; a man can have two cars but will tire of having two breakfasts. Production methods in agriculture can be improved greatly, but product improvement is comparatively slight and does little to increase consumption—in fact, it may lessen it if the improvement makes it more nourishing per unit. Alone among the major sectors of the economy, agriculture cannot raise itself by its own bootstraps after a saturation level is reached. At best it can hope that some other industry will find a synthetic use for its products and drag it along with it. Improvements in agriculture's own productive measures, moreover, have the same effect that they have in most industries: They increase productivity per man hour, and if the demand for the product fails to rise, they reduce employment.

The one way that farmers might have hoped to at least keep abreast of the rest of the economy was in combining to restrict production sufficiently to hold agricultural prices up through scarcity. This did not occur in agriculture because the many independent farms made this sector an example of classical "pure competition" on the producer's side. Added to their difficulties was the fact that industrial concentration did occur in the industrial and commercial operations that bought from the farmers and transported farm products— grain mills, meat packers, railroads, and ultimately, chain stores. To this disadvantaged segment of society that had always held an honored place in American mythology, the political order offered a solution in the form of countervailing power. Farmers who could not seem to organize economically organized politically. With the help of those who felt sympathetic to their cause and those who saw in a lagging farm sector a drag on the entire economy, they succeeded in getting legislation and governmental action that protected and raised their price structure [45] by purchasing and storing excess production, paid them for restricting acreage, and gave them further assistance by providing rural electrification, mortgage loan guarantees, and other services that they did not have the economic power to command. Because of the inherent economic problem of agriculture described here, these programs have been costly and often unsatisfactory, and the problem is yet imperfectly solved. The programs have benefitted those farmers whose operations were most advanced and most nearly consistent with the high level of technological development that characterized the rest of the economy while keeping many highly uneconomic farm operations barely in existence. They have not brought general prosperity in agriculture.

Agriculture is a vital part of the economy, and the assistance given to farmers was more than an act of generosity. It was part of the general tradition handed down from mercantilist times of government aid and furtherance to economic activities deemed of importance to national wealth or the general well-being of society. Another and important manifestation of that tradition is seen in state enterprises of the type that provide what was referred to in Chapter 1 as social overhead capital—costly, long-term, and sometimes unremunerative projects of great usefulness and value to substantially all other segments of the economy, or to the population at large. In this class fall public education, public health, postal service, roads, national parks and other recreational services, and more recently, public power projects, many types of basic and applied research, and support of the arts. Government undertakes such projects partly in order to promote aspects of them that might be undervalued in the market (such as the humanities in teaching) and partly to speed a development for social purposes. Thus a hydroelectric plant may be built by government before a region has reached a stage of industrial development sufficient to make the venture attractive to private capital. The Tennessee Valley Authority (TVA) is just such a case and had the added purpose of rescuing a desolate area from further deterioration.

With the growing costs of certain types of advanced technology and the frequent international implications of their use, there are now appearing in American capitalism new types of mixed government-private enterprise. The Communications Satellite Corporation (Comsat), is one such case, and modified forms of government-private cooperation occur in the aerospace industry and atomic power as well. Government funds there pay for research and

---

[45] This action, incidentally, had precisely the effect that rigid prices in many other industries have had: By restoring a margin of profit, it permitted expenditures on capital improvements (most of which arose out of research findings by the U.S. Department of Agriculture, which, given the straitened condition of farming as an industry, had become the chief source of innovative techniques). As a result, agricultural productivity rose sharply. The number of man hours required per hundred bushels of wheat harvested, for example, fell from an average of sixty-seven in 1935–1939 to an average of twelve in 1960–1963. *Statistical Abstract of the United States,* 1965, Table 924, p. 646. This, of course, only made the farm problem worse.

development projects that have both military and civilian uses, and government agencies oversee and sometimes carry on the work. This is regarded with concern by many who see in it a combination of public and private power in a highly technical and often secret field. There is in fact a problem of this nature, for there exist industrialized areas in the United States, such as in California, where whole local populations are dependent for their livelihood upon decisions made jointly by government and contracting firms, whose deliberations are kept from public scrutiny for security reasons, real or claimed. At present this is forcing increasing attention on the role of Congress as the overseer of governmental administration. However, the Congress, too, is enmeshed in the complex of forces, for its members are often closely allied with the participating firms.

In short, public and mixed enterprise in a capitalist economy pose problems for the control of economic and political power, but are otherwise not inconsistent with capitalism. They represent a desire to press forward somewhat faster than the market is able to proceed. In Western countries where industrial development came late and received a great deal of State support to speed it, the very large proportion of economic activity of this type has led to the designation of a variant of capitalism called state capitalism. Germany is regarded as the prime example of this system. Beginning in the time of Bismarck, State-owned railroads and public utilities, municipally owned banks, mixed public and private enterprises of all sorts, and even the more recent example of the astonishing Volkswagen concern have demonstrated the State's interest in rapid development. Whether particular examples of public enterprise are to be regarded as State capitalism or State socialism is much more a matter of intent, as expressed in the objectives of the system, than it is a simple question of ownership.[46] This point will become a little clearer when we turn to the analysis of socialism in Chapter 3.

Programs to help those who have been hurt or defeated in the economic struggle have from the beginning been a feature of governmental action under capitalism and, because they are a reflection of liberal humanitarianism, are a common feature of both capitalist and democratic socialist countries. Just as the competitive market struggle provides disproportionate rewards for a few, it provides disproportionate penalties as well. Not only (or even always) are the genuinely lazy and inept penalized, but also those whose skills are displaced by a changing technology and those who are thrown out of work by the failure of the firms by which they were employed. The harsh doctrines of Social Darwinism never took such firm hold in England or America that the general population was willing to see some starve in the midst of plenty. In the United States public welfare services were a function of the states until

---

[46] Whether or not the enterprise is a State monopoly does make a difference, however. See page 73. Some mention should probably be made at this point of government loans to business, which are akin to the activities described here, but generally do not qualify as "social overhead capital."

the depression of the 1930s when the superior financial resources of the Federal government were called upon to assist. By matching grants of funds, the states were aided in some programs, while other newer forms of financial assistance were given in the form of federal or federally guided insurance programs [47] to cover retirement, support of dependents of a deceased worker, unemployment, industrial injuries and diseases, and (later) permanent disablement, and medical care.

The interest of the people in helping the distressed and disadvantaged throughout government has been expressed in many forms other than welfare payments. It was shown in a massive way in the great public works projects and work relief programs of the Great Depression. It is among the motives that lie behind public housing (beautifying cities and reducing crimes are others). It is demonstrated in more recent ways still in the Manpower Retraining Program designed to assist displaced workers in learning new skills, in the effort to breathe new economic life into the Appalachian region, in the poverty program of President Lyndon B. Johnson, in the Job Corps (and, of course, in its international predecessor, the Peace Corps), and in disaster area loans. The political order has in all capitalist countries carried duties of this sort.

It is this collection of programs for the disadvantaged that now bears the general designation (often intended as a term of opprobrium), "welfare state," and that is held by some to be antithetical to capitalism. But is it so? These are programs and policies by which the State has assumed an economic function of raising the lowest standard of living for mankind from one of starvation, homelessness, and disease toward one of sustenance, shelter, and health. In a capitalist system, even though the cost of this must be borne by those whose own level of living is above the minimum, it is not so great as to eliminate higher gradations of wealth and income toward which those on the lowest level may strive. Even the recent proposals for a guaranteed minimum income do no more than this and are felt by some conservative economists to be likely to prove less costly than the multitude of present assistance policies.[48] Thus, while the welfare state may be for socialists a first step in the direction of a hoped-for equality, for capitalists it can be no more than an expression of the humaneness that their system never meant to deny.

[47] These were patterned on insurance partly to remove from the recipients the stigma of receiving aid. Because the employer, or the workman and employer both, made payments to the funds out of payrolls and wages, it was felt that there would be little or no damage to the individualistic pride of the workman when the occasion came to "cash in" on the benefits. Unlike private insurance, however, there were no actuarial reserves accumulated at the start. They are self-supporting on a current basis only.

[48] See, for example, Report of the National Commission on Technology, Automation, and Economic Progress, *Technology and the American Economy,* Vol. I (February, 1966), pp. 40–41. The method proposed is a "negative income tax" which, like the present income tax, would be scheduled in such a way as to retain incentives. It would ensure that increased earned income would not be totally cancelled by a reduction in the income-supplement payments. For the conservative favoring view see Friedman, *op. cit.,* ch. XII.

Countering the Business Cycle. The concern of democratic government for the welfare of the poor under capitalism proved to be the opening wedge that introduced the largest and most important change in the relation of the political to the economic order that has occurred, and one that, if successfully carried out, bids fair to eliminate the most serious defect that the system has displayed. For out of the patchwork of measures that were utilized to correct and ease the strains of the Great Depression of the 1930s, there emerged a new general policy—one of smoothing out the great swings of business activity that had brought alternate prosperity and depression, and of maintaining a level of employment that would guarantee to substantially every willing worker an opportunity to earn his own living.

For many years it had been noted that economic growth did not occur in a regular and sustained fashion, but followed a step-like progression in which each sharp advance was succeeded by a decrease in economic activity that brought falling prices and unemployment. At first attention was focused on the price changes, and capitalistic governments established central banking and currency controls designed to eliminate these. It was reasoned that if more money and easier credit were made available when prices were falling, the impulse to spend the money would bring them back up again. The Great Depression, however, seemed to show that this sort of remedy was not enough.[49] Furthermore, it was a frightening and shocking experience with 13 million people unemployed in 1933—a quarter of the total labor force—and a drop in the gross productive output of the nation to only slightly over half of what it had been in 1929. Wages fell dramatically, banks closed, and the welfare funds of charities and of state governments were strained beyond their capacity to alleviate the general distress. A rash of emergency measures was enacted, including many that have been discussed before, but the country was not brought fully out of the depression until the massive demands of the Second World War set the industrial machinery moving again full blast. Meanwhile, attention had become focused on the problem of full employment, following the insight offered by the *General Theory* of John Maynard Keynes.

It is time now to try to understand the economic phenomena with which Keynesian theory deals. The picture of the market economy that has been presented so far is an oversimplification which omits an important step: It was stated that production responds to consumer demands registered in the prices people are willing to pay for goods. Actually, however, there is a great deal of guesswork involved. If it appears that people are anxious to obtain a product, entrepreneurs must guess the amount by which they must increase their plant to supply it. If the product involved has never been on the market before, the basis for judgment is shaky indeed. Moving one step backward in the process, the industries that produce the industrial machinery used in

---

[49] Central banking and currency controls and the rest of the set of governmental actions that constitute what is called monetary policy have not been abandoned on this account. They are still universally employed and useful.

supplying new plant and equipment must also guess how much other industries will want of their products. Because the market is a competitive one, there is a general tendency for all of these guesses to be too high, each competitor hoping to capture a larger segment of the market than his fellows. Then, when the demand for the resulting products falls short and fails to absorb all of them, production is cut back and investment in plant slows or stops until demand catches up, after which the whole cycle is repeated. That is, it does start again *if there is money available to spend for new plant and equipment.* If there is not, of course the economy will simply stagnate, or continue at a lower level of production. Now, money must be *saved* to be turned into investment uses, and herein lies the problem Keynes identified. The slowing down of the economic machinery reduces incomes, throws people out of work, and causes savings to be drawn on just to keep people alive. It also cuts down business profits that might be saved and used for investment. If a depression is bad enough, as that of the 1930s was, there may be insufficient savings left to start things moving again. The problem happens at the top of the economic cycle also. When everybody is making money on a grand scale, more people save, and more money is saved than can be used in investments in plant. The unused savings simply accumulate, or are used to skyrocket shares in the stockmarket, but they are not used to purchase the goods that are being produced in too great supply, with the result that the boom fails and the economy starts its downward slide again.

What can government do about this? Quite a number of things. It could, of course, take over the regulation of the economy by directing and allocating production in such a way that no more will be produced than will be bought, and seeing to it that people will buy by placing in their hands the exact amount of money they need. It can go even further, and operate the economy entirely, giving people goods rather than pay in precisely the proportions that will use up everything that is made. In capitalist societies, however, and in others that maintain the market for at least part of their economic activity, other means are used. Most of these boil down to the *use, primarily, of market processes themselves in such a way as to leave people their freedom of choice,* by having the *government* buy and sell, invest and save, tax and make payments to the public in such a way as to counteract the forces that lead to "boom and bust."

In the first place government can try to help businessmen improve their guesswork. This is one of the principal purposes of the Employment Act of 1946,[50] which established the President's Council of Economic Advisers, one of the main duties of which is to issue reports on the state of the economy as a guide to business decisions (and to unions in framing their wage objectives). Secondly, it can increase its own rate of investment when private investment is slack, giving employment to more people, and thus putting money in their

[50] Note that the word *employment* is the key one in the title of the act. The purpose is the helpful one of trying to ensure enough jobs for everyone.

hands that they will be ready to spend or save as the situation warrants. Thirdly, it can use its taxing and borrowing power to "mop up" savings when they are too high, and put the money, through its own investments and purchases, and through welfare payments and the like, into the hands of people who, because they are not rich enough to save, will spend it. This is merely the simplest possible outline of the tools available to government that can be used for this purpose, but it suffices to show their nature. They involve no production controls, no allocation of resources, no licenses and permits to build or to expand, and so on. The harshest power employed is that of taxation, which still leaves a person free to do what he will with what is left. If properly handled, it is expected that these techniques will lead to a *sustained high level of aggregate demand,* which is simply an economist's way of saying that everyone has both money and a willingness to spend it, a condition that is obviously very much in harmony with an objective of ever-increasing abundance.

This rather lengthy excursion into economic theory was essential to show the consistency of Keynesian economic policies with capitalist traditions. It is now possible to outline a few of the specific governmental actions that have been taken pursuant to them in the United States. Fortunately, a number of the policies that were already in existence by the mid-1930s, and that had been adopted for various reasons of charity and necessity, happened to fit the purposes of stabilizing the market admirably. The welfare programs, particularly those of the insurance type that covered very large numbers of people and paid them when they were thrown out of employment or disabled, such as Social Security, Workmen's Compensation, and Unemployment Compensation, had the automatic effect of placing money in the hands of those hardest hit by a recession and most likely to spend it to sustain the demand for consumer goods. Conversely, the graduated income tax, which was adopted in 1913 to help make up the revenue loss caused by a cut in tariff rates and had been continued to pay the increasing costs of government in the First World War and after, automatically took more money out of people's hands when their incomes were high (and they were more likely to save), and less when times were hard and the important thing was for more people to have money to spend.[51]

In addition to these, however, the government has had to prepare itself to throw its economic weight deliberately in a direction opposite to that taken by the market. This has meant, first of all, that government had to be an impor-

---

[51] The graduated feature of the income tax, which causes a higher *percentage* of a person's income to be taken as his income rises, was originally adopted on the simple grounds that it was fairer to ask the rich to pay more, proportionately, than the poor, because they could afford it more easily. Socialist countries use a steeply graduated tax specifically for the purpose of leveling incomes, but it is notable that the United States recently *reduced* the steepness of its graduations, partly because it was felt that they distorted investment decisions too much, and partly because there simply was not that much revenue received from the higher brackets to make it worthwhile.

tant buyer and employer in the market, sufficient to affect it measurably. This was achieved, fortunately, or unfortunately, largely as a consequence of the demands of international politics, specifically war and preparation for war. United States Government purchases of goods and services in 1965 accounted for slightly under 10 per cent of the entire Gross National Product (GNP), with approximately 75 per cent of that amount being made up of purchases for national defense.[52] Civilian employment in the Federal government amounted to over two and a half million persons, with total federal, state, and local employment exceeding ten million. Government is by far the single largest buyer, employer, landowner, borrower, and investor in the economy. On the basis of this, and following the analyses made constantly by the Council of Economic Advisers, it is intended that government will adjust its economic activities to counter and correct swings in the market, spending and investing when others do not spend, and saving and paying off its debt when others do.[53] Whether or not these policies will in fact be pursued with sufficient vigor to eliminate for all time disasters such as that of the 1930s no one cares to predict. The intention to do so, however, has been declared by both national political parties, and their own fortunes certainly depend on it.

Government is not alone in developing ways to reduce the problems of guesswork that contribute to the business cycle.[54] Another change in the nature of business entrepreneurship has produced a generation of men who are more cautious (and, incidentally, more attentive to problems touching the general interest of society) than their predecessors. They also face a greater uncertainty in the market in which an affluent public is less driven by predictable needs in its choice of goods to buy than by whim or changing taste in luxury goods. To counter this, the new entrepreneurs (to a far larger degree than in times past) employ advertising, which attempts to direct consumer tastes and make them more predictable, and market research, which tries to discover in advance the potential market for a product to enable the producer

[52] This is not to say that defense accounted for 75 per cent of the federal budget. The figures used here are for actual purchases of goods and services and exclude transfer payments such as welfare grants, aid to state and local governments, interest on the national debt, and business subsidies.

[53] The size of the federal debt is often an object of concern to observers of these policies, and it does seem that political leaders find it more difficult to reduce spending than to increase it. Economists generally point to the fact that the debt has not kept pace with the productivity of the economy, and that corporate (and private) debt also rises as the economy grows.

[54] It should be stated that the foregoing analysis, because it was concerned with explaining certain governmental policies, did not exhaust this subject. A contributory cause of irregular growth is the uneven rate at which invention takes place. New inventions produce spurts that then taper off until another important discovery is made. Because government now is also the chief spender for research (on military hardware that often has civilian applications and on atomic energy, medicine, and agriculture, for example), it may be that these fluctuations will be reduced by government action also.

to avoid building too large a plant. Whatever feelings one may have about these developments from the point of view of taste and propriety, they do have a stabilizing effect. [55]

Supplanting and Controlling the Market. If the impression has been given that the overwhelming majority of governmental actions affecting the operation of the United States economy has tended to avoid supplanting the market as regulator of economic life, that impression is a valid one. There are, however, fields in which society has not wished the ordinary economic processes to take their course. Some of these have been described already, and there are others in which the market has seemed so clearly unable to function in a form that would produce the benefits expected from it, that it has been supplanted entirely. In addition, and finally, there has been the shattering experience of war, which appears to change many values, and which certainly has induced nations to set aside, temporarily at least, the values that support a capitalistic system.

To take the first subject first, the most general examples are found in laws regulating working conditions: health and safety regulations and minimum wage and maximum hours laws. All of these are subject to bargaining between labor and management, but public policy has established limits to the bargains that may be struck. Similarly, safety regulations have been imposed on public carriers to prevent the pressures of competition from leading to undermaintenance and possible loss of life, and banking and insurance reserve requirements and deposit insurance ensure the stability of financial institutions. The free market in land has been restricted by zoning regulations that serve to exclude business and industry from areas reserved for residential use. Businesses that do incidental damage to health and beauty through air and water pollution or by leaving the land open to erosion may in some states be forced to bear the costs of preventing or correcting that damage.

The foregoing merely set bounds to the operation of market forces and alter the competitive pattern by increasing the costs of doing certain types of business. More stringent, but still in the category of controls rather than suppressions of the market, are licensing procedures that restrict entry to certain professions and businesses (and that are often favored by those already engaged in the occupation concerned) and are supposed to provide assurance that minimum standards of competence have been met. Finally, there are

[55] In a widely read and justly famous book, *The Modern Corporation and Private Property* (New York: Macmillan, 1932), Adolf Berle and Gardiner Means pointed to another change in entrepreneurship—the separation of business management from business ownership. This, it was felt, would take the incentive for innovation out of private enterprise and also would require a redefinition of the meaning of property. Because that redefinition is already incorporated in the analysis in this book, there seems no point in expanding on it. As to the incentive, the recent trend in giving stock options to higher management has tended to restore the unity of entrepreneurship and ownership, at least sufficiently to eliminate the incentive problem.

regulations of competitive businesses because there is some quality about the business that would make competition extremely destructive and wasteful. Radio broadcasting is regulated because the airways would be chaotically "jammed" if they were not allocated by some responsible agency. Oil production is regulated because too-rapid drawing off of a deposit results in only partial recovery.[56]

The areas where competition does not seem to work are those of what are called *natural monopolies*. There is considerable danger in using this term, for at one time railroads were regarded as monopolies, a position they no longer occupy because of the technological development of the internal combustion engine that produced first the truck and later the airplane. Technically a monopoly exists when a single seller commands the entire supply of a product,[57] but because other goods may serve as substitutes, however imperfectly, and technical developments may render obsolete the good in which the monopoly is held, true monopoly must be one of the rarest and shortest-lived phenomena in the entire landscape of a capitalist economy. Nevertheless, gas, electric and water utilities, telephonic and telegraphic communication, air and rail, and to a lesser extent, water and road transportation have all tended either to be regarded as natural monopolies, or to be regulated by licensing and franchise procedures so that they were given monopolies (often at their own request, in fact). They are then regulated as to price, quantity and quality of service, and often labor relations as well—all features that a competitive market would regulate itself if it existed—or they are taken over entirely and operated as public enterprises.[58]

War is the great disrupter of the economic as well as other aspects of society, for in wartime a nation's goal of self-preservation takes precedence in people's minds over more personal wants and desires. Individuals will set aside their careers, many of them quite voluntarily, and risk or even invite death for this cause. It is not surprising, therefore, that the demand for free choice of consumer goods, free changing of employment, free search for innovations, and so on, should be subordinated to the needs of national defense.

---

[56] The principle of regulation in cases of this sort is generally strongly supported by the businessmen concerned, although the details and types of regulation may be fought bitterly. This sort of regulation usually reinforces an oligopolistic situation and facilitates stabilization of the market.

[57] There is also a phenomenon called monopsony, or a single buyer, but the only example of this outside the case of a corporate subsidiary in a vertical combination is the Federal government itself as purchaser of military and space hardware. Both terms apply equally to products, services, and factors of production.

[58] Lest this be misinterpreted, it should be made clear that there is considerable validity to the short-run view of monopoly. A customer who is already tied into the local gas company's lines and has a gas furnace and a gas stove is in no position to shop around for a lower bid from the local electric company. He is locked in and must buy gas at the current price until his furnace and stove wear out or the price differential grows so great that it pays to change.

In place of the standards of the market in directing production are substituted the governmentally made and generally popularly supported controls that increase production for war and suppress competing types of civilian production. Wage controls, job freezes, price controls, raw materials allocation, rationing, and so on, are not the conditions of capitalism—but then neither is war.[59] The result of a war is the temporary supplanting of the market economy by an economy of command that is, as our history showed, substantially its opposite. Of course the supplanting is not complete, and the habits of invention and competition are not lost during the period of hostilities. It was not, therefore, entirely beside the point for Americans to boast of the success of their economy in defeating the Axis Powers in the Second World War. However, the reason lay in the productive basis and the prepared skills that existed in the United States, and not in the fact that the market guided the mobilization for war.

Summary. Despite the really remarkable number of points of contact between the economic and political orders in American capitalism, the general nature of them with the understandable exception of war supports our view of the United States as a thoroughly capitalist nation. By and large the market is left as the guide to production and the register of people's wants; governmental action merely supplements it and seeks to keep it from damaging excesses. The decentralization of economic power that underlies the concept of private ownership continues, although the decentralization is less than that envisioned in the theory of pure competition, and is certainly weakened by the new mixed enterprise developments in the fields of military production, aerospace, atomic power, and communications. The economic decisions of American society are still made largely outside of the political order, at least insofar as the allocation of resources to civilian production and the very important matters of prices, profits, wages, rents, and interest are concerned. Government action to affect these (including interest, through central banking operations and handling of Treasury borrowings [60]) has remained largely permissive in nature, and despite not infrequent national emergencies caused by strikes, the temptation to substitute compulsory arbitration for the pulling and hauling of the collective bargaining process has been resisted. Finally, competition based on the expectation of gain remains as the motivating force in the economy, however much transformed by the development of the corporation, the growth of unions, and the other phenomena that have marked the evolution of capitalism.

[59] In a later chapter we shall deal with the conclusions reached by some theorists that capitalism leads to war.

[60] The very complex subject of monetary controls has been omitted from this analysis because a detailed description did not seem necessary. As was pointed out earlier, monetary controls and central banking are universally practiced as part of the government's stabilization program. Interest rate controls and credit restrictions are the most stringent and come closest to actually setting "prices."

Evaluation of Capitalism

Abundance. How well has this system succeeded in fulfilling the objectives with which our analysis began? On the matter of abundance the answer is apparently clear: The United States has the highest per capita income of any nation in the world,[61] clearly exceeding the others, as shown in Table 2.

Table 2 Seventy-two Countries Classified by Size of Per Capita National Income, 1962 (in U.S. Dollars)

Per Capita Income	Country	Per Capita Income	Country
$2450	1. United States	$200–299	36. Yugoslavia
			37. Portugal
$1400–1999	2. Sweden		38. Nicaragua
	3. Switzerland		39. Albania
	4. Canada		40. Ghana
			41. Jordan
$1000–1399	5. New Zealand		
	6. Australia	$150–199	42. Turkey
	7. Denmark		43. Honduras
	8. West Germany		44. Libya
	9. England		45. Iran
	10. France		46. Peru
	11. Czechoslovakia		47. Colombia
	12. Soviet Union		48. Tunisia
	13. Belgium		49. Malaysia
	14. East Germany		50. Syria
	15. Norway		51. Guatemala
	16. Iceland		
		$100–149	52. Morocco
$700–999	17. Finland		53. Communist China (1959)
	18. Netherlands		54. Rhodesia and Nyasaland
	19. Hungary		55. Ecuador
	20. Austria		56. Brazil (1960)
	21. Israel		57. United Arab Republic
	22. Poland		58. Paraguay
			59. Ceylon
$500–699	23. Ireland		60. Philippines
	24. Italy		
	25. Romania	$50–99	61. Thailand
	26. Bulgaria		62. Sudan
	27. Venezuela		63. Nigeria
			64. Kenya
$400–499	28. Japan		65. Congo
	29. South Africa		66. India
	30. Chile		67. Pakistan
			68. South Korea
$300–399	31. Greece		69. Tanganyika
	32. Spain		70. Uganda
	33. Mexico		71. Indonesia
	34. Cuba (1958)		72. Burma
	35. Argentina		

Adapted from *Economic Systems in Action,* 3rd ed. by Alfred Oxenfeldt and Vsevolod Holubnychy. Copyright by Holt, Rinehart and Winston, Inc. All rights reserved. Used by permission of the publisher. Comparisons of this sort, based on currency exchange rates and conversions of national income concepts into a common form, are not reliable as to detail or magnitude of differences between living levels in the countries listed. They do give a rough approximation of relative position, however.

[61] Actually Kuwait (not shown in Table 2) has a higher per capita income statistically speaking, but this is because of oil royalties and is not shared even remotely in the sense that a per capita figure implies.

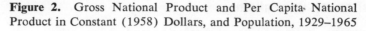

Figure 2. Gross National Product and Per Capita National Product in Constant (1958) Dollars, and Population, 1929–1965

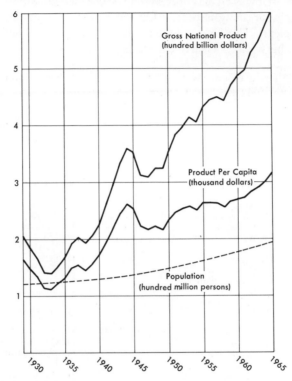

Source: U. S. Council of Economic Advisers, *Annual Report,* January, 1966, Appendix C, Tables C–2 and C–15.

It is also noticeable that in the second highest per capita income group is Switzerland, a small country substantially lacking in all of the specifically economic advantages of the United States (natural resources, a huge domestic market), but one that stands with the United States as a nearly completely capitalist society.

On the question of whether or not the abundance is *increasing* at what might be deemed a satisfactory rate, a more cautious answer must be given. In absolute terms, the wealth of the nation has been increasing at an irregular but impressive rate throughout the period for which good economic statistics exist, as shown in Figure 2. The frightening decline in productivity that took place during the Depression, however, and the higher rate of increase that has marked productivity in other nations since the Second World War have caused doubts to be raised concerning the ability of the capitalist economy to sustain a high rate of growth once a rather comfortable affluence has been achieved. As shown in Table 3, many nations have improved their output at higher rates since the Second World War. There are some indications, however, that

Table 3   Index Numbers of Industrial Production, Selected Countries,
1938–1964

(1958 equals 100)

Country	1938	1948	1953	1957	1960	1962	1964
United States	33	73	97	107	116	126	141
United Kingdom	62	73	88	101	113	114	127
USSR	23	40	58	91	122	146	169
Canada	32	62	84	101	108	120	138
Czechoslovakia	31	33	64	90	124	143	148
France	53	54	71	97	110	121	135
Greece	44	32	62	90	114	129	154
India	56	64	74	97	121	139	162
Italy	43	44	70	96	128	153	167
Japan	58	22	61	101	149	193	248
Mexico	41	53	68	95	117	129	158
Netherlands	49	56	79	100	122	133	151
Norway	47	58	80	100	114	125	142
Portugal	—	—	68	94	116	134	162
West Germany	53	27	66	97	119	132	149
Yugoslavia	29	43	53	90	131	150	201

Compiled from United Nations, *Statistical Yearbook*, 1965, Table 52, pp. 159–170.

tend to dispel these doubts. In the period 1960 to 1965, a new and radical upswing has been observed with an average growth rate of 4.5 per cent per year for the period.[62] Many of the trends that were supposed to account for a tapering off, specifically a decline in the rate of population growth and a drying up of new investment opportunities, have been reversed. Population in the United States, which seemed to be leveling off in the 1930s, has resumed, not merely as a result of the "baby boom" after the Second World War, but in a sustained fashion ever since. Invention and risk-taking have been spurred not only in the new fields of atomic power, electronics, and drugs, but in quite unexpected places. Such unpromising fields as cosmetics and the sale of miscellaneous articles for use in the home, including brushes, cleaning solutions, waxes, and the like, have witnessed the rapid growth of new, or previously small firms that have had astonishing successes. Their principal techniques have not been product innovation, but improvements in marketing—an element that our discussion of the function of advertising in an affluent society pointed to as of increasing fundamental importance for the economy.

A point that might occasion surprise is the fact that the capitalist method of economic organization has not, in the United States at least, diverted an unusually large share of the growing national wealth from employees and given it to stockholders, landowners, and business proprietors. Among countries whose shares of the total national income are analyzed by the International Labour Office, the United States ranks third in the total shares

[62] In the latter part of the period it rose even higher, but this was partly attributable to the demands of the war in Viet Nam, and may not represent a rate that would have been achieved under peaceful conditions.

given in wages and salaries and other forms of compensation to employees. As is the case with most statistics giving international comparisons, these are not reliable as to detail, but relative position shows the United States and Canada ranking at the top with the considerably more socialized United Kingdom, Sweden, and Norway:

Table 4 Compensation of Employees as Per Cent of National Income, 1963 (Top Five Countries) *

United Kingdom	74.6%
Sweden	72.7
United States	72.1
Canada	68.2
Norway	67.6

* Omitted are Puerto Rico (69.8 per cent), because of its special relationship to the United States, and two countries not reported in 1963, but which earlier reported percentages within the range covered by the countries in this table: Algeria (70.9 per cent in 1959) and Panama (69.1 per cent in 1961). Compiled from International Labour Office, *Year Book of Labour Statistics,* 1965, Table 24, pp. 597–600.

Less impressive is the performance of the economy in extending its benefits to all segments of society. A continuing trouble spot lies in the effects of technological displacement, and this has been exacerbated in recent years by the development of automation. The new economy requires fewer workers in many industries to provide an increasing output, and it is more demanding of higher skills than it is of unskilled labor. Table 5 shows the changing complexion of the American labor force from 1900 to 1966.

Those without skills find it increasingly difficult to find employment, and a recently increasing rate of high school drop-outs has added to precisely this

Table 5 Occupational Distribution of the American Labor Force, 1900–1966

	Per Cent of Labor Force	
Occupational Classification	**1900**	**1966 (March)**
Managerial and Professional		
Professional, technical, and kindred	4.3	12.9
Managers, officials, and proprietors (except farm)	5.8	10.2
White Collar		
Clerical and kindred	3.0	16.0
Sales	4.5	6.6
Blue Collar and Service		
Craftsmen, foremen, and kindred	10.5	12.6
Operative (semi-skilled) and kindred	12.8	19.0
Laborers (unskilled) except farm and mine	12.5	4.7
Household and other service	9.0	13.2
Farm		
Farmers and farm managers	19.9	2.9
Farm laborers and foremen	17.7	1.9

Source: The 1900 figures from U.S. Bureau of the Census, *Occupational Trends in the United States: 1900 to 1950,* Bureau of the Census Working Paper No. 5, 1958, Table 2, p. 7. The 1966 figures from *Statistical Abstract of the United States,* 1966, Table 323, p. 229.

segment of the labor force. In addition, the decay of once-important employment industries such as coal mining has brought economic blight to entire regions of the country. Unemployment hovered around 5.5 per cent, or four million unemployed, from 1960 to 1964, only falling below 4 per cent in 1966 as a consequence of a sustained boom to which the Viet Nam war was a contributing factor. These matters have not gone unnoticed in the political order, however, and increasingly greater effort is being made to extend training to those who need it and to seek new industries for regions where old ones have declined. Under the impact of the Manpower Development Training Program, begun in 1962, Federal funds for adult vocational and technical training increased sixteen-fold in three years, nearing the half-billion dollar mark in 1965. Relief for depressed areas has been instituted, and a variety of experiments has been undertaken in the so-called war on poverty.

Looking at the broader pattern of income distribution, the picture is much brighter. There has been a distinct leveling upward, as shown in the following table:

Table 6 Per Cent Distribution of U.S. Families Having Given Money Income in Constant (1964) Dollars, 1947–1964

| | Per Cent of Families | | |
Income Level	1947	1955	1964
Under $3,000	31	24	18
$3,000–4,999	31	24	17
$5,000–6,999	19	24	20
$7,000–9,999	12	18	23
$10,000–14,999	} 7 {	8	16
$15,000 and over		2	6

Adapted from *Statistical Abstract of the United States*, 1966, Table 473, p. 337. Table lists families only, not unrelated individuals.

Put another way, the average incomes received by the lower income groups in the nation have risen at a markedly higher rate in terms of constant dollar buying power than those of the higher income groups:

Table 7 Increase in Average Family Income, United States, 1935–1962

| | Per Cent Increase in Average Income (1950 dollars) | | |
Rank by Size of Income	1935/36 to 1941	1935/36 to 1962	1941 to 1962
Lowest fifth of households	23	120	79
Second " " "	28	136	84
Third " " "	36	131	70
Fourth " " "	33	115	62
Highest " " "	18	74	48
Top 5%	13	47	30
National average	25	98	59

Adapted from *Statistical Abstract of the United States*, 1965, Table 465, p. 340.

The cause of this does not lie in the graduated income tax, which is not deducted in these figures, but reflects such factors as higher wages gained in collective bargaining and in the enforcement of minimum wage laws. In addition, there has been a decrease in the number of hours in the work week, which is a way of distributing the benefits of affluence to the lower economic strata. This decline is not paralleled as closely in the number of hours worked by responsible management personnel. Certainly, the over-all performance of the capitalistic economy has not denied the promises of abundance held out for it, given the guidance that the political order has offered.

Freedom *Versus* Power. The objective of freedom of choice with its concomitant purpose of restraint of arbitrary power has been met only partially. Economically, the range of choice in occupation, investment, and consumer goods is unparalleled. Americans are often accused of a deadening conformity, and the example most commonly cited is the automobile. Even leaving aside all imported car styles, however, the range of choice is almost too broad. The lower price ranges of 1966 models included 57 body styles of Plymouths, 52 Fords, 50 Chevrolets, and 26 American Motors cars. To gain some idea of the magnitude of choice, Ford offered its models in 44 colors, Plymouth offered four different transmissions throughout its line, and engine choices and optional features such as air conditioning and radios made it at least conceivable that no two identical cars would be sold.[63] It can be argued that the purpose thus served is trivial, but it is a reflection of the market principle that popular desires, as reflected in consumer buying choices, shall determine production. Capitalism responds to those desires, whether one chooses to call them trivial or not. It thus fulfills its own objectives and serves its own values possibly at a cost to values that noncapitalistic societies would prefer. It may be noted that where consumer choices do not reflect urgent public needs, the political order may still undertake to supplement them by regulation. The weakness of consumer demand for safety features in automobiles is a case in point. Congressional legislation aimed at requiring safety standards for car manufacturers sought to meet this problem in 1966.

The question of power is more disturbing. American industry displays a high degree of concentration, as does also American labor through its union organizations. Substantial agglomerations of economic, social, and political power exist in the hands of a relatively small number of managers, owners, and labor leaders, as well as in government. The number of mergers among American corporations, after a long period in which it was believed that concentration had substantially reached its limit, has begun to rise again.[64]

[63] William Kilpatrick, "Which 1966 Car is for You?" *Parade,* October 24, 1965, pp. 6–7. It is worth noting that when the American companies found that they had misjudged their market by a failure to offer a "compact" car in the mid-1950s, they reversed their stand and met the demand with a flood of new models. Advertising was not enough to defeat consumer choice.

[64] The latest merger movement, which began to pick up speed in the mid-1950s, is one of diversification. Instead of either horizontal or vertical acquisitions, giant corporations are now acquiring firms that bring them new product lines.

The nature of the problem is apparently clear. Some five to six hundred corporations control about two thirds of American industry.[65] Approximately 30 per cent of all nonagricultural employees are members of the 130 unions affiliated with the AFL-CIO. The decisions made by these giants could thrust the economy into inflation or depression, or bring it to a halt through work stoppages or shutdowns. They make the principal decisions on the directions new investment will take. Individual firms could and sometimes do destroy the economies of cities by moving their operations elsewhere. To add to the problem, the stockholders, numerous as they are, no longer actively control their companies, and the largest stockholders, the pension funds, trusts, and insurance companies, generally refuse to exercise their voting control to hold management accountable. (If they did, they would still represent highly concentrated control.) Does this mean that these concentrations of economic power can and do control American society?

Curiously enough, it is Professor Berle, whose earlier worries on the point have been mentioned, who supplies the negative answer. Restraint of economic power comes partly from the fact that it is not monolithic—that within the economic realm in markets, wage negotiations, and the like, power is restrained by countervailing power, overseen by government agencies that attempt to see to it that no one achieves a monopoly of any form of power. More important, however, is the central fact of capitalism itself, the separation of the institutions for wielding economic power from the institutions of government that wield political and military power. Berle likens this to the separation of powers in the American Constitution. People whose demands are not heeded in the economic order can make them heard in the political order, as the catalogue of government restrictions, regulations, and interventions described in this chapter has shown. The economic giants operate within the framework of what he calls a "public consensus" of which, however indefinite may be its prescriptions, they are most clearly aware. That consensus establishes limits that serve to confine the exercise of economic power largely to the purposes for which it was established: the pursuit of economic growth. When those limits have been violated, that consensus has been enforced by government through revision or reinterpretation of the law, and neither corporate managers nor the labor union officials can and do ignore it.[66] Experiences

[65] Estimated by Adolf A. Berle, Jr., *Power Without Property: A New Development in American Political Economy* (New York: Harcourt, Brace, 1959), p. 53. Much of the ensuing discussion is based on Professor Berle's incisive thought as displayed in this highly readable little book.

[66] As a sidelight, even stockholders, impotent as they are, prod management with reminders of its public responsibility. At the 1965 Annual Meeting of one of the nation's largest corporations, management was asked to reply to questions about keeping its facilities in harmony with the beauty of the countryside, avoidance of air pollution, conservation of the company's own domestic reserves in the interest of national security, and the morality of trading with the Soviet bloc. Conversely, the chairman of the board gently rebuked one shareholder who seemed to be suggesting that the company provoke the United States into war to protect its foreign investments.

such as the seizure of the steel mills by President Truman in 1952 and government intervention in the railway labor dispute in the 1960s indicate that neither labor nor management will be allowed to use its power in a way that will interrupt the basic flow of economic activity. Increasing evidences exist that corporate managements, particularly the managements of the larger corporations, are actively concerned with their social responsibility in the performance of their corporate functions, however much they might privately wish that this were not added to their other cares. The readiness with which American industry responded in 1965 to President Johnson's call for a limitation on foreign spending to help the balance of payments suggests a combination of willingness to accept responsibility and a fear that it will otherwise be enforced. Similar calls to both labor and management to avoid inflationary wage and price rises have been given increasing attention as the willingness of government to follow up a voluntary request with firm action has been demonstrated.

An area in which this pattern of separation and restraint is weakest is the troublesome one of the aerospace industries, atomic research and development, and the other elements of the "civil-military complex." Here there is a power problem that has not been solved, and it is notable that one of the elements of difficulty is its involvement in the international competition for scientific prestige and the military demand for secrecy. As was stated earlier, war is no friend to capitalism, and cold war is not different from "hot war" in that respect. The absence of separation between the two orders in this field is, however, the underlying problem and although it is largely confined to one sector of the economy, that sector is the most rapidly advancing one in technology. The political processes in the United States are not accustomed to this burden of responsibility, but they will need to develop effective checks over this growing cluster of power.

If, in capitalism, government is a restraint on economic power, so also do economic organizations serve to restrain governmental power. Through the organization of interest groups and the mobilization of popular support, business and labor both can on occasion, veto contemplated government action. The veto plays a large role in political activity under capitalism, especially in America.[67] The American political system facilitates its use by its own fragmentation. A veto is, however, a characteristic expression of capitalism's presumption against any increase in government activity above the level already undertaken.

But the limitation of governmental power does not take place only through lobbying. It occurs through the electoral system and public opinion as well. The funds exist to oppose the government of the day, and the private media

[67] The effect of "veto groups" in weakening central power and leadership in American society is well discussed by David Riesman (who authored the term) in *The Lonely Crowd: A Study of the Changing American Character* (New Haven: Yale University Press, 1950), pp. 242–255.

of communications are at least as often critical of public officials as not. No power center is, in fact, safe from the possibility of attack by critics financed out of funds accumulated in private enterprise. Not so long ago great foundations that bear some of the illustrious names from American industrial history —Rockefeller, Ford, and Carnegie among them—were subjected to congressional investigation on the grounds that they were supporting research and writing that was sharply critical (and alleged to be subversive) of the American political system and the economic system as well. It is through their support of the foundations and of great private universities where academic freedom is held sacred, and through the individual support of unpopular and even unlikely causes, that capitalist managers and owners help maintain a climate of critical discussion that holds the state accountable for its actions, and holds the wielders of economic power themselves accountable also.

The goal of freedom is, then, not badly served, although there is far less decentralization of power than might have been expected at the start. The political order, too, plays a much greater role in preserving that freedom than was suggested in the outline with which we began.

Rewards and Recognition. The least measurable of all of the objectives of capitalism is that of reward according to merit, for merit is an ethical standard and will be judged on a slightly different basis by each observer. What can be measured is the degree to which capitalist society affords opportunities for workers to change jobs and rise to higher (or fall to lower) occupations. In this, American experience is impressive. Of all men twenty-five to sixty-four years old in the active labor force in 1962, less than one quarter were in the same occupational class as their fathers. Even more striking is the fact that nearly three quarters of them had changed their occupational category since their first jobs.[68] As may be seen in Table 8, there is literally no limit to the possible rise or fall of an American worker. Some of those who began their working careers in even the lowest occupational categories rose to the top of the occupational hierarchy, and some who began at the top ended as common laborers. In most cases only a small minority of those who started in a given job remained there. American mobility rates are not, as we shall see in Chapter 3, markedly different from those in other countries at a comparable level of industrialization. However, that they are as high as they are suggests not only a system that discriminates on the basis of ability rather than heredity, but one in which positions of leadership, and therefore of power, are not likely to remain in the same families from generation to generation. The immediate *cause* of high mobility is apparently industrialization, but the significant finding here is that, contrary to the claims of Marxists, capitalism does not stifle mobility under a rigid class structure.

[68] U.S. Department of Commerce, Bureau of the Census, "Lifetime Occupational Mobility of Adult Males, March, 1962," *Current Population Reports,* Series P-23, No. 11 (May 12, 1964), pp. 1, 3.

Table 8 Occupational Mobility in the American Labor Force, 1962:
Selected Starting Occupations Compared with Current Occupations
(Males 25 to 64 Years of Age—Figures in Thousands)

Starting Occupation (First Job Held):	Total with indicated starting occupation	Managerial and Professional		White Collar		Blue Collar and Service				Farm		Not in experienced civilian labor force *
		Professional, technical and kindred	Managers, officials and proprietors, except farm	Sales	Clerical and kindred	Craftsmen, foremen and kindred	Operatives, (semiskilled) and kindred	Laborers, except farm and mine	Household and other service	Farmers and farm managers	Farm laborers and foremen	
Farm Laborers and Foremen	5,704	111	403	103	156	977	1,124	542	328	1,101	**398**	461
Household and Service Workers	1,523	115	169	40	76	244	319	126	**302**	6	7	119
Laborers, Except Farm and Mine	5,231	301	528	175	258	1,122	1,226	**740**	348	102	65	366
Clerical and Kindred Workers	4,229	619	960	384	**744**	485	414	119	187	50	9	258
Sales Workers	2,430	277	717	**378**	246	257	305	56	73	21	1	99
Managers, Officials and Proprietors, except farm	719	123	**347**	53	38	55	37	16	13	12	2	23

Boldface figures represent workers in the same occupational group as that in which they started their working lives.
* Includes members of the armed forces and persons no longer in the active work force. Those temporarily unemployed are included in the figures for their normal occupation when employed.
Adapted from U.S. Department of Commerce, Bureau of the Census, "Lifetime Occupational Mobility of Adult Males, March, 1962," *Current Population Reports*, Series P–23, No. 11 (May 12, 1964), Table 2 p. 8.

Further substantiation of mobility in American life, and an indication that it is, if anything, increasing, comes from a comparison of the education of fathers and sons in 1962. In that year, 43 per cent of men fifty-five to sixty-four years old exceeded the educational level of their fathers, while 62 per cent of the younger group, twenty-five to thirty-four years old, did so.[69] Because education correlates closely with earnings and occupational level, this change is most significant. The occupational figures are statistical indications only and do not prove that merit was the principal cause for occupational rise and fall. However, the conclusion is not unreasonable that the capitalist system of the United States does meet the test of providing wide opportunities very well.

Other Social Values.   What have been the effects of capitalism on the outlook and values of society? Here, too, we are on grounds that tempt us to ethical judgment, but there do seem to be some discernible tendencies. Capitalism does not seem to have weakened the traits of generosity and concern for the underdog that were remarked on earlier. In the early years of the Depression, charitable giving actually increased as a percentage of personal consumption expenditures while incomes fell, and it remained high until federal welfare programs began to take hold. At their lowest, contributions never dropped below 71 per cent of their highest previous level (which was attained in 1930), whereas consumption expenditures themselves dropped to 59 per cent of their 1929 high. Since 1935, religious and charitable giving has grown steadily, reaching $10.6 billion in 1964.[70] As national income has risen there has been a small, but perceptible tendency for a larger proportion of it to go to charity. Thus, private charity continues even while an increasing part of government spending goes to fulfill the older functions of charity, and while even further government funds are being spent for foreign aid. As citizens as well as individuals, Americans have retained their capacity for generosity, it seems, and have found it not incompatible with capitalism.

Charitable contributions and welfare and international aid programs alone do not reveal the degree to which the tradition of concern for the disadvantaged has survived, for it is registered even more strongly in the hordes of young people who have marched and demonstrated for the rights of the Negro and other downtrodden minorities. However much they may feel that they are rebelling against the social system, their actions are the clearest possible expression of values that that system has preserved and fostered all along— not only care for the underdog, but disdain for and impatience with political authority as well.

There are other facets, however. The values supported by capitalism have

[69] U.S. Department of Commerce, Bureau of the Census, "Educational Change in a Generation, March, 1962," *Current Population Reports*, Series P–20, No. 132 (September 22, 1964), pp. 1–2.

[70] *Giving USA: A Compilation of Facts Related to American Philanthropy*, 1965 ed. (New York: American Association of Fund-Raising Counsel, Inc., 1965), p. 5.

moved only slowly to eliminate the taint of racial prejudice. It should not be necessary to point out that the institution of slavery, through which race prejudice was impressed upon American life, is not a capitalistic phenomenon, but a feudal, and even antique social pattern. The impact of it on both North and South, however, has been too great to be eradicated as readily as the religious and nationality prejudices that have steadily fallen away, and whose decay was so clearly reflected in the election of the Irish Catholic John F. Kennedy to the Presidency in 1960.[71] There are also some values that seem to have lessened their hold over time. The spirit of community cooperation and neighborly helpfulness has tended to be transformed into a function of specialists. Perhaps this is a consequence of the depersonalized relationships that accompany urban living and large-scale industrial organization, but the signs are very much in evidence that, except in the more rural areas, an American is more likely to call for help from a plumber, carpenter, electrician, or garage mechanic than to ask or expect it from his neighbors or passers-by. The emphasis on self-reliance may lead to this, but there is an uglier side as well. The recently reported cases of people refusing to assist others being attacked by assailants on the street or in subways and busses represents among other things a turning over to the police of a specialized function of protection and help and the abandonment of the same as a personal, individual responsibility.

It would be erroneous to ascribe any one or all of the characteristics discussed entirely or even largely to capitalism, for to do so would be to accept the idea of economic determinism. They are mentioned here as examples, however, in relation to the theme that runs throughout this book: The economic system is a part of the social system, and the values of both will find accommodation in time. It is clear that this analysis could be carried on considerably further, if space would permit.

Capitalism and the Developing Nations

As was indicated at the end of the first chapter, a secondary purpose of this book is to relate the study of the "grand alternatives" to the underdeveloped nations of the world. Our observation of capitalism will conclude with some applications of the lessons learned to this area.

Looking at the objectives and the social and political conditions that have seemed congenial to capitalism, it is apparent that some are lacking in underdeveloped countries. These countries share the desire for abundance, of course,

---

[71] Less widely remarked, but of nearly equal significance, was the fact that the Republican candidate in 1964, Barry Goldwater, had a Jewish grandfather, although the candidate himself is a Protestant. This fact was known, but appeared to have no effect on his nomination, and little, if any, on the campaign. To this may be compared the vilification of Franklin D. "Rosenfeld" during his four campaigns. Roosevelt, of course, is a name of Dutch, not Jewish, extraction, but this did not seem to deter the bigoted in his day.

but it is doubtful that there is any particularly strong feeling about freedom of choice, because of the lingering traces of traditionalism. For the same reason, a concept of reward on the basis of merit alone is at least not shared by the wielders of traditional authority, however much it may have affected the more Western-oriented segments of the population. These countries need time to change, and time is one commodity they do not have to spare.

Social conditions are especially unfavorable. Where a Westernized elite has taken over, there is a gap between segments of the native population, which tempts the new rulers to exploit their backward fellows, as the freed American slaves have done for so long in Liberia. This gap will tend to become both social and economic in nature, creating a class structure and a sense of class feeling that is clearly different from the fluid conditions in which American capitalism thrived. If a substantial population of ex-colonials remains the situation is even worse, for a parallel structure of race and economic class results, caused by the normally greater prosperity of the Western-oriented colonials. From these observations one seems forced to conclude that the best prospects for capitalist development lie in countries from which the ex-colonials have totally departed, and in which either the bulk of the population is educated and Westernized, or conversely almost entirely un-Westernized, so that there is no exploiting class large enough to maintain itself. In the latter case, of course, development would likely be unbearably slow.

The political problem for most of these countries is the lack of popular understanding of, and feeling for democratic government. Authoritarian rulers find it difficult indeed to tolerate competing powers and nonofficial decision-making, and this is what capitalism pre-eminently demands. To the extent that democratic procedures prove unworkable, these nations will tend toward authoritarian governments and an economy of command to match. Whether this is done benevolently or exploitatively will make no difference so far as capitalism is concerned: It will not be present in any significant way.

If the values and the social and political conditions present a rather bleak outlook for capitalism, the economic conditions are little better. The poverty that characterizes most of them hampers them at the start with an abnormally low level of aggregate demand and gives little incentive to the entrepreneur to offer his wares. Entrepreneurship is largely lacking in the native population, not because of any racial inferiority, but because the social conditions that produce it are lacking. The entrepreneurial functions that are exercised there are typically performed by non-natives—invading, colonizing, and trading populations such as the whites in Africa and the Chinese throughout Asia. Finally, the economies of these nations are generally marked by a widespread domination of monopoly, often in the hands of the same non-natives just referred to. Competition must be introduced to make capitalism work, but the power of the Westernized or non-native elite is often enough to call governmental power to their aid in resisting competitive intrusions.

Are there any measures that capitalist nations can take that might serve to change these conditions in capitalism's favor? Yes, but the prospects of their being undertaken or succeeding are slim. No amount of mere propaganda can shift people's attitudes into a flat contradiction of reality, if that reality is an ever-present starvation. In order to gain the optimistic outlook that under-girds capitalism through the vicissitudes that threaten it and the growing pains it causes, a people must be able to actually see progress happening. This means massive aid, aid on a scale that will run ahead of the population growth and pour purchasing power into the economy in an impressive and widely distributed fashion. Efforts must be made to promote native, and native wants-serving industries, rather than the extractive and trading ventures that are normally chosen by non-native capitalists because of their ability to earn the currency of the capitalist's home country. Only a successful domestic industry will give any assurance of the sustained growth that brings capitalism's promises to fruition.[72] Finally, and the catalogue will end here not because all aspects have been covered, but because enough has been shown for our pur-poses, the foreign capitalist must be prepared to withdraw in orderly fashion just about at the time when his ventures have proved most lucrative. He must leave the blossoming economy in native hands, so that no cause for economically irrelevant (that is, purely nationalistic) resentment against the owners and managers of industry will be given, and class feeling will have no clear object on which to fasten.

Capitalism, then, seems to be a system of rather limited application in the modern world, with only a few countries presently espousing it unreservedly and with no great prospects for additions to their number in societies not yet matured. To say this, however, is to overstate the case. Capitalism did dom-inate the Western world for about a century, and it still plays a part in the economies of most of the developed nations. Why it has been partially sup-planted in them, and what these countries are trying to do thereby, is the substance of the next three chapters.

[72] Enlightened American and foreign businessmen are beginning to foster native cap-italism by providing capital to native industries. A prime example is the Adela Invest-ment Company, which is supported by 120 major firms in Japan, Europe, and North America and provides capital for Latin American native enterprises. Standard Oil of New Jersey is also engaged in promoting the local economies of Venezuela, Colombia, and Jamaica with minority equity investments and technical help.

3 / Socialism[1]

In the United States capitalism found a congenial environment from the start, brought widespread and rapid increases in prosperity, and created relatively little social dislocation, because a rigid and hierarchical social structure had not taken root there, except in the South. Europe was not so fortunate, and the growth of industry produced not only capitalism, but broad movements of unrest and resentment against the strains and distortions that its introduction wrought in the social and economic fabric.

From these movements there arose a new politico-economic ideology, socialism, founded upon many of the same aspirations and expectations of human betterment that underlay the liberal tradition in capitalist thought. It was, however, directed against abuses that attended capitalist industrialization in a political and social environment far less fluid and adaptable than that which existed in North America.

Modern socialism, then, like capitalism, was an outgrowth of the Industrial Revolution. Its reference was to the economic and political organization of

[1] The discussion of socialism is beset with a problem of nomenclature. Economic theorists apply the term, *socialist,* to economic systems characterized by public ownership of the means of production. Thus they include the Communist bloc nations in general theoretical discussions of socialism, and often decline to include countries like Norway and Sweden (which have or have had socialist governments), on the grounds that their economies are only partly in public ownership and are, therefore, at most, "mixed." Common usage (which this book employs) distinguishes between socialism and communism roughly along the lines represented by socialist and communist *parties* in a Western democracy. Communism is the doctrine espoused (in varying forms) by the Soviet Union, Red China, and their associated parties and satellites. Socialism, in the terms used here, refers to the Western, evolutionary, democratic parties and movements in the socialist tradition, and to the ideals and doctrines they espouse. From time to time the phrase *democratic socialism* will be used instead of simply "socialism" as a reminder of this distinction.

industrial society. Yet its protest was against conditions of life that were only partly caused by the rising capitalistic system. It protested, as well, against the lingering trappings of feudal and aristocratic society that were slow to disappear, and that even now survive in vestigial form in the cultures of many European countries. From this fact arise three important characteristics of socialism: First, its doctrines vary from country to country in accordance with the differing conditions against which protest was made. Secondly, it includes elements of protest against social and political conditions that are not of capitalist origin, but are of much longer standing; in this, it shares a heritage derived from social protest throughout the ages. Thirdly, it has changed its main emphasis over time as those conditions themselves have changed.

All three of these characteristics are shown in one of the more important recent works on socialism, *The Future of Socialism,* written by one of the intellectual leaders of the "right wing" of the British socialist movement, C. A. R. Crosland.[2] Read as a whole, this book displays to a remarkable degree an emphasis on noneconomic questions; indeed, the final section of the author's chapter of conclusions is entitled, "Cultural and Amenity Planning; and the Declining Importance of Economic Problems." The chief thrust of the work, based upon the changes that have occurred in Britain in the last several decades, is toward the elimination not of economic inequalities but of the class privileges that still survive as carry-overs from preindustrial times, and that have, in Britain's unique social system, become merged with the privileges arising out of economic inequality. Crosland wrote in an effort to promote revision of socialist doctrine to accord with the current state of British life. It is this continuous willingness to change and adapt that poses the chief difficulty in an attempt to define the doctrines and beliefs of modern socialists.

The Development of Socialist Ideas

One consequence of the mixed nature of socialist protest is the fact that, while there is general agreement in naming the leading figures of socialist thought in the nineteenth and twentieth centuries, there is none when it comes to naming the first socialist. This designation has been placed upon men as divergent in thought and time, for example, as Jean-Jacques Rousseau and Jesus of Nazareth. Because, however, we have identified socialism as a modern ideology, we shall start with François Noël Babeuf, who at least reminds us that he has a philosophical heritage by his adoption of the pseudonym, "Gracchus."[3] Although his actual contribution to socialist theory was slight,

---

[2] Rev. ed. (New York: Schocken Books, 1957). Although frequently cited here, this writer should make it clear that Crosland does not represent the thinking of his party, but only that of its "right" or moderate wing.

[3] The reference is to Tiberius and Caius Gracchus, brothers, who were Roman Tribunes in the second century B.C., and who were associated with land reform and other measures for the betterment of the poor.

and he wrote and acted before the Industrial Revolution in France, he was in many ways representative of some very pervasive currents in socialist belief and feeling.

Babeuf was the leader of a short-lived conspiracy that attempted, in 1796, to carry the French revolutionary ideals of equality and liberty to their ultimate conclusion in the abolition of ownership of property and the establishment of what he called the True Republic. His thought was heavily influenced by Rousseau, but he stood, not for a return to nature, but for the employment of all the productive resources of his own time to give men equal living standards at whatever level the technology could produce. It is this that makes his writing specifically modern and applicable to an industrial age. Babeuf had no clear plan for achieving his Republic, but he voiced hopes and longings that have been expressed time and again in socialist writing when he decribed this happy state that would bring the disappearance of

> . . . all crimes, tribunals, prisons, gibbets, and punishments; of the despair that causes all calamity; and of greed, jealousy, insatiability, pride, deception, and duplicity—in short, of all vices. Furthermore (and the point is certainly essential), it will put an end to the gnawing worm of perpetual inquietude, whether throughout society as a whole, or privately within each of us, about what tomorrow will bring, or at least what next year will bring, for our old age, for our children and for their children.[4]

Here Babeuf painted a picture that, however firmly rejected in principle by the so-called scientific school of socialists as "utopian," [5] has remained a part of the popular mythology of socialism. It was an appeal directed to those aspects of the life of the poorer classes from which they were most anxious to escape. It was an optimistic vision—a vision of progress—but not one to be achieved by individual self-betterment. Rather, it required the building of a new society by cooperative effort.

Babeuf's principal experience had been with the evils of a landowning feudal aristocracy. It remained for his successors to declaim against the horrors of industrial life. Of necessity, the scene now shifts to England where the factory system was quickest to take hold. The English Industrial Revolution was accompanied by some of the most severe social dislocations that attended any of the early industrializations. Some recent efforts have been made to show that the plight of the factory workers at the time (1790 to 1830)

[4] The selection is from Babeuf's defense at his trial for conspiracy to overthrow the government, February to May, 1797, translated by Ronald Sanders in *Socialist Thought: A Documentary History*, Albert Fried and Ronald Sanders, eds. (Garden City, N.Y.: Doubleday Anchor Books, 1964), p. 68. Babeuf was convicted and died on the guillotine.

[5] In fact, not even the "scientific" socialists were able to exclude this element from their thinking, for like all reformers, they, too, had a vision of a better world, that they hoped to see become reality.

was at least no worse than that of the poor among the agricultural population,[6] but this tends to miss the point. The dislocation was caused by the enclosure movements that affected the rural population in the first instance and led them to crowd into the cities seeking work. What horrified the more sensitive among the English of all classes was the effect of seeing so many poor crowded together in the cities instead of dispersed in the countryside. And it was, in fact, the more well-to-do among the British who provided the chief voices of a distinctly British socialism and who took action to ameliorate the condition of the poor. The latter, lacking the vote (which they had tried in vain so far to obtain) were dependent on paternalistic champions, of whom no better example can be given than Robert Owen.

Owen was born in 1771, the son of a saddlemaker, and rose by his own efforts to become the owner of a small cotton-spinning mill at the age of eighteen. At twenty-eight he became part owner and manager of the largest mill in Scotland, at New Lanark. In that capacity he devised and operated a community in which he attempted, by education, high wages, and careful supervision of his workmen, to improve both their condition in life and their moral outlook. From there it was but a short step, which he took in about 1817, to attempt to organize cooperative communities of workers in England, and later, the United States. Despite having made a profitable success out of the operation at New Lanark, he came to regard profit as an evil unnecessary to production and hoped to reform social life by emphasis on morality and cooperation in the education of the young.[7] His cooperative movement, then, was more than an effort to provide fair shares. It was a moral and social reconstruction of society based on the belief that human character was largely formed through training and was perfectible by means within man's own control. He looked toward a new world in which harmonious cooperation would replace competitive struggle and men would come to recognize their interdependence—their reliance on one another—in society. Aside from the operation at New Lanark and a handful of other brief-lived cooperatives, Owen failed to achieve his hoped-for reconstruction. Through his writings, agitation, and influence with prominent public officials, however, he was able to affect the trend of social legislation and the adoption of factory laws that provided some protection for the workers. In this he was by no means alone, for there were many in British society willing to do battle for the disadvantaged, and who felt, with Adam Smith, that "no society can surely be flourishing and happy, of which the far greater part of the members are poor and miserable."[8]

[6] See, for example, the last two essays (by T. S. Ashton and W. H. Hutt) in *Capitalism and the Historians*, F. A. Hayek, ed. (Chicago: Phoenix Books, University of Chicago Press, 1954).

[7] In his later years Owen, after discouraging experiences with his communities, participated in the trade union movement, then in a variety of other causes culminating in an intense interest in spiritualism. It was as the founder of cooperative socialism in England, however, that he left his greatest mark.

[8] *Wealth of Nations*, Book I, ch. VIII.

English socialism was much affected by the concern for the workers displayed by those outside of the working class. Despite the really abominable conditions of lower-class British life throughout most of the nineteenth century and the strong sense of class-consciousness that still pervades its society, there has been less bitterness and sense of class war in the British movement than there was in France and Germany. Important, also, has been the contribution of the middle and upper classes to socialist theory—best represented by the Fabian Society, most of whose active members have been in at least tolerable financial circumstances. These two factors help account for the degree to which British socialism has been among the most "revisionist" of all the European movements and the most imbued with "conventional" morality. The fact that the British movement had, through the Fabians, access to men of power in the political system also lessened the need for extremism and violent action to express its demands. But it was neither the inchoate thought of Babeuf nor the paternalistic idealism of Owen that gave socialism its distinctive vision. That came from the last of the three great Western European powers to industrialize, Germany, in the thought and writings of Karl Marx.[9]

The intellectual heritage of Marx, like that of Babeuf, was drawn from before the Industrial Revolution in his own country. Steeped in the ideas of a group of philosophers known as "Neo-Hegelians," he, like they, sought to find in the complex web of history a single explanatory principle to give it meaning. He took from Hegel the idea that history was a process of advances in stages marked by conflicts that destroyed the old in order to make way for the new. But where Hegel had viewed all history as directed and determined by the stages of growth of a "world spirit" or *ideal,* Marx "stood him on his head," and identified the *process of technological change and innovation* as the moving force in history. History, according to Marx, was directed by changes that occurred in the forces of production. Each stage of man's development was determined by the particular form of production—simple farming, small-scale manufacture, and so on—that existed at the time. This was so because the form of production required a particular set of social relations to make it operate. Small-scale manufacture, for example, required the individually owned factory, which placed workers in subjection to a single capitalist employer. These social relations were the basis for the formation of classes—the exploiting and the exploited—which were naturally antagonistic toward one another and whose conflict was the principal content of history. In particular, this conflict was to eventuate in a revolutionary overthrow of the capitalist system and the establishment of a *classless* society in its stead. Upon this was founded that particular branch of socialism known as Marxism

---

[9] Marx had such an influence on the whole body of socialist thought that it would be impossible to discuss democratic socialism without him. For this reason, he is introduced in this chapter, rather than Chapter 4, which deals with communism. As we shall see, quite divergent strains of thought have developed out of his writing, and those who claim to follow his views have modified his theory greatly.

or "scientific socialism." This later was divided into the two streams represented by Russian and Chinese communism and their controlled parties in Western and developing countries on the one hand, and Marxist social democratic parties on the other.[10] But Marx had an impact beyond the particular schools of his followers, for he crystallized Socialist resentment against inequalities by relating it directly to *class structure*. From the time of his writing, class became a commonplace in the language of socialists of all descriptions, where it had been merely an occasional reference before. For Marx, history was to culminate in a classless society; for all socialists, the obstacle to the equality they sought became not mere individual *inequality*, but *class*.

Marx' writing is an extraordinary study in contrasts. He erected an imposing logical structure, purporting to describe in coldly scientific fashion the laws of historical development and the sources of economic and social power. Yet the words he used were impassioned and inflammatory; they lent themselves far better to the cause of Marx, the revolutionist than to that of Marx, the scientific philosopher. It is no wonder that his influence has long survived the failure of his predictions and the disproof of much of his reasoning. The course of historical development, as Marx saw it, followed laws of its own. Although human wills were active in it, the decisions men made were forced upon them in such a way that they could not decide or will otherwise. In essence it ran something like this:[11] The destruction of the feudal order, which was violently symbolized in the French Revolution, was accomplished by a newly emerged class, the bourgeoisie, under whom a new development of the technology of production was occurring. Unable to pursue this development effectively under the repressions of feudalism, they had thrown the old order off and established the bourgeois state, which was perfectly adapted to the form of economic organization, the small factory system, that the new technology required. The technology was the underpinning and the controlling force that shaped the rest of the structure. The factory system, with the capitalist owner in control and the workers subject to his direction, provided the best means of organizing the relations between men in the productve process. The State, finally, was the necessary instrument of the owning class—the bourgeoisie—to keep the workers—the proletariat—at their tasks.

At this point an economic theory enters, mostly derived from David Ricardo, asserting that the only measure of the value of a product is the labor that went into making it. The capitalist subsists on profits that he gets in a

[10] Marx called his theory communism, in order to distinguish it from the "unscientific" socialisms of his day. This designation was picked up by the Russian movement and its followers, whereas the evolutionary Marxists preferred to stress the tie between Marx and the rest of the socialist movement.

[11] Because it is not necessary to the purposes of this book to describe Marx' theory of history in full, only that part covering the capitalist period and the communist revolution will be given.

curious way: For each of the factors of production he uses, he must pay at least the value of the labor required to make it available. But labor itself is available at only as much cost as is needed to keep a man alive. The capitalist, then, can employ labor for a wage that is only enough to provide subsistence but, once hired, can work his workers as long as he needs to in order to gain his profit. Every hour worked beyond the minimum that would provide the value of a subsistence wage produces "surplus value" for the capitalist. So far, everything looks rather pleasant for the capitalist. But at this point competition is encountered. Under pressure from his competitors the capitalist must do two things: Introduce technological improvements in his productive processes and keep wages as low and working hours as long as he can. Both of these he must do if he is to cut costs and meet competitive prices. Despite these efforts some capitalists lose, and others grow richer and build larger and larger industrial empires as time goes on. Thus driven, the capitalist keeps on improving the technology of production, despite the fact that, unlike human labor, machines produce no surplus value. They can only add to the value of the merchandise produced, the actual cost of their purchase and maintenance. The more machines, the fewer jobs there are, and the more successfully wages can be kept down. But the lower also are profits, and the more intense the competitive struggle. One by one the weaker firms succumb to the stronger; ownership is concentrated in fewer hands. The capitalist class is reduced in size, and the proletariat grows. The new methods of production no longer "fit" too well with the bourgeois pattern of society. They produce monopolies instead of competition; they breed overproduction and depression; worst and most dangerous of all, they require large factories instead of small, and crowd the workers closer and closer together, making them aware of one another and of their common plight. Increasingly the State is relied on as the coercive arm of the bourgeoisie to hold the workers in subjection. Finally, realizing their numbers and their misery, the workers revolt, take the now fully developed technological apparatus from the hands of the last remaining capitalists and operate it themselves. The State then serves for a time as the vehicle for a "dictatorship of the proletariat" to suppress the remnants of the defeated bourgeoisie, after which, no longer needed because there is no one to keep in subjection any more, it withers away.

One must pause and stand in awe, not only of the fact that Marx predicted industrial concentration long before it actually took place, but of the breath-taking inevitability of the whole series of events. It is this that Marxists regard as the "scientific" aspect of Marxism. Here there is no soft do-gooder setting up a utopian community; here is the course of history laid bare!

Yet the verbal raiment in which Marx clothed his theory is of quite a different description. The exaction of "surplus value" from the workers, which is the life-blood of the system, is given the name, "exploitation"; capital is likened to a vampire, and capitalists are expropriators. The struggle between the capitalist and the proletariat classes, which is inevitable, becomes a holy war of the oppressed against the blood-sucking oppressors. *Das Kapital,* which was a massive historical study of capitalism, becomes indistinguishable from the *Manifesto,* which was a revolutionary pamphlet. Marx' theory was based upon faulty economics and even worse sociology.[12] However, he had focused attention on a number of ideas which, extracted from their theoretical context (as ideas always are when they are popularized), seemed to carry conviction when applied to the social and economic conditions of life in various countries of the West.

The prime example of this is in his concept of class. Social stratification is a phenomenon that is manifest in varying degrees of intensity from one country to another. As has already been suggested, the people of the United States are not very conscious of rigidities in the social structure that might tend to divide them into classes, but most European peoples are.[13] It seems fairly obvious that clear divisions of society into social classes—the kinds that tend to prevent those born into a low social position from rising higher—are not phenomena born of capitalism, but are survivals from traditional society that have become adapted to and merged with the differences in wealth that occur in capitalism. Marx, however, had argued that class inequalities were as natural to capitalism as they were to feudalism, and that they would not disappear until private ownership of the means of production itself disappeared. In this, he had provided a link between the socialists' yearnings for equality, their distaste for the ugliness and misery of factory conditions, and their consciousness that, whatever the reason, the social structure *was* rigid, and there *was* antagonism between those who regarded themselves as superior and those who felt more lowly placed within it.[14]

The emphasis on classes had another effect upon socialism in general, although more so on the Continent than in Britain. Despite the fact that there were members of the more favored strata of society who might espouse Marxism because of intellectual conviction and moral distaste for the inequalities of opportunity and recognition that society offered, the concept of class struggle tended to be a self-fulfilling prophecy. Parties that espoused Marxism could hardly be acceptable to the classes they denounced, and such political parties, as they arose, drew their membership largely from the working

[12] For a penetrating analysis of the strengths and weaknesses of Marx in these two fields, see Joseph A. Schumpeter, *Capitalism, Socialism and Democracy,* 3rd ed. (New York: Harper & Brothers, 1950), chs. II, III.

[13] Class feeling is relatively weak in Scandinavia, which helps to explain both the ability of Scandinavian socialist and nonsocialist parties to work together, and the mild and revisionist nature of Scandinavian socialism, which is nevertheless regarded as being derived from Marxism.

[14] Marx' stress on the relationship between mechanization and unemployment under capitalism was another point that struck a responsive chord, especially in England. There the Luddite movement had already demonstrated popular fear of joblessness by destroying machinery in the mills. Even today we face similar fears brought about by automation.

classes. The political system tended to become split into socialist and "bourgeois" parties and the solution of political questions was rendered difficult because of the lack of a common ground on which to reach agreement. This held so long as workers' parties cleaved to a fairly consistent Marxist line. Indeed, a number of the continental parties, convinced that bourgeois democracy was a sham, declined to participate in coalition governments right up until the "Popular Front" governments of the 1930s. By denying themselves governmental power and leaving it in the hands of parties devoted to capitalism and often run by rather short-sighted capitalists, they fed their own belief in the reality of the class struggle.[15]

Finally, Marx had, almost unwittingly, tied the humanistic aspirations of utopian socialism to the bitter antagonisms of the class struggle. He never undertook to describe the society that would emerge after the communist revolution. Aside from the references to the "classless society" and the "withering away of the State," [16] he left, as it were, an empty frame to be filled with whatever idyllic picture the mind of man could contrive. What he did say was that the harsh miseries of the factory and the hatred of class against class were leading inevitably to this—that the struggle was for a good purpose and was justified despite the apparent harm that was done. Because he really did not define the goal, he gave all socialists an appearance of a common objective that allowed them to meet together, despite differences about means, and to influence one another in its pursuit. That they could not stay together once the difference of means became important is no matter; [17] his vagueness on the goal allowed his influence to penetrate the thinking of those who could not accept the whole body of his theory.

It is largely in their sharing of a glittering and ill-defined vision of an egalitarian future society, and in their outrage at the condition of industrial man under capitalism, that one can find common ground among all of the disparate groups that went to make up the socialist movement and that joined together from time to time in international associations to further the workers' cause. There were anarchists—followers of Proudhon in France and of

[15] German socialists (and some in other countries) were so alienated from their government after the Bismarckian repressions that many of them actively advocated refusal to serve their country in the First World War on the grounds that this was a capitalist war, of no concern to the workers. After the fall of the German Empire in 1919, they were compelled by circumstances to accept governing responsibility, but were so little prepared for cooperation with the other democratic parties of the Weimar Republic that they were unable to govern in crisis. The bulk of French socialists declined to serve in cabinets until 1936. British socialists were an exception to this for reasons discussed earlier: they developed a class-oriented party without substantial "class war" feeling and, thus, without a strong tendency to alienation.

[16] This image comes actually from Friedrich Engels, Marx' collaborator.

[17] Marx himself, as leader of the international socialist movement, was the most intolerant of differences of all his contemporaries. He was able to dominate the First International (1864 to 1876), but considerable revisionism entered the Second (1889 to 1923).

Bakunin and Kropotkin in several countries—who agreed with Marx that the State was an instrument solely of oppression, but who felt that the "Great Vision" would become reality merely by obliterating all political authority. There were the followers of Ferdinand Lassalle in Germany who, rather than destroy the State, demanded universal and direct suffrage to give the workers control of it and make it serve them. There were syndicalists, largely French, and guild socialists, their milder English cousins, who hoped to reorganize society in the form of worker-run industries.[18] There were the cooperativists—heirs of Owen—and the Fabians, those idealistic but pragmatic and empirical, step-by-step remolders of society, who combined a humane concern for the workingman with a patronizing and at times puritan desire to improve him.

Finally, there were the revisionists—heirs of Marx himself—who accepted Marx' thesis, while recognizing that his predictions of actual historical development had failed. Gradually under their influence, the Western stream of Marxism turned from revolution to the ballot box for the achievement of the classless society. Some of them, such as Jean Jaurès in France, were the actual leaders of their parties, whereas others, like Eduard Bernstein in Germany, remonstrated with their compatriots at some remove. In the end their efforts were successful in producing a modified brand of Marxism that stood with the champions of liberal democracy against both the totalitarian extremism of the Right, and the new Moscow-dominated Marxist (communist) parties of the Left. It is this, along with moderate socialism in the British tradition and its counterparts elsewhere, that makes up the mainstream of democratic socialist thought today.

The interplay of ideas among proponents of various schools of socialism has had an impressive effect in bringing them toward a common ground, but perhaps the most significant recent influence has been the actual participation of socialists in the governance of their countries. The years since the Second World War have seen socialist governments in power at various times in England, Sweden, Norway, Denmark, Australia, and New Zealand and socialists serving as essential and responsible members of parliamentary governing coalitions in a number of other countries. A few socialist parties had shared governing responsibility even before the war. Because socialism originated as a protest movement, its ideas concerning the best methods of actually running a political and economic system were largely formed in a vacuum. Experience in government has modified socialist ideas markedly, as already shown by the reference to the work of C. A. R. Crosland at the beginning of this chapter. Even on the Continent and in parties that have not yet held majority power, such as the Social Democratic party (SPD) of West Germany, much of the rigidity and most of the harshness of Marxist doctrine have disappeared. It

---

[18] The chief spokesman for syndicalism was Georges Sorel, and for guild socialism, G. D. H. Cole. Both movements lasted only to the end of the First World War, and Cole went on to become one of the leaders and, ultimately, president of the Fabian Society.

could not be said that the goals of the movement have been abandoned, but the means by which socialists now seek to implement them are greatly changed, as we shall see.

The Objectives of Socialism

As should be evident from the foregoing, socialism arose as a humanitarian response to the oppressive and degrading conditions of European life in the nineteenth century. In this respect, it was allied to the whole liberal tradition of reform and pursuit of social justice, an alliance that was shown not only in its ultimate relaxation from the illiberal and intransigent posture that Marx had urged on his followers, but also in the continued presence of liberal humanitarians in and at the fringes of the movement. The goals of socialism are widely shared in Western culture. In some countries, indeed, they are so similar to or at least consistent with the generally agreed-upon values of society that governments dominated by nonsocialist parties, seeking to serve those values, have undertaken policies that were perfectly consistent with what socialists would have done, had they been in control.[19]

The world a socialist seeks to build is one of equality, cooperativeness, harmony, order, and sharing. One senses that he is not greatly confident that economic life will be abundant,[20] and he is determined that none shall enjoy an undue and unearned advantage in the use of what there is. For similar reasons, he is intolerant of waste, whether of human resources or of materials: He emphasizes planning both for the opportunity it offers to direct production into activities he feels are desirable and for the benefits he expects in the elimination of errors of overproduction in some lines, unnecessary duplication of facilities, and the general waste that occurs when a firm, having miscalculated its chances, fails and throws its workers and its productive facilities out of work. In his society there is freedom from want and from economic oppression, and an absence of aggressive and competitive hostility. Private individuals lack the power to control the lives and economic welfare of others. It is, in its fullest sense, a *community,* in which all participate gladly and help one another. Each does his part for the good of the whole, and not because of a nagging fear that he will starve if he does not or because of a selfish hope for gain that will enable him to lord it over his fellows. The socialist's world is a

[19] Cases in point are the four major nationalizations (Port of London, London Passenger Transport Board, British Broadcasting Corporation, and Central Electricity Board) that were done in Britain before 1945, three of them by the Conservative party and one by the Liberals. Even in the United States Norman Thomas points proudly to policies his Socialist party once proposed that are now law. Most of these, however, are not uniquely socialistic in nature; they include such things as social security and aid to education.

[20] By no means all socialists would agree to this, but at least until very recently abundance has ranked lower as a realizable objective among socialists than such things as social justice and equality.

more orderly place than the capitalist utopia, and the virtues it favors are the milder ones of kindness, cooperativeness, mutual concern, and dedication.

It is noteworthy that an attempt, such as the one here, to describe the ideal world of a socialist relies only partly on affirmations. Inevitably there creep in negations of conditions that the socialist sees, or feels that he sees, in capitalism. The reactive and reformist nature of socialism accounts for this, and the aspects of capitalism against which socialism reacts are not mere caricatures, but actual conditions that have existed and often do exist in capitalist societies. Most socialists do not deny the achievements of capitalism, but they concentrate understandably upon areas in which existing capitalist systems have failed to achieve conditions approaching the capitalist ideal sketched earlier. Indeed, there is some evidence to suggest that the strength of the socialist movement, and the degree to which it is doctrinaire and even revolutionary in a given country, is inversely related to the degree to which capitalism in that country has attained its own objectives, especially that of abundance.[21] Certainly the weakness of the socialist movement in the United States suggests this. Lest too great a stress be put on this interpretation, however, it should also be recalled that the success of socialism is at least equally closely related to the compatibility between the values it supports and those of the culture in which it arises. Again the example of Great Britain is instructive, and that of the Scandinavian countries as well. Here are found the strongest *and* the least doctrinaire socialist parties in the world.

Accepting the fact that socialist objectives are at least partially framed in reactive terms, we may now proceed to state them. As in the case of capitalism, the list will be kept small in order to concentrate on those most central and most highly ranked. Three prominent objectives appear to be common to all branches of socialism today: *Social control of economic power, substantial social equality,* and *a cooperative and harmonious society.*

Social Control of Economic Power. To the socialist, capitalism has meant principally the abuse of great power by private individuals whose power was derived from their control over the economic destinies of other men. Marx, it is true, praised the material achievements of capitalism, but for all socialists that achievement has been insufficient compensation for the degradations and the suffering that workers have endured in mines and sweatshops at the bidding of callous owners and their agents. It is not necessary at this point to argue the question of whether abuses of this sort were really widespread, or whether or not the workers were really worse off in the sweatshop in comparison with working as tenant farmers or farm laborers. It is important only that it is a humanitarian sense of outrage that examples of these conditions can and do occur in a capitalist system that motivates socialists and provides their first

[21] Seymour Martin Lipset, *Political Man: The Social Bases of Politics* (Garden City, N.Y.: Doubleday Anchor Books, 1963), pp. 45–53. Lipset also indicates, however (pp. 53–57), that *rapid* economic development is similarly productive of extremism.

objective. Crosland himself best expresses that outrage when he lists as the first ideal of socialism, ". . . a protest against the material poverty and physical squalor *which capitalism produced.*" [22] In order to correct such abuses, socialists propose to place economic power in the hands of the community, represented in most cases by the political order.[23] Only if the community has the power to direct the conditions of employment, they feel, will social justice result.

Socialism's objection to private economic power rests not only on the possibility of its abuse against workers, but also on three further grounds: that it tends to divert production from socially desirable uses into ones that are frivolous and harmful; that it tends to count as costs of production only those charged to the private owner and not the social costs that arise when land is laid bare, or air is polluted, or people are thrown out of work as side effects of economic development; and that it tends to rob democracy of its meaning, by giving undue political influence to its possessors, destroying the political equality on which democracy depends. The third of these is closely related to the question of equality in general, with which the next section deals, but the other two will be commented on briefly here.

Private economic power means, in part, private decisions guiding the allocation of resources to production. We saw in our earlier discussion that this included both the ability of the private entrepreneur to choose what he could produce, so long as there were buyers, and the ability of consumers to influence production through their choices in the market. The private owner or manager will direct his efforts toward the fields of greatest profit. To the socialist, the expenditure of vast sums in producing luxury goods for those who can afford them and the mass production of trivial or even harmful products, such as cosmetics, comic books, and liquor—while useful social services such as education, housing, and recreation suffer neglect—are indefensible, and so innately a part of the capitalist system that the system must be replaced if the balance is to be redressed. In this, the socialist makes a distinction, consciously or unconsciously, between human wants and human needs, and feels that the latter will be served better if the community, and not private persons, control productive resoures.[24]

Crowded slums, polluted streams, smog, hillsides laid open to erosion by strip mining and timber-cutting, sprawling suburban developments, and ugly and garish commercial areas find few defenders anywhere. To socialists, these are among the ineradicable social costs of capitalism—costs that are borne

[22] Crosland, *op. cit.,* (Italics are mine.) p. 67.

[23] The major socialist parties favor giving it to the State, although some variants of socialism, notably cooperative socialism and guild socialism, would choose a smaller unit: the local community and the workers' organizations, respectively.

[24] This reflects the attitude that there is not an unlimited future supply of resources, for the argument rests heavily on the idea that a choice must be made between alternative uses of what is at hand. The distinction between wants and needs is not made in capitalism. See Chapter 2, p. 47.

by the community while the corresponding rewards go to the private power-wielders whose undeviating pursuit of profit causes them. Regulation to re-impose those costs upon owners, as we saw was done in capitalist societies, is not regarded as sufficient, because it usually does not come until much damage has been done and is never complete. The solution, then, is seen in removing the power to do such damage from private hands in the expectation that no community, acting as a community, would do such things to itself.

Substantial Social Equality. The goal of equality is both an affirmation and a reaction. It is socialism's link with social protest in the past and its ideal-ized picture of the future. It is the heart of the socialist's struggle against class privileges and against the great inequalities of income and wealth that occur under unbridled capitalism. Finally, it is the direct counterpart of the capitalist objective of recognition and reward on the basis of merit, placed in a social context in which that recognition seems permanently denied by an unbending class structure. Where a capitalist sees the possibility of replacing a fixed ordering of classes by a fluid, but diversified social structure, the socialist implicitly accepts the Marxian assertion that class is an integral part of any society in which inequalities of wealth and property exist. Where the capitalist asks only for equality of *opportunity* the socialist seeks equality of *condition*. We can see here the importance of experience in the selection of goals.

Socialist attitudes toward equality have undergone change in recent years. Formulated in the abstract, the goal of equality was an absolute and was applied to the sharing of the social product as well as to matters of social status. The Marxian formula, "From each according to his ability to each according to his needs," and the various utopian and anarchistic plans for the total abolition of private property were all developed relatively early. With the exception of a number of experimental utopian communities, however, all of them failures, socialists in power have done little more than attempt to reduce extreme inequalities by taxation and redistribution of wealth. Whether or not the goal of absolute equality has been abandoned, the emphasis has shifted to a focus on social rigidities that arise from hereditary right, educa-tional advantages, and other phenomena only partly economic in nature. Most socialists today accept the use of differential rewards to provide incentives, although they may bemoan the fact that people have been so trained and edu-cated that these are necessary. Equality is not to be "absolute," but "substantial."

This modification of the objective should not lead one to the conclusion that it has become unimportant. On the contrary, the ideal of equality is the most enduring and central rallying point around which socialists can unite. Even in a society that gives substantial benefits and protection to the workers, the presence of severe class distinctions can keep a socialist movement alive and vigorous. It speaks to the frustrations of laboring men who feel that they are not receiving their just recognition as human beings and as constructive contributors to national well-being. An important result of the modification, however, has been to make the goal less specifically economic and more social. It has led to different sorts of demands upon the political order than had been made formerly. The emphasis has shifted from equality of reward to equality of treatment and recognition.

Not to be omitted in the discussion of equality is the modern socialist's commitment to democracy. Just as "free enterprise" has been used as a synomym for capitalism by its defenders, so also do socialists occasionally use the phrase, "economic democracy." Socialist parties themselves frequently bear the name *Social Democratic,* rather than simply *Socialist.* Democracy cannot be fully achieved, they feel, until inequalities of social power are eliminated. Although the earlier Marxian assertion that "bourgeois democracy" was a sham has been proved untrue by the success of workers' parties in gaining political power, the socialist remains disturbed by the ability of the economically and socially powerful to exercise their influence in a democratic political order. The knowledge that the weak, by organizing, can match the power of the strong is not for them a sufficient solution to the problem of political equality, nor is the countervailing power of the democratic State a sufficient answer to the economic power of private wealth.

A Cooperative and Harmonious Society. The third goal of socialism is, in a sense, a summary of the hopes entertained by socialists for the society they are trying to build. It looks toward the utilization of the kindlier aspects of man's nature to provide the motivation for economic well-being and effective social organization. Unlike capitalism, which looks for a harmonious result to emerge from the operation of the competitive market, socialism establishes harmony and cooperativeness as explicit goals in themselves. To replace the constructive forces that arise from competition for unequal rewards, the socialist looks to a heightened sense of public service and an increased emphasis on the brotherhood of man. Some earlier versions of socialism expected this to be achieved outside of the framework of the nation-state, but present socialist movements, although not abandoning their aspirations for international harmony, have concentrated on employing the strength of community feeling within a nation to further this objective. Indeed, from being the least nationalistic of all political groups, some socialist parties have altered their attitudes and policies to become stronger proponents of distinct national identity than their bourgeois opponents. Since the Second World War the German Social Democratic party has been more concerned with reunifying Germany than have the Christian Democrats; the Labour party in Great Britain refused to join in Conservative moves to enter the Common Market in the early 1960s.[25]

[25] There were, of course, particular reasons for each of these attitudes. The SPD could expect a great increase in strength through the joining with its counterpart in East Germany, and the Labour party feared the effects on wages and employment that might follow joining the Common Market.

The willingness of socialists to accommodate their objective to the conditions of nationalism highlights the similarity between this goal and the sense of community feeling and common purpose that exists in varying degrees in all nations. Because the goal is explicit, and not merely subsumed, it is well adapted to countries in which the sense of the community is strong, and in which there is a disdain for, rather than an admiration of aggressive individual behavior. These attitudes may exist even in a highly stratified society, such as the British—a fact that helps explain the acceptance of socialism there and the relative absence of strain experienced during the alternations of the Labour and Conservative parties in power. A sense of the community is implicit in the ideals of *noblesse oblige* that are (along with class consciousness itself) a part of the British heritage from feudal times. It is also present in quite different traditions—the Rousseauean ideal of the General Will and the concept of the organic State—that are found in other European countries.[26]

Thus this last objective strikes a responsive chord in cultures that might be resistant to the achievement of the other two and conforms to broadly felt humanistic aspirations in the world at large. Countries that place a high value on those aspirations and on a sense of common purpose within the nation are not loath to adopt some of the policies associated with socialism, particularly if their experience with capitalism has tended to emphasize the latter's harsher qualities.

The Operating Principles of Socialism

The means by which socialists have sought to achieve their objectives have altered with time and experience, for socialism has had to be experimental in its efforts. Ideas formulated when out of power have been adapted by socialists when in power, with the general effect of making the socialist program into a less drastic reconstruction of society than it was in the hands of its originators. Looking at the programs of the major Western socialist movements today, we may distinguish three underlying principles common to substantially all of them: *Social ownership or control of basic industries and financial establishments; subjection of the market to governmentally fixed standards of social value through planning and controls;* and *conscious adjustment of governmental policies to promote economic and social equality.*

Social Ownership.   Historically, the dominant operating principle of socialism has been the social ownership and direction of the physical means of

[26] Rousseau is regarded as the proponent *par excellence* of the idea of the community, for he envisioned it as having but one will, to which all particular wills must conform. The organic State concept, found especially in German thought in the Hegelian tradition and sometimes in the British conservative tradition, portrays the State or the community as an organism of which the various individuals in their several vocations represent the different organs and parts.

production: land and capital. Although the importance of this principle has diminished greatly in the last two decades, as we shall see, public [27] ownership of basic industries and central financial institutions is still a part of the socialist program in most countries.

Social ownership offers the most general means for the achievement of socialist objectives. It removes the controlling economic power from private hands and transfers it to the community. By denying to individuals the right to own productive resources, it eliminates both the major basis of inequalities of wealth and the chief sources of great inequalities in income: rents, interest, and profit. By allowing the community to direct the employment of resources, it seeks to ensure that the decisions regarding them will be made in the spirit of cooperation and common betterment, rather than in the interest of the individual owners. It was expected that all of these results would follow total socialization of productive property, and although in the mainstream of socialist thought total social ownership is no longer advocated, these reasons still provide support for such public ownership as is attempted.

In one branch of modern socialism, social ownership still occupies its original central position. This branch is the *cooperative movement,* which has considerable strength in Scandinavia and a lesser following in Great Britain and elsewhere.[28] Cooperativism is unlike the other forms of socialism in that it rejects the State as the best representative of the people's interests. It seeks to achieve "economic democracy" through bringing the purchasers of goods (in a consumers' cooperative) or the workers (in a producers' cooperative) into the management and decision-making processes of the enterprise. With the divergences of interest between the owners and entrepreneurs on the one hand and the customers and employees on the other eliminated, cooperativists hope to bring about the disappearance both of arbitrary use of economic power and of gross inequalities of wealth and income.[29]

For the bulk of socialists, the State is the instrumentality through which social ownership is to be achieved or through which, in the absence of ownership, public control is to be exercised. In response to some of the problems that have been revealed in the practice of State ownership, which will be

[27] In normal usage, *public ownership* means government ownership. In the usage employed here, that common meaning will be observed, and the term social ownership will appear when the broadest possible meaning, including cooperative ownership, is intended.

[28] This includes the United States, where it is less an ideological movement than a means by which certain producers and consumers can share in the profits of the enterprises with which they do business.

[29] A form of socialism in which *public* ownership plays a commanding role is that called *municipal socialism*—municipal ownership of local public utilities, transportation systems, and the like. This type of public enterprise is undertaken in most instances (especially in the United States) for nonideological reasons and is not properly considered a manifestation of a socialist movement. In many cases it might with equal appropriateness be called *municipal capitalism*. For this reason, it is not treated further in this book.

described subsequently, State control over essential entrepreneurial decisions has become increasingly acceptable to socialists as a substitute for ownership. This has led to a greater emphasis on the other operating principles as a means of achieving equality. Economic power can be restrained and placed in the hands of the community without transferring ownership, but this still leaves the problem of unequal wealth and income to be solved.

What are the industries for which public ownership is still frequently advocated? In general terms they are those regarded as basic to the economy and include transportation, communications, fuel and power, and the most widely used metals: iron and steel. In addition, socialists usually insist upon public ownership of the central banking and credit institutions and, occasionally, of insurance, mineral rights, and land. Taken together, these constitute the areas in which the exercise of economic power can have its most far-reaching effects. The removal of them from private hands or the subjection of them to close regulation eliminates the strongest centers of private economic power and is intended to ensure that decisions made regarding them will be in the interest, not of profit, but of benefit to the community. Through public ownership, resources can be allocated to activities that are deemed socially useful and, if in short supply, denied to those whose use of them is considered trivial or wasteful. The ability of the owner of a greatly needed natural resource or facility to enlarge his profit by raising price and restricting supply can be permanently taken away. In addition, public enterprises can serve as examples to set standards for the whole community in the treatment and remuneration of workers. And, finally, public ownership, whether cooperative or State, of competing businesses in various other sectors of the economy can be employed to force price reductions on private enterprises in the same fields.

Essentially, then, public ownership of basic industries and financial establishments is offered as a means of transferring the bulk of economic power to the community and of restraining (partly through the threat of further nationalizations) arbitrary exercises of power in the portions of the economy left in private hands.

Planning and Control of the Market. As we have seen, planning and regulation are not absent from a capitalist system, and the former, especially, is being given increasing attention by both government and business in an effort to even out business fluctuations. But their function there is corrective and supplementive of the market processes. Under socialism their purpose is more central: They serve to reduce further the range of discretion for the exercise of private economic power; they are used to ensure the widest possible sharing of the material benefits of the economy; and, more importantly, they establish an independent standard, *social value,* as a counter to the market standard of value that directs the allocation of resources to production under capitalism.

Precisely what is the difference between the two standards of value? Essentially it is the one between wants and needs discussed earlier. The market method of evaluating alternative uses of the factors of production, which relies on the individual buyer's personal decisions concerning the goods and services he wants to have, is regarded by socialists as incompatible with the objective of a cooperative and harmonious society and the objective of equality for two reasons. In the first place, because people enter the market as buyers with varying amounts of wealth, it gives a wealthy man a larger "vote" in allocating production than a poor man. If total resources are limited, then the rich man's wants may divert some production from the poor man's needs. Secondly, the market choice is made on a purely individual and selfish basis. The potential buyer is not required to make a choice between the provision of a luxury for himself and an essential item for someone else or for the community as a whole. He could not make that choice if he wished to, for there would be no guarantee that, if he forebore to buy, another man would or could buy what he required.[30]

What the socialist seeks to do is to provide for a choice, or relative evaluation of potential use of resources, that will be made by men acting *as a community,* judging the community's needs and seeking to fulfill them. He sets an ethical standard of value that is not measured in exact monetary terms and seeks to have society, acting through the political order, determine whether, say, new housing is more urgently needed (socially more valuable) at the moment than new cars. This establishment of an order of priorities is part of the function of planning, and controls are to be used to impose the standards set in the plan upon the market.[31] Illustrating another way, and more concretely, we noted that a consumer-dominated market may be characterized by great variety in the products offered, as manufacturers seek to satisfy buyers' whims and fancies. This variety, however, involves a greater drain on resources than would standardized production. The new British National Plan makes specific reference to an intent to reduce product variety in order to save on imports and to increase production for export—purposes that are of great importance to the community as a whole.[32] The socialist feels that unless men are impelled to take each other's and society's needs into consideration in the making of fundamental economic decisions, a cooperative and harmonious society cannot be achieved, and fundamental social purposes will be neglected or ignored altogether. The way to achieve this is to supplement the atomistic decision-making of the market with the collective decision-making of the plan.

---

[30] Of course, a rich man could, instead, give his money to a charity. This, however, is not the immediate choice that the market itself offers. As we have seen, capitalist countries make this type of decision through government also, but instead of controlling the market, the government *enters* it as a buyer of social goods and services.

[31] In this particular section the word, *control,* is used in its most general sense, to include direct control through regulation and indirect control through such devices as subsidies and penalty taxes.

[32] *The National Plan,* Cmnd. 2764 (London: HMSO, 1965), p. 47. The plan goes on at this point to suggest ways of inducing manufacturers to be "public spirited" and forego part of the home market in order to increase production for export.

The fact that the promotion of equality is a part of socialist policy automatically makes it a part of planning as well, because governmental policies are integrated with and stated in the plans. In some ways, however, planning and controls make their own distinctive contribution to equalization. Regional plans intended to disperse industry and thus even out employment opportunities and wage scales do this, as do plans affecting national wages and incomes policies. Finally, specific controls may have an equalizing intent, such as those designed to foster the standardized production of "utility goods," which were a feature of immediate postwar British economic regulations. (These, however, were mostly of wartime origin and were also for the purpose of ensuring an adequate quality and quantity of goods while conserving resources.)

Does the adoption of planning mean that the market is not allowed to function at all under socialism? Quite the contrary. In abstract discussions of socialist economics that were predicated on total public ownership and in discussions of communist economics there have been occasions when this was assumed, but Western socialists no longer advocate (if indeed they ever seriously did) the total elimination of the market.[33] The standard of "social value" is, as suggested here, rather imprecise. It is useful in setting priorities for giving attention and support to parts of the economy while holding back others, but modern socialists do not propose to abandon consumer choice altogether or even largely. Many of the controls used, as will be shown later, are in the form of inducements and penalties that shape the market to conform to the priorities established in national plans. Where the market itself is assumed to meet reasonably well the needs of society, it is to be left free. Only where it is felt to not do so, do socialists advocate intervention. The standard of social value is *imposed on,* rather than *substituted for* the market.

Planning and controls are also, and increasingly, being used in socialist economies for promoting economic growth and stability and for other purposes that have their counterparts in capitalist economics. Their distinctively socialist functions are the ones just described, however.

Promoting Economic and Social Equality. The third operating principle of socialism provides a criterion by which all government policies are to be judged and a function toward which certain of them are to be oriented. Because socialists today accept the continued existence of some private enterprise, of partial market regulation of the economy, and of differential incentive rewards for persons, government policies must be designed to pre-

---

[33] Communists are also turning increasingly to the use of the market, or more properly, a modified and simulated form of the market, for the regulation of aspects of their economies, as will be shown in Chapter 4. Curiously, much of the discussion of the economics of socialism in which total public ownership has been posited has hinged on the question of finding ways to create a publicly owned economy that would duplicate the effects of a market in serving consumer choice! See Oskar Lange and Fred M. Taylor, *On the Economic Theory of Socialism,* Benjamin E. Lippincott, ed. (Minneapolis: The University of Minnesota Press, 1938).

vent extreme inequalities of wealth from developing. They must also work to eliminate pre-existing disparities. Consequently, socialist tax policies, welfare programs, business regulations, and the like have as either a collateral or a direct purpose the redistribution of income, the suppression of extraordinary gains, or the recapture of large accumulations of private wealth to prevent inequalities from passing from generation to generation. None of these would have been necessary had the original plan of total public ownership and absolute equality been maintained (except that they would have been needed in the transitional phase), and not any are now intended to produce absolute equality. They are designed to keep wealth and income differences within what are regarded as tolerable limits in terms of economic well-being and social power.

More recently attention has become focused on policies that might attack other forms of social inequality. Differences in levels of education and in the quality of the education gained are recognized as having marked effects on class consciousness and on economic opportunity. Housing and living conditions that breed apartness and that emphasize economic disparities have been given attention. Unequal cultural opportunities that tend to create different styles of life in different classes have been reduced. Opportunities for consultation between management and employees have been sought as a means partly at least to reduce the difference in status that obtains between those who make guiding decisions and those who carry them out.

The pattern of governmental policy in socialism is intended to avoid conditions that create and foster inequality and to promote actively conditions that suppress it, within the limits of the necessary incentives to advancement that the system requires in order to produce optimum effort.

The Practice of Socialism

Describing the practice of socialism is somewhat more difficult than was the same exercise with respect to capitalism. Most Western nations have experienced at least a period of time in which their economies were almost entirely capitalistically organized. Democratic socialism, on the other hand, has been only partially adopted anywhere, and the degree to which it has been adopted is the subject of disagreement among competent scholars. There has resulted a tendency to portray certain countries as offering a "middle way" between capitalism and either communism or one of the earlier and abstract forms of socialism, in lieu of identifying any country as a clear example of democratic socialism in action. Crosland himself, after surveying his own country (Britain), arrived at the conclusion that it was no longer capitalistic; but he declined to give a name to its present system.[34]

The difficulty is compounded by the fact that measures we identify as "socialistic" may be taken either by a country dominated by an avowedly

[34] *Op. cit.,* ch. II.

socialist party, or by a nation whose values closely approximate those that underlie one or more of the socialist objectives. This is particularly true of measures which provide the political order with control over the economic order without necessarily promoting economic and social equality. In doing this, a nation is merely reasserting the pattern that existed before capitalism— a pattern that it may not have wholly abandoned, and one that is consistent with a paternalistic or an organic form of community, rather than with the egalitarian community of the socialist ideal. We must face the uncomfortable fact that neither party names nor programmatic labels are a sound guide. As to parties, those that uphold socialist doctrines in England, Australia, and New Zealand are called Labour parties, whereas the equivalent in Canada is called the New Democratic party. In France the socialist party is called the French Section of the Workers' International, whereas the so-called Radical Socialist party is, in the well-known aphorism, neither radical nor socialist! As to program, it has already been pointed out that four major nationalizations in England were carried out by the Conservatives and the Liberals. In France, postwar nationalizations and the start of national planning were the product of a coalition of parties prominent in the wartime resistance in which the communists and socialists played a major part. Subsequent governments, whether including the socialists or not, have maintained the nationalized industries in government hands and have continued the series of national four-year plans to the present day. In Scandinavia, by way of contrast, majority socialist governments have refrained from pressing nationalizations of industry even to the point that the British Labour party did in 1945 to 1951.

These apparent contradictions and confusions arise partly from the different national courses of socialism, partly from the abandonment of abstract ideology by socialists once they have come to power, and partly from the compatibility of socialist values with national values in many countries. In the last of these three conditions attempts to reform the capitalist system have quite naturally taken a course consistent with socialism, even if no explicit intention to introduce socialism as a system has been voiced.

Because our purpose is to understand the nature of socialism as one among several consciously chosen alternatives, it is probably best to concentrate our attention on practice in movements and regimes that are avowedly socialist. Some examples, however, will be drawn from countries where practices have originated under socialist governments and been continued by successor non-socialist ones. In both categories Great Britain will provide the bulk of the examples. There a socialist party came rather suddenly into power with a clear program that it proceeded to carry out. It was followed by a thirteen-year rule by the nonsocialist Conservative party that did relatively little in the way of dismantling its predecessor's work and that relinquished control to the socialists again in 1964, giving us a remarkable case study in congruence of socialist with nonsocialist values in the same country.[35] Britain also affords us

[35] Norway's socialist government was succeeded by a "bourgeois" government in September, 1965, but there is as yet little evidence of policy change.

most useful material because the Labour (socialist) party's program of nationalization was the most extensive of those introduced after the Second World War, and because the question of pragmatic adaptation of policy to changing conditions has been openly debated among its members.

Social Ownership. Social ownership of the means of production has come about in various countries for reasons that are only partly related to the ideology of socialism. In Scandinavian countries, where it has mostly taken the form of cooperative, rather than governmental ownership, a combination of belief in cooperativism in principle and simple pragmatism seems to have underlain it. Consumer cooperatives in Sweden, for example, date back to about 1850. They fairly rapidly became associated in a national organization, the Cooperative Union (KF), the purpose of which was to provide mutual support and furtherance of the cooperative idea. In about the 1920s, KF and its associated cooperatives began to establish production affiliates, often as a means of attacking monopoly positions that had been gained by private cartels. In this way, consumer cooperatives became the owners of factories producing electric lamps, chemical fertilizers, vegetable oils, and margarine.[36] Today, KF and its affiliates produce foodstuffs, clothing, furniture, textiles, rubber products, plastics, paper, and a variety of other items, most of which are sold through its 5,800-odd stores and restaurants. It also has an insurance affiliate, Folksam, which claims to insure one half the Swedish population. Producers' cooperatives have been actively promoted by the Norwegian and Swedish governments in agriculture and fishing as a means of strengthening the "countervailing power" of producers in these sectors of the economy.

State ownership—public ownership in the usual sense of the term—has arisen in many countries, as we have already seen, simply because only the State has had the necessary capital resources to carry out major and central projects, such as railroads and electricity supply. In Scandinavia, despite the fact that public ownership was part of the Marxist ideology with which the socialist movement there began, the preceding has been the principal basis upon which State ventures in hydroelectricity, railroads, communications, and the like have been undertaken. The actual reasons, then, have been substantially the same as those used in capitalist countries for the provision of social overhead capital. In addition, the State has become the owner of various enterprises for quite miscellaneous reasons. The Swedish tobacco monopoly, for example,[37] was undertaken in 1915 as a means of gaining additional revenue for the State and the liquor monopoly in order to control Sweden's alcoholism problem. Finally, the aftermath of the Second World War produced some nationalizations in the way of reparations and punishments. In this way

[36] The story of this period is told in admiring fashion by Marquis Childs in his *Sweden: The Middle Way,* rev. and enlarged ed. (New Haven: Yale University Press, 1938), chs. II, III.

[37] Sweden has recently ended its monopoly by permitting the private importation of tobacco products.

Norway obtained an aluminum plant and shares in a number of German-established firms (and France, similarly, nationalized the Renault automobile works that were confiscated from an alleged collaborator).

But it was in Great Britain that the most clear-cut pattern of socialist nationalization of industry occurred, and here was presented a remarkable example of a convergence of ideological and practical reasoning and of socialist and national values. It was, to begin with, a program clearly intended as the first step toward socialism from which others would follow. The Labour party, indeed, seemed almost apologetic in proposing only a specified collection of businesses for nationalization, instead of a wholesale and general program. Its election manifesto, *Let Us Face the Future,* hastened to remind the more radical supporters of the party that "Socialism cannot come overnight, as the product of a week-end revolution." Such as it was, the list covered a substantial segment of the productive and commercial enterprise of the nation.[38] Yet, the party rested on neither its ideology nor its majority in Parliament in pressing its case in the debates on the nationalization measures. Drawing heavily from reports of studies made under previous administrations, it presented practical arguments very similar to those the Liberals and the Conservatives had used in years past to justify public ownership of the London docks, London passenger transport, the central electricity grid, the British Broadcasting Corporation, and later, the British Overseas Airways Corporation and other specific enterprises. In short, they demonstrated clearly the common thread that ran through their proposals and the policies the nation had followed in the past. It is, in fact, fairly widely agreed that many of the same industries would have been taken into State ownership sooner or later by the Conservative party, had it been the winner in the 1945 election.[39]

As things proved out, the Conservatives, when returned to power in 1951, did denationalize iron and steel and part of road haulage but left the rest of the Labour nationalizations in force. Whether they would have nationalized the others themselves or not, they consented to leave them as they found them.

As our investigation of capitalism showed, the mere fact of ownership does not establish control, and the principal practical problem of social ownership

[38] Specifically, the firms and industries nationalized were the Bank of England, coal, electricity, gas, railroads, road, water, and air transport, telegraphic communications (already slated for nationalization under policies of the preceding government), and iron and steel. Compensation, generally regarded as fair, if not generous, was given the former owners. A few other public ventures were created (not nationalized) for assisting colonial development and industrial research.

[39] A jaundiced view of the whole set of proposals by a left-wing British socialist reflects the same general point. Mr. D. N. Pritt, in his study of *The Labour Government: 1945–51* (London: Lawrence & Wishart, 1963), p. 20, complains that the effect of the nationalizations was to leave efficient and profit-making industries in private ownership while nationalizing only inefficient ones, ". . . to the concealed delight of their owners and the relative disadvantage of the community, which would gradually become a sort of hospital for sick industries." The State had functioned as such a "hospital" under British governments for years. It was at precisely this point that Conservative party policy and socialism converged.

is the translation of it into control by the community. The development and complexity of the economic order has made it necessary, in socialist as well as in capitalist countries, for economic enterprises to be operated by managers especially trained in their operations. From this arises a danger that these experts will pursue an independent course divorced from the intent of the owners. Capitalism, being mostly concerned with the decentralization of economic power and the separation of economic from political power, could solve the problem merely by giving the managers themselves a share in the ownership. They would then be sufficiently motivated to maintain a high standard of performance and innovation and, thus, earn a profit both for themselves and the other stockholders. But socialism demands more; it requires that the managers be subject to decisions imposed from above by the community. This problem is not as acute in cooperative socialism, for the purpose there for each individual industry is not control by the whole community, but service to that part of it, the consumers or producers, that constitutes the membership of the cooperative. Control by a board of directors elected by the cooperative's members is the usual method employed, and because the standard of judgment on the management is reasonably clear—goods of the best quality and at the lowest prices possible in the case of a consumer's cooperative—it is not difficult for the management to be held responsible.

Where the State is the representative of the community as owner, however, a more difficult situation exists. Just as the economic order has developed its own specialized processes, so has the political order, especially in a democratic polity. So many questions are referred to popular consultation in a democracy that the addition of a multitude of economic decisions poses problems of determining just which sorts of economic questions do require reference to the people or to the political process. The British experience in this regard displays some of these problems.

In order to maintain the general management scheme that had been found most effective in the economic order for the direction of large enterprises, each industry nationalized by Labour was placed under the control of a public board (equivalent to a board of directors) chosen by a government minister [40] who headed that department of the government most nearly concerned with the industry's operations (the Minister for Fuel and Power in the case of the National Coal Board, for example). The minister was given a few powers to approve or deny certain types of board decision and a general power to direct the board on any matter of "national interest." He was not supposed to intervene in the day-to-day decisions of the board. In turn, the minister was to be responsible to Parliament for his actions, and the board was to submit an annual report that might be brought before the Parliament for general debate.

[40] A minister is the political head of a government department. He is a party official, a member of one of the Houses of Parliament, and is in most cases (at least insofar as the ministers charged with supervising nationalized industries are concerned) a member of the Cabinet.

Finally, decisions on new investment (expansion of facilities, and so on) were reserved to the Cabinet and Parliament. The entire system was intended to provide general direction by and accountability to the political order, and ultimately to the public itself, while maintaining the advantages of technical expertise in daily management decisions. Unlike France, which had national-ized many industries at about the same time, neither labor nor consumer control were contemplated, although advisory councils representative of consumer interests and joint consultation bodies to provide labor involvement in industrial decision-making were set up.[41]

In operation the system of controls proved to have some rather different effects than had been anticipated. The control over investment was effective and did permit the investment activities of the industries to be adapted both to the needs of the national plans [42] and, in some degree, to the counteraction of cyclical fluctuation in the market.[43] During the period of intensive controls that followed right after the war, the nationalized industries implemented materials allocations (but so did private industries under government regula-tion). There is even a suggestion that the National Coal Board has used its powers to subsidize certain sectors of the economy or businesses whose activi-ties the government sought to promote.[44] Parliamentary and ministerial super-vision, however, have proved less effective and less public, respectively, than many Labour supporters had hoped.[45] The difficulty is partly that the Parlia-ment does not have time to debate adequately the annual reports and other matters needing its attention and partly the unwillingness of the ministers to use their powers of general direction.[46] This reluctance seemingly arises from

[41] The French established tripartite boards, representing the government, consumers, and labor, but found that these tended to degenerate into quarrelsome factions. Ulti-mately they increased the government representation sufficiently to ensure government, rather than interest control. Nevertheless, a number of British socialists reared in the guild socialist tradition were (and are) unhappy at the British failure to give workers a larger role in industry decision-making.

[42] It is notable that in Scandinavia planning authorities regularly emphasize the fact that public investment, including that in State enterprises, is the only kind over which they have secure control for planning purposes. This, despite the existence, as will be described, of credit controls and building licensing.

[43] There has been some debate over the effectiveness of this, and the general view of economists seems to be that the countercyclical effort has been only partly successful because of the problems of forecasting and of making radical short-run changes in the level of investment in large fixed assets, which take time to get under way. A study by William G. Shepherd, *Economic Performance under Public Ownership: British Fuel and Power* (New Haven: Yale University Press, 1965), pp. 130–137, suggests that the results have been poor, and the effects on the industries themselves harmful.

[44] Graeme C. Moodie, in *The Government of Great Britain* (New York: Thomas Y. Crowell Co., 1961), p. 166, writes of ". . . supplies of fuel from the National Coal Board at low (and secret) rates."

[45] See the rather bitter criticisms in *Keeping Left,* by a Group of Members of Parlia-ment (London: New Statesman and Nation, 1950), pp. 29–31.

[46] By 1954 only one directive under the general power had been issued, and that one by a Conservative minister. See Eldon L. Johnson, "The Accountability of the British Nationalized Industries," *American Political Science Review,* XLVIII (June, 1954),

the unwillingness of both ministers and boards to publicize their disagreements and of the ministers particularly to accept public responsibility for board actions.[47] The upshot is that although ministers can and apparently do consult with the boards, recommend policy, and even threaten the use of directives, they have not done so under conditions that allow parliamentary and public review of what has been done. They have thus broken the connection between *political* or *governmental* control, represented by themselves, and *public* control, represented by open debate in Parliament.[48] In partial contradiction of the foregoing it is felt by some that the reluctance of ministers to issue directives has played into the hands of strong-minded boards and board chairmen and permitted them to maintain a greater independence of all governmental control than was consistent with what socialists intended.[49]

There is, thus, a possibility that nationalization has contrived something equivalent to the "managerial society" that is felt by some to represent the present state of capitalism, but with certain differences. In the first place, the profit-seeking motive is absent from the instructions of the boards,[50] whose

---

pp. 369–371; this article is a very useful review of the entire subject, the best in American publications.

[47] Under British parliamentary practice a minister may be subjected to questions in Parliament for actions taken by him or by subordinates subject to his direct control. These can be exceedingly embarrassing to the minister and to his party if some error in policy is revealed. In the case of the nationalized industries, the minister could point to the semiautonomous corporate status of the boards in refusing to answer questions, provided he himself had not issued a directive in the matter concerned. Of course, it was often possible for a minister to get a board to do as he wished by threatening to issue a directive, so that it is difficult to establish with any sense of confidence the exact extent of ministerial control.

[48] W. A. Robson, in his 1960 study, *Nationalized Industry and Public Ownership* (Toronto: University of Toronto Press, 1960), pp. 142–162, expressed great concern, feeling that ministerial control was, in fact, exceedingly close, despite its effective concealment.

[49] Mr. R. H. S. Crossman, a spokesman for the left wing of the Labour party, expressed the belief that the chairman of the great private chemical firm, ICI, was more amenable to government control than were some of the chairmen of the national boards. See his *Socialism and the New Despotism* (Fabian Society Tract No. 298), reprinted as "Planning for Freedom" in his book, *The Politics of Socialism* (New York: Atheneum Publishers, 1965), pp. 59–85.

[50] There has been some dissent to this. One writer, after pointing out that the National Coal Board and others are required to include among their costs the interest *and the retirement of the principal* of the bonds issued in compensation to the former owners remarked that, ". . . an economist might well be forgiven for thinking that this form of 'breaking even' conceals profit taking on a handsome scale." Quoted from A. Beacham, "Nationalization in Theory and Practice," *Quarterly Journal of Economics,* LXIV (November, 1950), p. 556. There were some grounds for feeling that the Labour government was anxious to prove the feasibility of nationalization by running the industries "in the black." It was the Conservatives in 1961, however, who established a policy requiring them, if possible, to make a return on capital equivalent to that in private industry. Scandinavian public enterprises, which are usually not monopolies, normally attempt to simulate the cost factors applicable in private industry in order not to be charged with unfair competition.

general mandate (and inclination) is to pursue the public interest. There has been little question that the management of the nationalized industries have been both able and public-spirited.[51] Moreover, they have not been compelled to compromise between a stockholder interest and the public interest, which somewhat vitiates the complaint that the government might be reluctant to call them to account. In the second place, there is direct government control over their investment programs, which is an aid to implementation of national plans. What has *not* occurred has been the vast centralization of economic power that might have been anticipated. The combined independence of both boards and ministers has made it difficult for government to direct the whole weight of the nationalized industries uniformly in a desired direction.

Two other results of nationalization may be noted briefly. Because, with the exception of steel, the industries nationalized were characterized by low or nonexistent profit margins, public ownership has had little effect in reducing the amount of private profit in the economy and has, thus, done little to promote equalization.[52] Labor relations have been improved, but not to the extent that was hoped, and workers have yet to show impressive signs of abandoning their traditional distrust of management, whether public or private. The sense of public service that is found in at least the higher management has not permeated to the operatives or, in an important way, to their union leaderships. In some ways the great concentration of management that took place in combining many separate firms under single boards, as was done in electricity, gas, and coal, contributed to the continuance of a sense of estrangement. The workers could hardly feel that these large agglomerations were "theirs," even if they were suddenly shown more solicitude by the new management and were given places on consultative councils to help determine their working conditions and influence other managerial decisions affecting them.[53]

With such relatively moderate results from nationalization, and with in-

---

[51] But some socialists have worried about the development of a new elite of privilege springing up. See Crossman's essay cited earlier.

[52] One consequence of this has been some Labour party' consideration of the idea of the State simply purchasing shares in profitable private enterprises in order to channel some of those profits into common hands. This proposal was put forth in a party pamphlet in July, 1957, entitled, *Industry and Society,* and has also been suggested by Mr. Crosland. Trenchant criticisms of it have also been heard, however, notably from W. A. Robson (*op. cit.,* pp. 480–485) who has long been an authority in socialist circles on the subject of public ownership. Robson points out that the State would thus become committed to increasing, rather than reducing, the profit margin. Since returning to power, the Labour party has not implemented this proposal.

[53] The size of these new industrial giants (the National Coal Board had in 1954 three times as many employees as had the General Motors Corporation in the United States) also hampered the ability of the consultative councils to work, for the labor unions brought together under one employer by the nationalization of a multitude of separate firms found themselves engaged in jurisdictional disputes. They were thus ill-organized to give their members a sense of effective representation on the councils. See Johnson, *op. cit.,* p. 382.

creasingly effective work being done in the planning and regulation of private industry, much of the drive has gone from the nationalization movement. Socialists on the moderate or "right" wing, such as Crosland, moreover, have come to entertain real doubts about the compatibility of a State monopoly with the freedom that socialists also cherish. As he suggests in connection with the British Broadcasting Corporation, there is a danger to personal independence when there is a monopoly employer of a certain type of talent.[54] They are also a little more impressed than formerly with the usefulness of competition in private industry in encouraging initiative.[55] For their part, even "left-wing" socialists seem to have retreated from a position of seeking national monopolies to one of recommending government acquisition or development of individual enterprises and promotion of cooperatives competing with private firms in various fields, as is done in Scandinavia. They also are ". . . less concerned about who owns a factory, and more about who manages it and how, and whether it is working according to socialist plans."[56] At its 1960 conference the Labour party adopted a statement regarding nationalization that perhaps sums up the present socialist position in England and is probably a bit more favorable to nationalization than the socialists of other countries would be:[57]

It (the party) is convinced that (its) objectives can be achieved only through an expansion of common ownership substantial enough to give the community power over the commanding heights of the economy. Common ownership takes varying forms, including state-owned industries and firms, producer and consumer cooperation, municipal ownership and public participation in private concerns. Recognizing that both public and private enterprise have a place in the economy, it believes that further extension of common ownership should be decided from time to time in the light of these objectives and according to circumstances, with due regard for the views of the workers and consumers concerned.[58]

On its return to power (by a very slim majority) in 1964, the Labour party took preliminary steps to renationalize steel, but no other industries. As of the

[54] Crosland, *op. cit.,* p. 319.

[55] *Ibid.,* p. 322. Crosland actually goes a great deal further than this, showing grave doubts that nationalized industry could be flexible enough to survive in competitive markets such as the export market.

[56] *Op. cit., Keeping Left,* p. 28. The authors of this pamphlet included R. H. S. Crossman, Ian Mikardo, Barbara Castle, and Harold Davies, among others. Remarkably, they made no specific mention of an industry or firm for which they were prepared to recommend nationalization.

[57] The German Social Democratic party, for example, has in recent years taken the line that it would introduce the Scandinavian model of socialism if it came to power. As we have seen, this involves a smaller amount of nationalization than exists in Britain.

[58] Quoted in Harold Wilson, *Purpose in Politics* (Boston: Houghton, Mifflin Company, 1964), p. 264.

1965–66 session of Parliament they had not completed the renationalization, but with a new and enlarged mandate won in the 1966 election, they have announced their intention to proceed with it.

Planning and Control of the Market. The socialist regimes that found themselves in power in Europe after the Second World War inherited an extensive set of controls over their economies that had been developed to mobilize and sustain production for war. Even neutral Sweden had been unable to avoid the effects of the market distortions caused by the conflict that had raged all about her. In view of the destruction caused by war, the interruption of trade, and the clear danger of inflation, no one supposed that these controls could be eliminated immediately, but socialist governments undertook to try to transform them into planned programs for guiding the peacetime economy. Plans were developed to meet the immediate needs of stimulating production for export while restraining domestic production and consumption, and longer-range planning was begun designed to ensure that future investment would go primarily toward socially useful, rather than frivolous purposes. The impulse to planning was enhanced by the recognition that materials were scarce and were likely to remain so for some time, and that the essential thing to do was to ensure that maximum social advantage was obtained from what was available.

In a very real sense the experience of Britain, Sweden, and Norway in the decades since the war is indicative of the extent *and the limits* to which democratic socialists are willing to go in curtailing the free action of the market and freedom of individual choice in order to achieve the objective of a cooperative, harmonious, and essentially orderly economic society. Starting with a full panoply of "physical" [59] as well as fiscal and monetary controls and powers of taxation and subsidy that could be used to influence and direct the economy, they all gradually altered the pattern from one of compulsion toward one of persuasion, and from detailed toward rather general and limiting controls, often accompanied by promotion instead of restraint. This they did partly in response to popular resentment against detailed State interference, and partly in recognition by socialists themselves of the problems that controls posed to the enjoyment of liberty.

The systems for planning in Norway and Sweden differ somewhat from that in Great Britain, although the intent and "tone" are similar. The interruption of socialist rule in the last-named by thirteen years of Conservative governments has injected some practices common to nonsocialist planning, largely copied from France.[60] In the first two, long-term plans of four or five years'

[59] The term *physical controls* applies to such things as rationing, licensing, and other controls that have a prohibitive effect, rather than merely tend to induce conformity to objectives.

[60] The Conservatives discontinued most of the Labour government's planning activities after taking office, although the annual *Economic Survey,* which was the vehicle for

duration are established, and annual economic budgets adopted, both of which fix planned rates of growth, investment, and consumption, and state the expected and desired allocation of investment among sectors of the economy. The British do not employ the annual economic budget but, instead, rely on periodic reviews of the long-range plan. There are important differences between socialist plans and those employed in communist countries, for the former are far less specific, less binding, and less "official" than the latter. They are not adopted by the legislature, and they serve as guides for private businessmen's decisions as well as for governmental policy-making officials. Perhaps the best indication of the approach taken in democratic socialist planning is contained in the following rather lengthy excerpt from the British National Plan, adopted by the Labour government in 1964, which appears under the heading, "The Nature and Purpose of Planning."

. . . Our economy, like most others in the modern world, is a mixed one. The Government element is important; public spending is a large part of total expenditure; for this reason the Government must raise large sums in taxation; a large part of the basic industry of the country is carried on by public corporations; the Government are able to exercise authority in many other fields. All this gives the Government great economic power and influence. They intend to use this to secure faster growth and national solvency.
. . . Most manufacturing industry and commerce is, and will continue to be, largely governed by the market economy. But this does not necessarily, and without active Government influence, bring about the results which the nation needs—for example, sufficient exports to pay for our imports and other overseas expenditure. Also, the forces of competition often operate too slowly. Then again, where productive units are large and investment decisions have to be taken two to five years ahead, competing companies tend to bunch their investment, holding back and moving forward together, producing surplus or over-stretched resources. There is, too, little doubt that inadequacy of investment in British industry has resulted in increasing home demand being met by a greater flow of imports than the economy could afford.
. . . Sometimes Government action may be required to strengthen the forces of competition, for example, by reinforcing the legislation against restrictive practices or providing for more disclosure in company accounts.

Labour's annual plans, was continued as a guide to problems of balance of payments and countercyclical policy. (It was replaced by the National Plan under Labour in 1964.) By 1957, however, the Conservative government had found it necessary to set up a Council on Prices, Productivity, and Incomes, which was to give guidance concerning wage negotiations and price changes in order to avoid inflationary effects. (It was not particularly successful and was replaced with stronger machinery when Labour returned to power.) In 1962, a National Economic Development Council was created, following an intensive study of the French system, and marked the acceptance by Conservatives of the need for a planning agency that would set target growth rates, a practice that had been abandoned ten years before. The French system, which the Conservatives refrained from copying exactly, is described on pages 222–224.

In other cases, such as the regional distribution of industry, and transport, important social costs arise which are not expressed in market prices; and positive Government action is required to supplement market forces. Each case must be judged on its merits. Care will be taken not to destroy the complex mechanisms on which the market economy is based. The end product of both co-operative planning and the market economy is an internationally competitive industry; and in securing this aim they complement each other.[61]

In all three countries, representatives of management and labor are consulted in the process of drawing up plans, but the responsibility for plan formulation lies clearly with the political order, and specifically with the Cabinet of the country concerned.[62]

Socialist planning in practice is essentially a process of reconciling predictions of the future shape and growth of the economy with certain economic and social goals that the planners would like to see fulfilled, and that are somewhat different from what the expected outcome would be if no planning or controls were undertaken. There is enormous detail in the published plans of the various countries using the planning mechanism, including manpower supplies, output levels, productivity, and investment for each industry. Most of this, however, is required simply to give accuracy to the forecasts made and to pinpoint those particular fields in which conscious directed effort must be made to achieve the larger goals set in the plans. Planning does not descend to the level of the individual firm. The emphasis in the plans is primarily on economic growth, full employment, stability, stimulation of exports (all three countries are heavily dependent upon international trade), and allocations for social purposes. Attention is likely to be paid to problems of regional development—aiding sections of the country that are suffering from unemployment or underdevelopment—and to housing, as one sector of the economy most often in need of stimulation and of great importance for improving living conditions, especially in the lower economic classes. Insofar as a goal is set for private industry, which it is expected to fulfill, it is usually first stated in broad terms—an increase of 7 per cent per year in investment in manufacturing industries, for example—and then broken down in more detail to show how this can be done, and which industries are expected (and are likely to be able) to make the largest contribution. By stating the government's intention to aid and promote certain rates of growth, by showing how this relates to the expected demand for the output of the industries concerned, and thus by giving some assurance that what is asked for is both feasible and reasonably safe to try, the plan serves to aid businesses and give them some

[61] Cmnd. 2764, pp. 2–3.

[62] There has been more formal machinery involving consultation of private interests in the planning process in Britain than in the other two, but such consultation takes place in all of them on an informal basis at least. Norway had an Economic Coordinating Council from 1947 to 1954, which was an advisory body including labor and management interests, but it seems not to have functioned well and was abandoned.

confidence in making their investment decisions. Equally, however, the detail does suggest an intention on the part of government to see to it that performance lives up to expectations. In the words, again, of the British Plan:

> . . . Forecasts are also a useful control device. If an industry falls below projection it will be valuable to discover why. In some cases (*e.g.,* if consumers' preferences have been wrongly forecast) no action by Government may be indicated. But in other cases (*e.g.,* if it is due to the failure of productivity to rise) it will serve as a useful warning signal for action by industry, by Government, or by both in co-operation.[63]

All in all, there is some unavoidable ambiguity in the meaning of the plans. There is apparent clarity promised in this statement from the Norwegian long-range plan for 1966–1969: "For some sectors the figures are to be regarded as a prognosis of developments during the Programme period, e.g. in shipping. In other sectors the figures express the Government's plans." [64] Yet there is a mixture of language used throughout the plan in which the term *forecast* or its equivalent alternates with the term *target,* or other words to that effect. The British plan also speaks of targets and "national effort required," but repeatedly refers to growth rates as forecasts. The resulting mixture of prediction and intention permits considerable flexibility in the implementation of the plans and is consistent with the type of devices used to carry them out, for these devices include a far larger measure of persuasion, inducement, and assistance today than they do of direct control, limitation, and prohibition.

Immediately after the war, of course, the controls used were extremely strict. The devastation wrought by war and the great pent-up demand for consumer goods made it necessary to suppress the demand temporarily while rebuilding the nation's productive capacity so that, at a later time, the demand could be fulfilled without disastrous inflation. In Britain, not only were most of the wartime economic controls continued, but some were strengthened. Rationing and price controls (with subsidies where necessary to ensure production) governed most of the widely used consumer goods and fuels, and luxury goods were taxed at rates as high as 100 per cent of the wholesale price. Materials for industrial production were allocated, business investment and construction plans were subject to government approval and licensing, and even the wartime power to direct workers to remain in needed employments was revived by a Control of Engagement Order, issued in 1947.

The Labour government was clearly unhappy with the necessity to restrict consumer freedom of choice and to order individuals to remain in their jobs. Rationing was abandoned in most goods in 1948 and 1949, and the Control

[63] Cmnd. 2764, p. 3.
[64] Royal Norwegian Ministry of Finance, *Norwegian Long Term Programme 1966–1969* (official English translation of selected chapters) Parliamentary Report No. 63, 1964–65 (Oslo, 1965), p. 39.

of Engagement Order was rescinded entirely in 1950, after its use had already become very slight. Business controls, including licensing of new investment, import controls, materials allocation, and price and rent controls, were maintained longer and many of them were not dismantled until after the Conservatives had returned to power, but they had been declining steadily even under the Labour government, except for the emergency caused by the Korean conflict. It seems likely that the impression given by the Labour government immediately after the war was not a valid one as respects socialist intentions, and that even on an experimental basis the party might not have engaged in so wholesale a direction of the economy as circumstances forced upon it. Nevertheless, discussions within the movement subsequently indicated that the experience had shown the incompatibility of full planning and controls with the kind of free society that British socialists wanted.[65] Especially clear was the recognition that, in order to fully plan and direct the use of resources to production, the ordering of workers into specific jobs would be required, and this the party was quite unwilling to do again.

Present practice for the implementation of planning is to avoid direct physical controls where possible and to shape the allocation of resources by combinations of monetary incentives, subsidies, and penalties.[66] The consumer market for goods and services is left largely free, although high taxes, consumer credit restrictions, and occasionally sumptuary taxes on luxury items are used to hold over-all demand sufficiently low to release resources for increased investment. Price controls are maintained on a standby basis in Norway and Sweden (and the British Labour party requested, but did not remain in office to obtain them in 1951), but are used principally to restrict profits to a level consistent with productivity increases to avoid inflation, and to further the objective of equalization of incomes. Rent controls are usually kept, but these, too, are for purposes of equalization and are not intended to redirect the allocation of resources.[67]

Principal attention is given to influencing investment, for the decision to invest is the basic economic decision that allocates the resources of society to various purposes. When a firm builds a new factory, it is not only using materials and labor that could go to other purposes, but it expects to direct a future flow of materials through that factory, to turn them into some specific

---

[65] See, for example, the Labour party's pamphlet, *Plan for Progress: Labour's Policy for Britain's Economic Expansion* (London: Transport House, 1958), pp. 9–10.

[66] Even in the area of imports, where licenses and restrictions are relatively easy to administer and meet with less resistance than attends domestic rationing, there has been a tendency away from direct controls. In its attempt to solve the balance of payments crisis in 1964, the British Labour government used a 15 per cent selective levy instead of controls.

[67] Indeed, because they reduce profit expectations, they may slow investment both in repairs and in new housing, a fact that has required governments employing rent control to undertake simultaneous efforts to increase public housing or to subsidize private housing, or both.

product, and expects to continue to use labor on the site to operate the plant. As in capitalist countries operating on Keynesian principles, government monetary and fiscal policies are used to affect the general level of investment and employment, but more specific controls and inducements are used to ensure that investment will be made in the desired fields. In the public sector (the part of the economy consisting of government economic activity, including government-owned enterprises) there is obvious direct control of the pattern of investment. In the private sector, however, government must either induce or compel private owners to shape their investments to conform to the plan. This is done first of all through inducements: Special tax advantages to firms willing to invest at times and in fields favored by the government,[68] government subsidies for factory building, and tax advantages to producers of certain goods, which tend to cause them to enlarge their production and, possibly, build more plant for the purpose.[69] Government purchases themselves, of course, also stimulate certain industries and increase investment in them.

On the negative side, socialists have used two instruments principally to prevent excessive investment in fields given low priority in the plans: building licensing and credit rationing.[70] Building licensing, which controls all sorts of construction (and thus the enlargement of productive capacity) by requiring a permit from the government before starting, is used principally to require firms to locate new plants in low-employment and underdeveloped areas. It is also employed to shape investment, as has been done recently in Britain, by greatly restricting the types of building (factory, office, home) for which permits will be granted. Credit rationing is carried out (principally in Norway and Sweden) through annual or longer agreements worked out between the government and the banking system (much of which is government owned). These agreements are voluntary, and at best imperfectly observed, but they are buttressed by the extensive involvement of the government itself in the total credit supply. Through the agreements and through direct government

[68] Sweden and, more recently, Norway have developed a system by which companies may retain part of what they would otherwise owe in profits taxation, provided that they will deposit it in the Central Bank, where it remains "frozen" until the government releases it for investment. This is used for countering the business cycle, and it may be used selectively to specify the sorts of investment desired by government. Britain has a system of actual cash grants for certain types of investment.

[69] After its return to power in 1964, the British Labour government established rebates of certain indirect taxes paid in the course of manufacture of goods for export. This, it was hoped, would lure more manufacturing effort into the export trade.

[70] Earlier, control over the issue of securities (stocks and bonds) was used. These were not particularly effective, in Britain at least, because most companies use surplus funds from earnings for a large part of their expansion plans. Political and Economic Planning (PEP), *Government and Industry* (London, 1952), p. 214, concludes its review of this type of control with the observation that it ". . . has little influence on the volume of investment, and not much on its direction." This work, incidentally, is an excellent review of the whole set of immediate postwar Labour policies and their effects.

lending operations the balance between loans for, say, housing, imports, fixed investment (factories, and so on) and consumer loans can be shifted in the direction contemplated in the national plans.

A number of other implementing devices are used, which may perhaps be mentioned briefly. First, there is extensive government assistance through sponsored research, study commissions, and other mechanisms to assist industry in improving its methods and increasing its productivity. Secondly, there is, in Norway especially, considerable government involvement in wage settlements (partly because both labor and management are nationally organized and face each other in an annual over-all wage agreement). Finally, there are innumerable contacts for persuasion, information, consultation, and other means of gaining informal consent to the following of the national plan.

Although there has been a remarkable easing of the implementing control structure since the hectic days following the Second World War, neither the British nor the Scandinavian socialists have moved so far toward the use of market influences instead of direct controls in regulating their economies that their systems cannot be distinguished readily from capitalism. Their unwillingness to abandon freedom of individual choice is quite different from an aggressive defense of freedom of choice in principle. They all impose one general limitation upon choice—the dampening of consumption in order to enlarge investment—and they intend to control and direct the economies of their nations in a manner consistent with broad social purposes. They recognize that the imprecision of the standard of social value makes it undesirable to impose detailed control on individual firms. However, they are prepared (as may be clearly seen in the statements made in their national plans) to impose more stringent ones than they now employ if the semivoluntary ones fail to hold the economy within the broad outlines intended. This is well illustrated by the comments in the British National Plan concerning the new National Board for Prices and Incomes. This board has been established to review price and wage changes in individual industries to see if they are consistent with productivity increases. At the present time the board has no enforcement power and must attempt by negotiation to induce reductions on the part of unions or managements whose wage demands or price increases exceed the amounts warranted by improvements in productivity. In this regard, the authors of the National Plan have this to say:

> To be successful a policy for prices and incomes requires the co-operation of management and workers throughout industry. It needs to be accepted by all organisations and individuals concerned with prices and incomes decisions as being both in their own interest and in the interest of the community as a whole. The Government have made clear their belief that real and lasting progress can best be made if it is based on consent. . . . The essential need is to ensure that the policy acquires increasingly greater momentum, and the Government are continuing to discuss with both management and unions ways of achieving this. *The Government have made it clear that they will*

take any further steps which may prove necessary to ensure that the objectives are realised.[71]

It would, in fact, appear that the processes of consultation and persuasion between government and business in Britain (and to a lesser degree in Norway, where some friction has been evidenced, and in Sweden) have been so fully developed that there is far less antagonism in the relationship than there would be in the United States if so close an intervention were attempted. In a fairly meaningful sense, it can be said that the British government is a participating partner in economic decision-making generally, whether that participation is regarded as backed by the possible use of coercive powers or not. The consensus of observers is that a great part of the success of British regulation has arisen from the parallel self-regulation and restraint that British private enterprise employs when the government's intention is made known.[72]

Socialist economic planning and regulation in practice, then, does serve to impose a social judgment upon the market in its central function of guiding the productive process and selecting those aspects of production to which emphasis will be given. It does so, however, by means that allow some to "buck the tide" if they are willing to pay the penalty costs attached, and provided that they do not so far defeat the purpose of planning that the State finds it necessary to apply more stringent restraint. Socialists in power have regularly proved themselves unwilling to destroy personal freedom and individuality in the pursuit of harmony and cooperation. Most impressively, they have moved since the war to lay major stress on economic growth, looking toward a greater abundance in the future that might lessen the need for the controls that now exist.

Before leaving the subject of planning, brief mention should be made of one more important element in the total schema of socialist policy, and that is *amenity planning*. Although not central to much of classical socialist thought, town and country planning has been consistently among the policies favored by the Fabians in England and practiced by socialist governments in both Britain and Scandinavia.[73] British socialists are justifiably proud of the New Towns and other beginnings of comprehensive land-use planning that

[71] Cmnd. 2764, p. 68. Italics are mine. This has since been implemented by powers given the Secretary of State for Economic Affairs to suspend projected price and wage increases temporarily.

[72] See for example, J. C. R. Dow's description of the operation of direct controls (and the many unused loopholes in them) in the period 1946 to 1958, in *The Management of the British Economy, 1945–1960* (Cambridge: Cambridge University Press, 1964), ch. VI. It must be admitted that cooperation is not always forthcoming. In respect to the prices and incomes policy referred to above, more stringent measures have already proved necessary.

[73] Early utopian socialists, especially Charles Fourier in France, were fond of including physical specifications for their ideal communities, so that the element of land-use planning was not wholly absent from socialist traditions.

were initiated under the Town and Country Planning Acts of their first post-war government. It may be expected that increasing attention will be given to this aspect of Labour party policy in the future. It is directly related to the idea of a harmonious and orderly society, and represents an area that social-ists, as reformers by nature, are likely to promote more strongly the more nearly they come to achieving their objectives in other fields. The planned provision of open spaces, parks, recreational and cultural facilities accessible to all, and of decent and comfortable housing for the lower income groups, serves to equalize advantages of rich and poor also, thereby contributing to both of the major positive objectives of the socialist movement.

Promoting Economic and Social Equality. The two principal instruments of policy for economic equalization under socialism are taxation of the well-to-do and payments or services to the poor. Surprisingly, however, it is diffi-cult to distinguish the tax systems of Britain, Norway, and Sweden from those of other countries on grounds that are clearly related to ideology. Inheritance tax rates in Britain, although much written-about, are in fact only slightly higher than in the United States, whereas those in the Scandinavian countries are lower.[74] Britain, moreover, still allows wealth to pass from generation to generation by gift, because unlike the United States, gifts made more than five years before death are not taxable.[75] An old socialist favorite for equalization purposes, the capital levy (a heavy tax on private wealth that could conceiv-ably cause a considerable redistribution at one fell swoop), has been used in Norway once to recapture gains made in wartime. The nearest approach to it in Britain, however, was the so-called Special Contribution of 1948, which was used to cover an immediate crisis in government finances and (by intention) to counteract inflationary tendencies.[76] Recent discussion of the capital levy in Britain seems to indicate that it is no longer contemplated seri-ously, on the grounds that it would be too harmful to personal incentives.

Taxation of incomes at progressive rates (rates that take a larger *percentage* of higher incomes than they do of lower ones) has been adopted, as we have seen, by most governments simply on the grounds that it is assumed that maximum revenue can be raised this way with minimum hardship to the tax-payers. Top income tax rates in Britain and Scandinavia are probably [77] a

---

[74] This comparison is of *rates* only. Depending on the deductions made, the *effective* rates can be considerably higher.

[75] The Labour party has indicated its desire to correct this, but did not do so in its 1965 tax revision.

[76] The Special Contribution was levied on the basis of income tax returns already submitted, rather than on capital, but it is generally agreed to have been paid largely out of capital, given the existing high rate of income taxation.

[77] The comparison of tax rates between countries is extremely difficult and uncertain, because the effects of exemptions for dependents, different ways of calculating tax, and different definitions of taxable income all contribute confusion. Moreover, differences in standard of living may affect the real impact of a tax in unpredictable ways.

bit higher, and they certainly are reached lower down the income scale than they are in the United States.[78] They are, however, partly offset by the presence of other taxes that are *regressive* in their effect—that is, bear more heavily on persons of low than on persons of high income—such as sales taxes, excises on tobacco, and social insurance taxes, which have their equivalents also in the United States. Until such time as truly comparable studies are made showing the over-all effects of the taxation systems of different countries on individuals at varying income levels,[79] we must conclude that the chief proven effect of socialism on tax policy is to produce a higher general level of taxation to support social services and other government activities.[80] This is shown in Table 9, which compares the proportion of total taxes to Gross National Product in England, Norway, Sweden, Canada, and the United States.

Table 9 Taxes As a Percentage of Gross National Product, Selected Countries, 1964

Country	Taxes as % of GNP
Sweden	36.7
Norway	34.3
United Kingdom	28.6
United States	27.0
Canada	26.8

Calculated from Organization for Economic Cooperation and Development, *National Accounts Statistics, 1955–1964* (March, 1966), *passim*.

There are economists who see in this a danger to incentives and risk-taking, especially in small business;[81] but here, too, the number of other influences that might be at work is too high to permit a reliable judgment.

The most spectacular part of the British Labour government's equalization

[78] The top bracket rate as of the 1965–1966 budget in Britain was 91.25 per cent, and was payable on taxable income in excess of £15,000 ($42,000). In the United States the top rate is 70 per cent (to which should be added 7 to 10 per cent, approximately, for state income taxes in most states), but it applies only to taxable income in excess of $100,000 ($200,000 for married couples). Norway and Sweden use a combination of national and municipal income taxes and a tax calculated on the basis of owned wealth (but payable out of income), with the top rate reached at a taxable income of approximately $10,500 and $28,500, respectively. Both Scandinavian nations stipulate that no taxpayer must pay more than 80 per cent of his taxable income in such taxes in a given year.

[79] For an illustration of the present state of the art, see International Association for Research in Income and Wealth, *Income and Wealth: Series X: Income Redistribution and the Statistical Foundations of Economic Policy,* Colin Clark and Geer Stuvel, eds. (London: Bowes & Bowes, 1964), especially pp. 99–120.

[80] Tax policy is, after all, an object of intense political struggle and is usually a compromise containing innumerable concessions to particular interests, both in socialist and nonsocialist countries. Tax policy is also used to promote planning objectives, as noted earlier.

[81] See Roy Harrod, *The British Economy* (New York: McGraw-Hill, 1963), pp. 63–65, 78–79, for a concise and reasonably balanced statement on this and related points.

program was, of course, the new system of social legislation, including the National Health Service, comprehensive social insurance, and family allowances (payments to families on the basis of the number of children to be supported). These represent the socialist version of the welfare state. Like other parts of the Labour program, they were not really *innovations,* but rather *enlargements* of policies of previous governments. National health insurance and social security, both incomplete as to coverage, had existed since the early part of the century. During the war, moreover, a study initiated by the coalition government, and headed by Sir William (later Lord) Beveridge, had brought forth a report urging substantially the entire program subsequently adopted by Labour.[82] Taken as a whole, Labour's social legislation was designed to provide a minimum standard of economic well-being below which no person in Great Britain should be allowed to fall. Weekly benefits were given in cases of sickness, unemployment, or disability, and pensions were paid upon retirement. Medicines, medical, dental, and ophthalmic treatment, and hospitalization were made free, although individuals were allowed to continue to use private physicians if they were willing to pay the charges. The social insurance program is supported by a special tax, but the Health Service is paid for out of general revenues.[83]

With the exception of the National Health Service, which sharply altered the economic organization of medical services, the social welfare programs of Britain (and of the Scandinavian countries as well) differ essentially only in degree of coverage and, in most respects, amount from those that are part of the pattern of social legislation in capitalist countries. Even the Health Service is but an extension of the idea of social responsibility for the unavoidable accidents of life that underlies unemployment compensation, workman's compensation, and medical care for the aged in the United States. Characteristically, however, these programs are only a part of the whole corpus of policy in Great Britain designed to reduce economic inequality and eliminate the permanent advantage of the rich. Other aspects are found in food subsidies, the whole postwar rationing system, rent controls, public housing,[84] education, land policy, agriculture policy, and (as noted before) in town and country planning.

In education the main effort of the Labour party has been to try to widen

---

[82] *Social Insurance and Allied Services,* Cmd. 6404 (London: HMSO, 1942). The Conservatives, who headed the coalition that chose Beveridge (a Liberal) to make the study, appeared to dissociate themselves from the report, although they could hardly have declined to put some of its proposals into effect had they won in 1945.

[83] Under pressure of financial difficulties, the Labour government imposed fees for some services and appliances in 1951, and the Conservatives increased and extended them. Labour is presently pledged to return to a free system, and announced elimination of prescription charges in January, 1965.

[84] Both the Conservative and Labour parties of Britain stress active housing programs, but the latter concentrates on public housing principally. In Scandinavia there are public housing, publicly aided private housing, and cooperative housing all as part of the socialist housing effort.

the educational opportunities of children of lower class parents. A study made in 1949 had revealed that in the years immediately before the Second World War boys of the upper classes in the government school system had five times the chances of a liberal secondary school education [85] as boys from the lowest classes, and thirteen times the opportunity for a university education. To this disparity could be added the boys who attended the famous "public" (really private) schools who were drawn principally from the upper classes, and whose chances of a university education were even higher.[86] By legislation in 1944, under the coalition government (but the implementation of which fell largely to the postwar Labour government), a considerable enlargement of educational opportunities was undertaken. The continuation of socialist interest is evidenced by the appointment, in late 1965, of a royal commission to study means of providing greater opportunity for lower-class (poorer) children to attend the public schools.

Equalization also enters into British Labour and Scandinavian socialist programs to capture the windfall and speculative gains arising from the rise in values of land subject to development. The nationalization of land has been repeatedly advocated in socialist circles but has been abandoned, insofar as it applies to agricultural land, because of the resistance of farmers to the idea. In the first postwar Labour government, a tax intended to mop up the appreciation in the value of land slated for urban development was levied with every grant of permission to develop under the Town and Country Planning Act and related legislation. This was repealed by the Conservatives on the ground that it stifled incentives to carry out development projects. The new Labour government has moved to reinstate it partially, with further provision for the purchase by municipalities and the central government of developable land in their jurisdiction—a practice already followed in Norway and Sweden. This is tantamount to the socialization of urban land, although it does not affect existing developments, and it has the effect of eliminating one form of "unearned" increment or gain.

Most of the equalization effort has been directed at the extremes between the very poor and the very rich, but we might note in passing some indications that the socialist outlook does not ask sacrifices only of the wealthy. As a part not only of agriculture policy, but of union activity in Scandinavia, there has been a largely successful effort to bring agricultural incomes up to a level comparable to equivalent work in industry. There is in Norway, particularly, a great sense of solidarity within the labor movement that leads industrial unions to make common cause with agricultural labor in seeking a national wage settlement. Thus, they not only sacrifice part of their bargaining power

[85] This refers to the so-called grammar school, as opposed to secondary modern, and to technical schools, which are of lesser prestige and are not designed for university preparation.

[86] Jean Floud, "The Educational Experience of the Adult Population of England and Wales as at July, 1949," in *Social Mobility in Britain,* D. V Glass, ed. (Glencoe, Ill.: The Free Press, 1954), pp. 107, 114.

in behalf of their weaker brethren, but must be prepared to accept the resulting effects in higher food prices. Because the socialist movement embraces
the unions in Norway, this phenomenon can reasonably be associated with the
practice of socialism there.

One would have to catalogue very nearly the entire policy complex of the
government to describe the ways in which purposes of equalization, or at
least, the elimination of poverty enter into it under a socialist regime. Even
in its broadest aspects, as in the effort to curb inflation (because it lessens the
value of fixed pensions for the elderly, and so on) this policy motif appears.
Suffice it on this point to quote Francis Williams, former Adviser on Public
Relations to Clement Attlee in the first postwar Labour government:

> This determination to relate all policy, even when dealing with matters
> of the most urgent importance, to a long-term social purpose can be criticised
> as doctrinaire. To that the socialist leaders would reply that . . . [t]hey are,
> and know themselves to be, the administrators of a revolution, and as such
> must measure each decision they make by the requirements of that revolu-
> tion as they see it.[87]

It is probable that the effort to provide equality will continue to be a source
of innovation in governmental policy in the future. Already there is growing
emphasis on the provision of cultural opportunities that will tend to reduce
the obvious class differences in Britain. In Sweden, government assistance
now makes possible holiday trips for children and mothers in families that
could not otherwise afford it. Intensive concentration there on the cultural
and physical development of the young is evidenced in the extensive system
of day nurseries, child health services, and even the provision of temporary
domestic help to working parents. The term *cultural democracy* has now
joined *economic democracy* in the language of socialists, and the socialist
emphasis on investment planning has now been buttressed by increased attention to investment in "intangible human capital"—in the education and cultural development, as well as in the training of the young.

Evaluation of Socialism

Joseph A. Schumpeter began the third section of his analytical study of
Capitalism, Socialism, and Democracy [88] with the question, "Can socialism
work?" He answered it immediately: "Of course it can." The socialism he
described, however, was a far cry from that practiced in the countries we have
reviewed; it was modeled not upon the pragmatic, adaptive socialism of Britain and Scandinavia, but on the rigid scheme of total public ownership advocated by philosophical socialism. In his discussion, he pointed to dangers

[87] Francis Williams, *Socialist Britain: Its Background, Its Present, and an Estimate
of its Future* (New York: The Viking Press, 1949), p. 122.
[88] 3rd ed. (New York: Harper & Brothers, 1950), p. 167.

that might arise to liberty and indicated that the working of socialism in a free society might be difficult. He did, however, hold that the conjoining of socialism and democracy was possible.

But we need not concern ourselves with a philosophical model. Despite the very short time in which socialism has been practiced, the answer seems evident that democratic, pragmatic socialism is "working." Nationalized industries have been operated at least as successfully as they were under private ownership. Considerable enlargement of social services has occurred without bankrupting the economy, and it has been possible to achieve a large measure of political direction over the economic order without serious curtailment of individual liberties. Certainly the *political* liberties of free expression and dissent have been no less carefully preserved in Britain, Norway, and Sweden than in the United States. Moreover, the emphasis socialists have placed on growth has produced economic progress that appears likely to narrow, if not eliminate, the gap between their per capita output (a good measure of economic well-being) and that of the leading capitalist countries of North America, or so at least has been the case in Norway and Sweden, as shown in Table 10. Britain has lagged, but the lag is attributable more to the antiquated structure of British industry—which the Labour party has struggled to correct—and to difficulties encountered in getting British unions (which are organizationally independent of the Labour party) to accept some of the more austere growth–inducing policies than it is to any consequences of the socialist planning effort.[89]

Table 10 Per Capita National Product in 1964 and Average Annual Rates of Growth of Per Capita Real Gross Domestic Product from 1960 to 1964, Selected Countries

Country	Per Capita National Product in 1964 (U.S. Dollars)	Average Annual Growth Rate, 1960–1964 (%)
Norway	1,689	4.6
Sweden	2,292	4.7
United Kingdom	1,690	2.6
United States	3,325	2.7
Canada	2,269	3.2

Calculated from United Nations, *Statistical Yearbook*, 1965, Tables 19, 181, 183, 185.

[89] Indeed, it could be argued that the *incompleteness* of British planning was a factor, in that growth was not pushed vigorously enough. In this connection, it should be pointed out that the period covered by Table 10 and several other illustrative tables in this chapter is one in which the Conservatives were in power. This is inescapable, since comparative statistics (as compiled by international agencies that adjust them for comparability) have not, as of this writing, been prepared for the years since Labour's return to power, and to use the 1945 to 1951 period for this purpose would introduce distortions resulting from postwar readjustments. The impairment of the illustrative value of these tables by this factor is not as great as it might be, due to the continuance by the Conservatives of the major part of the Labour government's main programs, but one should bear in mind that the effects of socialist policies are better seen in the Norwegian and Swedish figures than in the British.

Critics of socialist economics point to the fact that close direction of the economy often leads to decisions that are uneconomical from the point of view of the market—that a factory built in a particular region as a means of spurring that region's economic development may be inefficiently located with respect to the market for its products, or with respect to an already-trained local labor force to employ, for example. To say this is merely to state the obvious, however. Certainly what is done in order to maximize certain social values will seem defective if judged by other social values, and the market standard of economic efficiency is no more than one possible standard of judgment of economic policy. As we have seen before, the market standard does not usually include all social costs in its calculations in any case, so that the argument of pure "economic efficiency" might not always favor the market choice.

That there have been restrictions of *economic* freedom that would be deeply resented if applied in countries such as the United States, there is no question, but it is inherent in socialism that economic freedom will be curtailed in the interest of serving the socially established goals of national plans. These restrictions have proved acceptable in cultures less insistent than the American culture upon the privately oriented rights of individual property owners, more concerned with the corporate development of the community and the obligations of members of society to society at large, and less confident of the prospect for indefinite future expansion without conscious direction of the process. Socialism has required denial of the free choice of a businessman to develop his enterprise as he sees fit, and it has even imposed restraint upon consumers as a means of ensuring the availability of resources to provide growth for future well-being. In most instances, socialists have avoided limitations on *variety* of consumer choice,[90] but aggregate statistics indicate a suppression of private consumption in the interest of increasing the flow of resources into investment. The relationship between consumption and investment expenditure in Britain, where socialist planning was incomplete, resembles that in the United States.[91] Norway and Sweden, however, do show fixed investment expenditure taking in the neighborhood of one quarter of the total value of productive output, whereas private consumption is held to below 60 per cent, as may be seen in Table 11.[92] In order to achieve this,

---

[90] In some cases, they have promoted and even required production of goods that private enterprise had failed to supply voluntarily. Cooperatives in Scandinavia, and the government in Britain, actively promoted the production of so-called utility goods and even utility bread—products that lacked frills and ornamentation designed to assist advertising of them, but that were made cheaply, of sound quality, and in the case of bread, of optimum nutritional value.

[91] The new National Plan, however, proposes a reduction in the proportion given to private consumption by about 2 percentage points and a corresponding increase in that given to fix investment, to be achieved by 1970.

[92] Also to be noted is the larger proportion of government expenditure on purchases of civilian goods and services associated with socialist governments, despite the fact that these figures do not include cash payments such as welfare grants.

socialists have been forced to limit the amount of money available for consumer spending by the imposition of sales taxes, by restricting consumer credit (time payment plans), and in some cases, by holding down wages (because wage earners tend to spend, that is, consume, a larger proportion of their incomes than persons in higher income brackets). Norway, in particular, has followed a policy of active wage restraint.[93]

Table 11 Percentage Allocation of Gross National Product to Various Types of Expenditure, Selected Countries, 1964

Country	Private Consumption Expenditure	Government Purchase of Goods & Services		Fixed Capital Investment	Other *
		Military	Civilian		
Norway	57%	3%	12%	29%	−1%
Sweden	57	4	14	23	1
United Kingdom	65	6	11	18	1
United States	63	8	10	17	2
Canada	63	4	11	23	†

* Includes inventory changes, net surplus or deficit in international trade balance and international investments, and (in the case of Canada) statistical discrepancy. Percentages do not add to 100 because of rounding.
† Less than −0.5 per cent.
Calculated from Organization for Economic Cooperation and Development, *National Accounts Statistics, 1955–1964* (March, 1966), *passim.*

Socialism, then (some would say surprisingly), has not been characterized by governments dedicated to serving every demand of labor and to suppression only of the capitalist class. Socialism has demanded effort (and sacrifice) on the part of substantially all segments of society in the interest of the common good as determined in the political order. The decline of the "class war" concept that underlay the earlier formulations of socialism, especially the Marxian variety, and the responsibility for the whole of society that socialists had to assume upon accession to power, has made them both willing and able to seek a balance between the desires of their principal supporters and the needs of the rest of the community.

Political and Economic Power. If a rough balance among *demands* made upon various segments of society seems to be emerging, what can be said about the structure of economic and political *power?* Has socialism achieved its objective of bringing about social control of economic power? The answer to this, if we take social control to mean control by the general public, must certainly be mixed. The picture presented by socialist countries today does not match easily with the vision of an economy made subject to the democratic will. Partly, of course, this merely reflects the difficulty in showing the impact of the public will on representative democracy generally and in defining the

[93] Norway's approach is described in Allan G. Gruchy, *Comparative Economic Systems* (Boston: Houghton Mifflin Company, 1966), pp. 324–325. Britain refrained from the use of coercive powers until the economic crisis of 1966 and has been decidedly less successful in holding wages down. This helps to explain the British figures in Table 11.

public will itself. Nevertheless, there are some tentative observations that can be made about the manner in which economic decisions are now made and about the forms and the employment of political and economic power.

To begin with, the economic power of private individuals has been reduced and circumscribed. The processes of socialist planning are a limitation on the range of decision open to the private entrepreneur and to the union leader. Nationalization, also, has in large measure taken the "commanding heights of the economy" from private hands, so that the very greatest potential sources of private economic power have been eliminated.[94]

The power that has been taken from private industry has been lodged, theoretically at least, in government, but it is at this point that the picture becomes somewhat less clear. In the first place, as was shown, the nationalized industries retain a considerable measure of managerial independence, and such political direction as is imposed upon them is often carried out beyond the public view. What results, then, is a combination of managerial and technical decision-making by the political leadership (the ministers) and the economic leadership (the boards and managers of the industries) that, although intended in the public interest, is not actually subjected in any clear way to public review and electoral decision. A marked difference exists here between the handling of nationalized industries' decisions and those made by private enterprise in a socialist state. In Norway and Sweden, for example, private cartels are permitted, but they must register with the State, and their agreements are published. The result of this publicity, especially as it affects pricing policies, is that many such agreements have been cancelled voluntarily.[95]

In a similar way, the studies and reports on price and wage rises made by the British National Board for Prices and Incomes and the Norwegian Ministry of Wages and Prices give more publicity to private economic decision-making, including union decisions (and therefore impose more impressive public pressure), than exists for State-owned enterprises. In a sense, then, the managers of public enterprises, especially public monopolies, receive some

[94] In the language of military strategy in a nuclear age (as opposed to the gunpowder-age image of "commanding heights") it might be suggested that the "capability" possessed by private holders of the "heights" might not be employable without risking annihilation anyway. Surely the owners and managers of basic industries in the United States do not imagine that they could try to dominate decision-making in the United States economy without encountering "massive retaliation." In this sense, then, if the private economic power eliminated by public ownership (and to be eliminated, if steel is renationalized in Britain) was largely illusory. One might add that "massive retaliation" including a measure of "overkill" (as registered by the stock market reaction to it) was used in 1962 against the United States steel industry in response to much less drastic action than the "commanding heights" image suggests. (Similar actions were taken in 1965 to 1966 against steel, aluminum, and copper in response to price rises the government opposed.)

[95] The agreements are also subject to disallowance by the State. A somewhat similar law exists now in England, passed by the Conservatives in 1956.

protection from *public* control in compensation for their subjection to *ministerial* or governmental control. Economic power is more centralized than it is under private ownership, but less centralized than it would be if managerial and ministerial independence did not exist in public enterprise.

The second element confusing the picture of public control of the economy under socialism involves the planning process. By intention the planning objectives under socialism are set by the political order, and the private sector of the economic order is merely consulted and instructed. In practice, however, in both planning and plan implementation, private interests may play a very large role. Like other forms of governmental intervention into a partially private economic order, planning is not neutral. It operates to distribute benefits and disabilities to both management and labor, and elicits therefore a response in the form of interest group representation that seeks to influence the planning process. The early postwar experience of the British affords an example that is probably extreme and, therefore, unrepresentative of the general pattern, but it does illustrate the point: Planning was carried out by consultations among representatives of the various economic departments in the government, each estimating the needs of the industries in the area of its concern. The Ministry of Supply, for example, acted as representative for the capital goods industries—including iron and steel, chemicals, engineering, and aircraft—and the Ministry of Transport represented railways.[96] Under the coalition government in wartime these same departments had acted as "sponsors" for their industries in the obtention of scarce materials. They had, therefore, built up close relationships with their "client" industries. They were in the first instances judges of their clients' claims, deciding just how much of their requests they could support, but in the actual planning process they became advocates.[97] Similarly, the process of allocating materials, which was one of the strongest of the physical controls used to implement the plans, was described in the following terms by one economist observing it:

> Ideally, perhaps, the pattern of . . . allocation would have sprung from the pattern of output the government intended. In practice, it was a result of a tussle between different [sponsoring] departments and sections of departments. Again, allocations to different firms had necessarily to be made according to some rule of thumb, and were in fact generally based on what different firms had used before the war.[98]

The strongly entrenched customs of consultation and compromise between government and private interests that characterize all three of the nations principally described in this chapter have permitted the representatives of trade unions, of large enterprises, and of economic associations—all of whom

[96] Ben W. Lewis, *British Planning and Nationalization* (New York: Twentieth Century Fund, 1952), p. 14.
[97] *Ibid.*, pp. 21–22.
[98] Dow, *op. cit.*, pp. 161–162.

are the principal wielders of private economic power—to influence the course of governmental planning and plan implementation. As a consequence, they continue to wield economic power even when that power is officially possessed by the political order. They wield it, not because of some right or title accruing to ownership, but because they lead and direct large social organizations, and it is felt just that they should be consulted. They do so, however, under responsible guidance by officials who are accountable through the political order, and they are no longer able to act arbitrarily, without consultation with, or permission from, these same officials.

One other apparent facet of the same phenomenon is seen in the great multiplication and concentration of interest groups in Britain and Sweden and in their increasing growth in Norway. The small size and relative homogeneity of these countries would lead one to expect that interests would be more completely organized than in the United States, but the degree of organization is somewhat surprising. In Britain, for example, the British Employers' Confederation, which already included firms that negotiated with 70 per cent of the employed population,[99] merged with the Federation of British Industries (which tended to represent larger firms) and the National Association of British Manufacturers (small and medium) to form one national organization, the Confederation of British Industries (CBI), to speak for employers. Interestingly enough, nine of the nationalized industry boards, including the largest employer of all, the National Coal Board, announced in early 1966 that they, too, were joining CBI. The National Farmers' Union represents 90 per cent of the farmers in England and Wales (the other parts of the United Kingdom have separate farmers' organizations); the Trade Union Congress (most of whose member unions are affiliated with, and form the major constituent element in the Labour party) includes approximately one half of the eligible workers; the Co-operative Union includes over 96 per cent of all cooperative societies; and the British Medical Association includes 85 per cent of its profession. Additionally, there are interlocking memberships (the National Farmers' Union was a member of the old Federation of British Industries) and a multitude of trade associations and other sectional interest groups, so that group organization tends to be both more intensive than in the United States and, for particular purposes, more specialized at the same time.[100]

Sweden displays a similar pattern,[101] to which must be added the Scandinavian practice of organizing the political party system to give the principal

[99] S. E. Finer, "Interest Groups and the Political Process in Great Britain," in *Interest Groups on Four Continents,* Henry W. Ehrmann, ed. (Pittsburgh: University of Pittsburgh Press, 1958), pp. 118–122 is the source of the figures given in this paragraph.

[100] Finer reports that Britain has 1,200 manufacturers' trade associations compared to an estimated 800 in the United States, despite the latter's larger size. *Ibid.,* p. 118.

[101] "At present, Swedish society is more completely organized than most Western societies." Gunnar Heckscher, "Interest Groups in Sweden: Their Political Role," in Ehrmann, ed., *op. cit.,* p. 157.

economic interests—labor, farmers, and business—each at least one party mainly responsive to it.[102]

It seems likely that growth of the economic power wielded by government and extension of political involvement in the economic order are bound to increase the response of affected interests in the form of organizing to press their claims to have that power used, if not to their advantage, at least not against them.[103] There is no reason for them to assume that their particular interests are safe in the hands of the political order, or that their interests are identical with those of the community, however well organized and well run that community may be. Furthermore, because the political order is committed to heavy intervention in the economic order, economic interests cannot afford the luxury of merely acting as "veto groups." Legislation, they know, *will* be enacted and policy made. They must organize effectively to shape it, or face the consequences, and this requires of them a higher level of activity than is demanded in a capitalist system. Intensive organization of economic interest groups and heightened political activity by private economic interests, then, is to be expected under socialism, and it does appear to exist.[104]

In general it would appear that democratic socialism as presently practiced has not succeeded in transferring economic power entirely from private hands to the political order. Rather, it has intertwined political and economic power in a fashion that certainly increases the importance of the former in directing the use of the latter, while at the same time inducing the holders of economic power to be more conscious of, and to seek more actively, a voice or influence in the political order. The fact that economic decision-making, including especially planning, involves highly technical questions makes the public at large able to enter the policy-making process in only the most general way. The leaders in the political order undoubtedly seek to serve the public and

[102] This practice, of course, antedates socialist government but is not unconnected with socialism, for the emergence of a socialist party with a strong labor and reform bias at about the turn of the century in both Norway and Sweden was followed by the creation (or, in Sweden, rebirth) of an agrarian party. Farmers had found their own interests ill-tended in the political struggles between the bourgeois conservative and liberal parties on the one hand, and the socialist parties on the other. See Maurice Duverger, *Political Parties: Their Organization and Activity in the Modern State,* 2nd ed., trans. by Barbara and Robert North (London: Methuen & Co., Ltd., 1959), pp. 234–238.

[103] This phenomenon in general terms as applied to the United States is discussed in David B. Truman, *The Governmental Process* (New York: Alfred A. Knopf, Inc., 1951), ch. 4.

[104] It must be stressed that the presence of a multiplicity of interest groups and a high degree of organization among them in socialist countries is not proof that socialism is the causative factor. There are too many other potential causes for it. What is suggested here is that there is a *logical* connection, and the practice does not refute the logic. Beyond that one cannot go with assurance. Further discussion of this thesis with specific reference to Britain and the United States is to be found in Samuel H. Beer, "Group Representation in Britain and the United States," *The Annals of the American Academy of Political and Social Science,* Vol. 319 (September, 1958), pp. 130–140.

possess the authority to make binding decisions effective upon the economic order. In making them, however, they are restrained from doing so either arbitrarily or in too great detail by a number of considerations: In the first place, they are conscious of the imprecision of their own standards for economic judgment and seek not detailed direction of the economy, but the promotion of a rather broad pattern of selective growth, accompanied by certain types of restraint. Secondly, they have found some instruments of control both distasteful to themselves and politically unpopular, especially rationing and labor directives. Thirdly, they have found the active cooperation of business and labor leaders useful in achieving conformity to their plans. They are anxious not to damage friendly relations by actions that would be regarded as harsh or arbitrary and that would, therefore, become most difficult and costly to sustain and enforce. They want and need the information and the technical advice that those same leaders of the private economic order supply and would be badly hampered if they had to work in an atmosphere of active hostility. Under such conditions they would be forced to do what most of them no longer desire: Take over and manage the entire economic establishment.[105]

For their part, business and labor leaders find themselves drawn into active consideration of the social and political effects of their contemplated actions (through their consultation in the planning process) and unable to act freely on their own judgment. Businessmen, and to a lesser degree labor leaders, face a political order clearly willing, if necessary, to impose its own judgment upon theirs. They find it necessary to seek permission for new ventures. They cannot avoid the political dimension of economic decision that inhibits both arbitrary use of power and (unless their proposals find support in the political order) radical changes in the existing arrangements for production and distribution.[106] They must intensify their efforts to exert political power.

Can this intertwining proceed without producing a new type of public-private technocracy from which the public is excluded as a controlling force? At present this does not appear to be the case. The relations between business, labor, and government are still better characterized as a struggle than as a process of harmonious consultation, and even the representatives of government are, as we have seen, divided in their stands. As in all functioning democracies, the leaders in the political order are conscious that they will be

---

[105] They could not gain popular consent to do so in any case. Recent studies show a strong majority opinion opposed to nationalization in most Western countries. See the studies reported in Seymour Martin Lipset, "The Changing Class Structure and Contemporary European Politics," *Daedalus,* XCIII (Winter, 1964), p. 282.

[106] Of course, the reverse is also true, for government may, and in Britain, especially does, apply considerable pressure for modernization and development of new product lines where an essential industry is lagging. This was evidenced in the efforts made by the British iron and steel industry to modernize in a futile effort to stave off nationalization after the war. Socialist governments have so far been less able to induce labor to accept innovation.

judged for re-election by their results, rather than for the technical considerations that entered into their decisions. The private participants, business and labor both, can and do make their appeal to public judgment in support of opposing political parties.

In fact socialism leads to very great reliance on the electoral process as the means of restraining the arbitrary use of power, both political and economic. Because both planning and nationalization reduce the effectiveness of business competition as a restraint upon economic power,[107] and because intensive consultation reduces the independence of business, labor, and government in relation to one another, the restraints that are found in capitalism are weaker under socialism, and must be made up either by self-restraint on the part of the participants or by reference to the electoral process. In this there does lie a possible danger, for it increases both the number of issues involved in an electoral decision and their technical complexity. It places a strain on the political order, which is already burdened by many economic issues, plus those involved in social regulation and international affairs.[108]

The Struggle for Social Equality. It is exceedingly difficult to offer a reliable measurement of the degree to which socialists have succeeded in their important objective of providing substantial economic and social equality. Socialism is, after all, a protest not merely against the fact of economic inequality, but against the "society of unequals" in which inequality becomes embedded and perpetuated in a class structure and in the sense of superiority and inferiority that the concept of class conveys. To be judged as having succeeded in having reached its objective, socialism must be shown not only

[107] Not only does planning inhibit competition (by substituting government allocation of investment opportunities for private venturesomeness), but it happens that all three countries (and most other European nations) are less inclined to prohibit monopolistic practices than is the United States, although they have taken recent steps in this direction. Some competition is maintained and is even enhanced when, as in Scandinavia, public and private enterprises exist in the same field.

[108] In the more distant future another problem may be encountered. Socialist planning to date has been governed largely by standards established within the context of capitalist accomplishments, and it is not unfair to say that the growth goals of Britain, Norway, and Sweden have, at least partly, the economic condition of the United States as their model. Just as under affluent capitalism consumer choice becomes more whimsical and arbitrary, and requires advertising to stabilize it, so also it may be expected that a socialist system under close political control would reach a stage of uncertainty of judgment in time. At what point, for example, should Norway and Sweden allow the percentage of national income allotted to private consumption to rise above its present level? At what point should freedom of consumer choice (presently patterned after the existing supply of consumer goods) be allowed to dictate the production of a good or service not presently enjoyed? How would such a decision be made, and what would be the recourse of the general public against a negative decision in so speculative an area? The possibilities are great that such an issue could be lost among others. The defeat of the Norwegian Labor party in 1965, for example, was seemingly unrelated to any of the policies the government had pursued for the preceding thirty years.

to have reduced disparities in income and wealth but also to have lessened appreciably the *feeling* of inequality. Yet the determinants of this feeling are many, and to identify a reduction of class antagonisms only with certain policies adopted by particular governments would be to do violence to reality. Such reduction has been observed in recent years in most of the nations of the Western world, whether governed by socialists or not. It is at least partly attributable simply to the improvement of the general standard of living—an improvement that has enabled the lower economic groups to achieve a consumption pattern much closer to that of the well-to-do than they could formerly enjoy.[109]

Inequality, then, is at least as much a cultural phenomenon as an objective one. A class structure can long survive the conditions that gave rise to it, and we must begin our evaluation with the recognition that cultural traits are slow to change, and socialist regimes have been in power for too short a time to have had a drastic effect on the cultural traditions of their societies. Because the problem of social inequality and class-consciousness is distinctly more acute in Britain than in Scandinavia, perhaps the effects of socialist policies, despite their partial interruption by a long period of Conservative government, can be discussed best in terms of developments there.

In objective terms, socialist policies have effected a considerable change in the distribution of incomes in Britain but have had only a gradual influence (largely because they have been incomplete [110]) upon the distribution of privately held wealth. The top one per cent of the adult population in Britain, which owned 56 per cent of all private wealth in 1936, still owned 42 per cent in 1956.[111]

Income redistribution has been achieved principally through the tax system and welfare services. As it happens, there have been noticeable changes both in the range of incomes *received* (before taxes) and in the net effect on incomes of governmental *redistributive* policies compared with the period before the socialists came to power. The former, however, seems to be an expression of the same phenomenon that has occurred in the United States: The tendency

---

[109] Lipset, *op. cit.,* "The Changing Class Structure and Contemporary European Politics," p. 272.

[110] The principal weaknesses have been in the failure to enact a tax on gifts to accompany the heavy estate taxation and in the absence, until 1965, of a tax on capital gains (both of which the United States has had for years).

[111] By comparison, the top one per cent of the United States adult population in 1958 owned 23.8 per cent of private wealth. British figures are from H. F. Lydall and D. G. Tipping, "The Distribution of Personal Wealth in Britain," *Bulletin of the Oxford University Institute of Statistics,* XXIII (January, 1961), p. 92, and the United States figures from James D. Smith and Staunton K. Calvert, "Estimating the Wealth of Top Wealth-Holders from Estate Tax Returns," a paper prepared for presentation at the Annual Meeting of the American Statistical Association, Philadelphia, September, 1965, p. 20.

for income disparities to decrease as over-all income rises.[112] The nationalizations and planning policies appear to have had little over-all effect on pretax incomes, because the industries nationalized were compensated for, and because the various incentives and penalties used to implement the plans at least partly counteracted one another.

Britain's taxing and public expenditure programs, by one estimate, redistributed approximately 8.8 per cent of the national income in 1937; by 1948 to 1949, under the Labour government, the proportion had increased to 13.1 per cent.[113] The effect of these was to reduce the disparity between high and low incomes and to "bunch" most family incomes within a narrow range, where the highest income received was no higher than ten times the lowest. This effect, and a comparison with the Untied States, is shown in Table 12.

Table 12 Effect of Taxation and Benefits on Income Distribution, United States and United Kingdom Compared

Country	Income Distribution Before Taxes and Benefits		Income Distribution After Taxes and Benefits	
	% Within Range *	% Outside Range *	% Within Range *	% Outside Range *
United States (1946–47)	62.6	37.4	74.7	25.3
United Kingdom (1948–49)	62.1	37.9	87.4	12.6

* Range is fixed such that the lowest income is no less than half the average family income, and the highest not more than five times the average. Per cent is of total *number* of incomes reported. Adapted from Allan Murray Cartter, *The Redistribution of Income in Postwar Britain: A Study of the Effects of the Central Government Fiscal Program in 1948–49,* (New Haven: Yale University Press, 1955), Table 38, p. 90. Copyright 1955 by Yale University Press. Reprinted by permission.

Not only has Britain succeeded in significantly altering the pattern of income distribution, but her people encounter nearly as good a chance to rise or fall in the occupational structure as is found in the United States. Although upward mobility in Britain is somewhat less than is found in America and downward mobility greater,[114] the gross mobility rate does not differ significantly.

[112] See Simon Kuznets, "Economic Growth and Income Inequality," *American Economic Review,* XLV (March, 1955) reprinted in his *Economic Growth and Structure: Selected Essays* (New York: W. W. Norton & Co., 1965), pp. 257–287. Kuznets points out that, at least in the more advanced economies, economic growth produces a narrowing of income inequalities even before taxes and social walfare benefits are computed.

[113] Allan Murray Cartter, *The Redistribution of Income in Postwar Britain: A Study of the Effects of the Central Government Fiscal Program in 1948–49* (New Haven: Yale University Press, 1955), pp. 79, 84. The comparable estimate for the United States in 1946–47 was 7.5 per cent. Interestingly enough, the difference was largely accounted for by the *size* of the fiscal programs of the two countries, for Britain redistributed 32 per cent of its tax revenues, whereas the United States redistributed 31 per cent, according to these estimates. These estimates should be treated with caution for, as indicated previously with respect to taxation, international comparisons are uncertain.

[114] S. M. Miller, "Comparative Social Mobility," *Current Sociology,* IX, No. 1 (1960), pp. 29–58. The Swedish pattern closely resembles that of Britain. Norway was not compared.

Neither country, however, can attribute its mobility rate principally to distinctive policies pursued by its political order for, as the authors of a recent comparative study say, *"The overall pattern of social mobility appears to be much the same in the industrial societies of various Western countries."* [115] There is little information with which to judge changes in these rates that might have occurred since the socialist policies were instituted.

By objective standards, then, Britain seems to have a reasonably fluid society and it has been made distinctly more equal in the distribution of incomes than it was before the socialists came into office. What, then, of class *feeling?* Paradoxically, class consciousness appears to remain high, and the British are far more willing and able to identify social classes and to rank themselves within them than are Americans.[116] Writers have frequently remarked on the distrust that exists between workers and management in Britain, and between classes generally, as suggested in the following passage from Mr. Crosland: [117]

> [Britain is] a society characterised by an exceptionally mature political democracy, growing economic prosperity, and a social order which apparently metes out social justice in a reasonable degree: yet still with an unreconstructed class system, productive of deep collective resentments. The apparent invulnerability of this system to changes in the sphere of income suggests that the classless society will not be reached simply by more redistribution of wealth.

There is also a form of class-consciousness that, rather than being antagonistic, is *deferential,* as suggested in the following two responses to interview questions asked by a Labour party member seeking an explanation of the party's loss in a recent election (they must have brought tears to the eyes of the interviewer):

> —There are only two classes, the bosses and the workers. I vote for the bosses; they give you the work and they've got the money.

[115] Seymour Martin Lipset and Reinhard Bendix, *Social Mobility in Industrial Society* (Berkeley and Los Angeles: University of California Press, 1959), p. 13. Italics in the original.

[116] A study in 1950 in two districts near London using open-ended questions about class (questions that asked the subjects to define the class structure in their own terms and then rank themselves) evoked the following self-assessments: "lower" or "poor," 9 per cent, "working," 36.6 per cent, "lower middle," 3.9 per cent, "middle," 37.2 per cent, "Upper Middle" or "Professional," 3.9 per cent and "upper," 0.2 per cent. Altogether, 96.1 per cent of the sample attempted self-assessment. See F. M. Martin, "Some Subjective Aspects of Social Stratification," in D. V. Glass, ed., *op. cit.,* pp. 51–55. A comparable study in the United States found 27.5 per cent unable to rank themselves while 62.3 per cent of those who essayed a ranking chose "middle class." See Nathalie Rogoff, "Social Stratification in France and in the United States," *American Journal of Sociology,* LVIII (January, 1953), p. 349.

[117] *Op. cit.,* p. 103.

—Labour's better for us, for the working class. But the Conservatives are better for the country as a whole. They're the party of businessmen; they're used to running things—they were brought up to it; and, after all what's the state except the biggest business of them all? [118]

Available indications on the current trend of class feeling in Britain are at best contradictory. Professor S. M. Lipset points to increased leftist agitation in the Labour party as suggesting increased tension,[119] whereas the authors of the study *The British General Election of 1959* viewed the increasing affluence and economic equality in British society as reducing the tendency of the working classes, at least, to maintain their self-identification: "At the bench a man may still be plainly working class, but in his new home, in his car, or out shopping, his social position may be more difficult to assess. He may well think of himself as a consumer first and only secondly as a worker." [120]

Table 13   Class Voting in the 1964 British General Election

Party	% of Total Vote	Social Class of Voters Middle Class (10%) *	Lower Middle (29%) *	Skilled Working (39%) *	Unskilled "Very Poor" (31%) *
Conservative	42.9	74.7%	60.7%	33.9%	30.9%
Labour	44.8	8.9	24.8	54.4	59.1
Liberal	11.4	14.9	13.7	10.9	9.1
Other	0.9	1.5	0.8	0.8	0.9
	100.0%	100.0%	100.0%	100.0%	100.0%

* Figure in parentheses represents proportion of total electorate falling in that class. Figures in column under each class heading show the way in which the members of that class distributed their vote among the parties. Adapted from D. E. Butler and Anthony King, *The British General Election of 1964* (London: Macmillan & Co., Ltd., 1965), p. 296. Copyright, 1965, D. E. Butler and Anthony King. Reprinted by permission of Macmillan & Co., Ltd. and The Macmillan Company of Canada, Ltd.

Certain it is, that the very nature of socialist politics makes it difficult to overcome class feelings, simply because the appeal of a socialist party is toward those who sense the existence of social discrimination against them. It is hard for a socialist party not to present the image of a class party seeking to wrest power from the dominant classes in society. Like socialist parties throughout Europe, Labour draws its voting support much more strikingly from a particular social stratum than do the nonsocialist parties, as shown in Table 13. Equally, its spokesmen—its candidates for Parliament—display a class origin markedly different, as measured by education (a good index of

[118] Ralph Samuel, "The Quality of Life," *Where? (5 views on Labour's Future)*, Fabian Tract 320 (London: The Fabian Society, 1959), p. 32.

[119] *Op. cit.*, "The Changing Class Structure and Contemporary European Politics," note, p. 276.

[120] D. E. Butler and Richard Rose, *The British General Election of 1959* (London: Macmillan and Co. Ltd., 1960), p. 15. Of course, the prosperity referred to occurred during the period of Conservative rule (and won the Conservatives the victory).

class in Britain), from the candidates of other parties. (See Table 14.) Both of these tend to accentuate, rather than overcome, class feeling in politics.[121]

Table 14 Educational Background of Party Candidates in the British General Election of 1964 (Figures are in percentages of all candidates for a given party having the educational background specified.)

Education	Labour	Conservative	Liberal
State schools only; no university training *	52.7	18.4	29.6
Private schools; no university training †	2.5	23.0	11.8
Total with university training	44.7	58.6	58.6
	100	100	100
Total with private school training (with & without university)	16.9	66.2	38.4

* Includes some who attended adult education colleges.
† Private school here means what the British call public schools. Attendance at one of these generally signifies higher social background than the State schools.
Calculated from D. E. Butler and Anthony King, *The British General Election of 1964* (London: Macmillan & Co., Ltd., 1965), p. 237. Copyright, 1965, by D. E. Butler and Anthony King. Used by permission of Macmillan & Co. Ltd. and The Macmillan Company of Canada, Ltd.

Eradication of class feeling will take time—time for the equalizing policies to have their effect on habits of thought. It will also require the elimination of visible and audible signs of class difference—styles of dress, speech, and bearing—that still survive in Britain in far sharper form than most Americans suspect.[122] It is to these, most particularly as embodied in their perpetuation by separate school systems and divergent cultural opportunities for the sons of the rich and the sons of the poor that the Labour party is now turning in its continuing effort to achieve an egalitarian society.[123] It has greatly tempered its class appeal over the years since the Second World War (as have most of the socialist parties of Europe, including the German), so that one may expect a gradual reduction of class consciousness over time. Nevertheless, the social pattern of inequality, which is in many ways the *raison d'être* of socialism and the chief source of emotional commitment to the socialist cause, is likely to be most resistant to reform.

Toward a Cooperative and Harmonious Society. From the foregoing it appears that the objective of a cooperative and harmonious society has not

[121] This records itself in the negative images the members of each party have of members of the other. Gabriel A. Almond and Sidney Verba show British Labourites and Conservatives regarding each other as selfish and ignorant to a much greater degree than American partisans do—*The Civic Culture: Political Attitudes and Democracy in Five Nations* (Princeton: Princeton University Press, 1963), pp. 125–126.

[122] Crosland points out that the character of Eliza Doolittle in Shaw's *Pygmalion* (*My Fair Lady*), with her extraordinary accent, is not looked on in Britain as improbable and farcical, as she is regarded elsewhere (*op. cit.,* p. 111).

[123] The Labour government announced the appointment, in December, 1965, of a commission to widen access to the socially prestigious public (really private) schools that are the chief perpetuators of a special culture for the British elite.

been achieved under socialism. Certainly none of the countries reviewed presents an idyllic picture of brotherhood and common cause. Class antagonisms, conflict and struggle of interests in the planning process, and the usual tumult of political campaigns indicate that divisive forces are still very much alive. Correspondingly, there is no useful evidence that the attitude of workers toward their jobs and toward management, especially in England, has undergone significant change. (It should be added that this statement applies equally to changes in all directions; the fears of opponents of the welfare state that workers would cease to strive have not found confirmation either.) Yet it should be noted that the exercise of political power by labor-backed socialist parties has completed the integration of the working classes into the political community that had, in the countries we have been investigating, been delayed in comparison with that same integration in the United States. The workers have received satisfaction in having been permitted access to political rule, and they have signified it by coming to terms with the existing political and economic structure, instead of seeking to overthrow it out of hand. There is, then, some easing of tensions as the result of the ability of the total community to absorb what could have been a most serious challenge, although it cannot be attributed to the practice of socialism as such. The general solidarity and sense of community that Britain, Norway, and Sweden display today is as much or more a part of the general culture of these countries and a consequence of the wartime experience of common sacrifice and effort (in Britain and Norway), as it is a product of socialism. In fact, it seems more than likely that it is these characteristics that have made socialism successful and permitted the controls desired by socialists to be imposed and accepted without bitterness and resentment.

The conditions that socialists in power have accepted, of course, have prevented a true experiment in reshaping the culture to achieve maximum stress on cooperative, rather than competitive, attitudes. They have left in existence a considerable part of the capitalist structure of industry, with its concomitant multiplicity and diversity of interests. They have declined to impose massive social retraining and propagandizing (such as communists and fascists employ) in order to reshape human personality and social values. They have maintained, in short, a *pluralistic* society with all that this implies in terms of personal freedom, individuality, and right of dissent. As democrats, as well as socialists, they have tempered their demands for orderliness and controlled development where those demands would require strict enforcement on specific individuals. They have relied instead on broader inducements and penalties that emphasized common goals but allowed a choice to conform or not to conform. They have not sought a tyranny of the majority or a "dictatorship of the proletariat," but have permitted the cleavages and disagreement on policy that are necessary for effective democracy.

They retain their hope for increasing cooperation, however, and continue to seek new ways to enlarge the area of agreement in policy-making, despite occasional discouragements.[124] If it must be agreed that socialist goals have not been fully achieved, it may also be admitted that those goals set a very high standard against which to judge performance, and a difficult one, given the gradualist and uncoercive measures that socialists have, in practice, chosen to employ. To return to the words quoted earler of Francis Williams, socialists "are, and know themselves to be, the administrators of a revolution," but they are committed as democrats, to most unrevolutionary means.

Socialism and the Developing Nations

Given socialism's emphasis on directed and stimulated economic development and the need for rapid development in the poorer nations of the world, it would seem that socialist doctrine and practice would be highly appropriate for these nations to adopt. And, indeed, many, if not most of the recently independent states of Africa and Asia have explicitly declared their intention to organize their political and economic systems on socialist principles. It would be a mistake, however, to assume either that Western socialism is an adequate model for them, or that democratic socialism will provide a solution to the enormous difficulties they face.

Socialism, as we have seen, developed out of a specific set of circumstances in the cultural environment in Western Europe. Its doctrines, framed in reaction to the conditions created by the emergence of a capitalistic economy in a postfeudal society, do not meet the particular problems that are most acute in African and Asian countries [125] and could be most misleading if they were so applied. Many of the less-advanced of them hoped to leap from a pre-industrial, nonacquisitive society to an industrial society without passing through the highly inegalitarian and acquisitive stages against which socialist ideology is directed. At the same time, however, and for perfectly sound reasons, they have accepted modern socialism's decreased stress on nationalization. They hope to take advantage of private initiative where it exists and to employ state enterprises in new and socially important industrial and developmental projects. In this, despite their intentions, they are likely to encounter sharply increasing differences in wealth and income between the private entrepreneurs and the masses.[126] If, in the name of equality, these

[124] Norway, for example, attempted to bring management and labor formally into the planning process by creating an Economic Coordinating Council in 1947, but found it too plagued with disagreements to be effective and abandoned it in 1954. Attempts to revive it in the 1960s were made repeatedly, and also failed.

[125] Because the political and economic situation in Latin America is distinctly different from that in Africa and Asia, the former will be omitted from this discussion. Space does not permit treatment of both.

[126] Although countries near the upper end of the scale in per capita income find income differentials *decreasing* in periods of economic growth, the reverse is apparently true for those near the bottom of the scale. The over-all standard of living is so low, moreover, that these differentials produce strikingly unequal patterns of consumption, likely to arouse envy. See Kuznets, *op. cit.,* pp. 274–284.

differences are attacked by taxation or confiscation, the incentives of a most useful segment of the population will be impaired, and the State will have to enlarge the area of its activity to maintain the intended growth.[127]

The doctrinal difficulties are in some measure recognized. Africans and Asians who have chosen socialism have done so not so much for its perfect applicability to their situation, but as the framework for the least objectionable means for rapid development. Such experience as many of them had of capitalism in the hands of colonial traders and extractive industries has not endeared them to that method, and their observation of the human costs that attended forced collectivization in Soviet Russia and China have so far induced most of them to shun the communist path.[128] Within that framework, however, there has been and will be considerable adaptation. African socialists, for example, although largely trained in European and American universities, have been developing their own brand of socialism in which, specifically, the class war basis of socialism is disavowed on the grounds that Africa is classless to begin with. Other doctrines have emerged, therefore, hinging on the supposed communal and cooperative native social organization.[129] There is considerable emotional force behind the development of a specifically African socialist ideology, for it accompanies African nationalism and the drive for a self-respecting African identity.

Like Western socialism, the African and Asian varieties are now wedded to nationalism or, in the case of parts of Africa, pan-Africanism. The development of a distinctive ideology is only a part of the process of disassociation from the former colonial powers with which Western socialists are, despite their best intentions and actions, linked in the minds of the new nations' leaders.

A practical problem that socialists in developing nations must face is the determination of what must and what must not be planned. The experience of India suggests that it is possible to plan and control too much. India has imposed more stringent controls over her private sector than has any developed socialist nation, occasionally with harmful results. In some areas initiative has been stifled, in others the controls keep inefficient firms alive

[127] See Jacob Viner, "The Economics of Development," in his *International Trade and Economic Development* (Glencoe, Ill.: The Free Press, 1952), and Paul A. Baran, "On the Political Economy of Backwardness," *The Manchester School of Economics and Social Studies,* XX (January, 1952). Both of these articles have been reproduced in a number of anthologies on underdevelopment.

[128] Castro, of course, did not, but for reasons that are interestingly discussed by Barbara Ward in *The Rich Nations and the Poor Nations* (New York: W. W. Norton & Co., 1962), pp. 131–132.

[129] These, however, have been challenged as being erroneous analyses of African economic society. See Igor Kopytoff, "Socialism and Traditional African Societies," in *African Socialism,* William H. Friedland and Carl G. Rosberg, Jr., eds. (Stanford, Calif.: Stanford University Press, 1964), pp. 53–62. This volume is a most useful compilation of a variety of points of view.

while granting windfalls to those that are better organized or more favorably located in the economic structure.[130] The private sector can be an area of great flexibility, filling in gaps in the economy that inevitably arise when there is much to be done at once and conditions are changing rapidly. India may have erred in yielding too greatly to the temptation to plan, which, both for socialists and for those undertaking rapid development generally, must be very great. There is also a tendency, which is not confined to socialists, to plan too ambitiously for heavy industry without adequate attention to other sectors, including education and agriculture. India has increased fertilizer production by over 900 per cent and has a comparatively good literacy rate. She has also given attention to cooperatives and cottage industries. Of the nations of Africa and Asia she is probably the most nearly ready for industrial development (except for her abnormally low level of per capita income). Yet she is under continuous pressure, including external pressure from both East and West, because of her symbolic position in the cold war conflict, to overcommit to heavy industry. Other nations share this pressure without being as favorably positioned to either resist or make the best of it.[131]

There is also the problem of social reconstruction. Socialists today are having their first experience in carrying industrial development from "scratch." As we have seen, this requires drastic changes in the social structure. Capitalists have rent society apart without conscious intention to do so and communists have done it ruthlessly and in premeditated fashion. The conscientious humanitarianism of socialists may deter them from pursuing the rigorous course that has so far been associated with industrialization. They mean to show the world a model of humane economic development, especially in India; it remains to be seen if they can.

Whether or not policies adequate to the occasion can be developed and enforced while retaining a democratic basis for the political order, however, is a more serious question. Certainly the Western socialist regimes were faced with the problem of popular discontent under tight controls, and their response was to ease the restraints, particularly those on consumer choice, that they had maintained after the war. For African and Asian socialists, popular discontent may prove most difficult to manage even when their policies are humane. Their independence movements fostered hopes and expectations among the populace that were often grossly unrealistic and that, even under tight economic direction, are not likely to be fulfilled soon. They may well find it dangerous to permit their achievements to be judged by the democratic process in the immediate future. Many of the new nations are nations in name

---

[130] P. T. Bauer, *Indian Economic Policy and Development* (London: George Allen & Unwin, Ltd., 1961), ch. IV.

[131] For a discussion of policies applicable to different stages of development, see John Kenneth Galbraith, *Economic Development,* Sentry ed. (Boston: Houghton Mifflin Company, 1964), ch. III, IV.

only: They lack the sense of the community upon which harmony and cooperation can be built and which can serve to hold a people together in the midst of political campaigns and policy disputes. Already it has proved apparently necessary to limit popular consultation by the device of establishing a single dominant party in a number of them and to attempt to control and guide union leadership so that it will promote the aims of the dominant party, rather than serve the demands of union members for wage increases and the like.[132] They do not feel that they can afford the luxuries of pluralism and organized dissent. Even though these devices are justified by socialist leaders on the grounds that they represent an effort to forestall the development of competitive interests within society, so that all will be imbued with the impulse to serve the common good, they also operate to weaken the possible checks against autocratic rule by the new political and administrative elites.

The real danger both to socialism (conceived as a gradualist, egalitarian, and permissive system for guidance of the economic order by the political) and to democracy lies in the fact, as pointed out by Professor Lipset,[133] that independence has brought the "democratic Left" into power "prematurely." Parties representative of the workers must apply the brakes to consumption and take the blame for suppressing wage and other demands for the immediate enjoyment of the fruits of economic development so that investment may move ahead of population growth. Socialist labor parties have done something like this in Norway and Sweden and have tried to do it in the United Kingdom, but only after their nations had long been unified and their political systems stabilized. In earlier times in the West these actions had been taken by the older elites who, having once been assigned the blame (and having done the job), were discredited and replaced by democratically chosen governments. If the present democratically oriented elites in the newer nations are discredited, the prospects for both democracy and permissiveness are, in Lipset's word, "bleak." Discredit may come, unfortunately, either for ineffective and inadequate control of the economy, leading to economic crises, or for too-effective control, leading to resentment at restrictions and austerity.[134]

Not unexpectedly, it would appear that Western socialist governments, anxious to sustain friendly socialist movements, must, like capitalist governments with equivalent aims, further their cause with sufficiently massive aid to make the native development programs effective and to minimize the aus-

[132] India is a major exception. Although her dominant party does have a sponsored labor union, it does not attempt to control all union organization and activity. Electoral opposition is also freely allowed and constitutes a real threat to the Congress party in some of the states of the Indian federal system.

[133] *Op. cit., Political Man,* pp. 82–86.

[134] That this is already happening is witnessed by the fall of six African regimes to military coups within six months toward the end of 1965 and the beginning of 1966, including the socialist regime of Kwame Nkrumah in Ghana, which managed to commit both errors at once.

terity that accompanies them.[135] It is doubtful that the foreseeable amounts of aid will permit native governments to relax significantly the degree of direction that they will need to impose on their economies, or that it will so improve living conditions that an early shift to a competitive political system can be risked. The alternatives to the survival of most of the present socialist one-party regimes, however, appear to be fairly well limited to one form or another of authoritarian political system—of which communism and fascism are the most prominent modern examples—ruling the economy by command. As in Western countries in the past, so also in developing countries today, both communism and fascism are fostered by the dislocations caused by rapid economic development, as we shall see.

[135] The Norwegian Labor government enacted a special 0.25 per cent income tax on its own people to sustain aid programs in apparent recognition of this need.

4 / Communism

Capitalism and socialism have reached their present form in societies characterized by party competition and free voicing of dissent within the political order. The presence of criticism and the ready availability of alternative choices before the electorate has doubtless had some effect in compelling a reasonably close correspondence between the expressed objectives of each and the methods used to achieve them, because too great a gap between expectation and reality could result in defeat of the government that allowed the gap to exist. Thus, capitalism seeks freedom and abundance by methods designed to release and stimulate men's energies; socialism seeks harmony and cooperation by methods of planning and sharing. In turning to the third of the great modern politico-economic systems, communism, one of the first things that strikes the observer is the vast gulf between the expressed ultimate goal and the stages by which, apparently, it is to be approached.

This quality has been evident in communism from its beginnings in the writings of Karl Marx. As we saw earlier, Marx looked for a world of peace and brotherhood to emerge from revolution and bloodshed. He saw a great economic machine being built up by oppression and exploitation under capitalism until it became capable of serving all of man's material needs, and then predicted the sudden transferral of this machine to the hands of society to be run without any of the oppression or compulsion that were needed to create it. Similarly, Soviet Russia and Communist China have lodged enormous powers in the hands of the State in order to achieve one day a condition in which the State and all of its paraphernalia of police, prisons, and propaganda will wither away. In a sense, then, communism appears to us with a "split personality" that we will have to use caution in analyzing. Where communists are not in power, the ideal of a free and abundant society toward which communists claim to strive is at the forefront of the doctrine. Where they have gained control of the State, what is chiefly manifested is a system of political domination of the economic order and a political order itself that is monolithic and closed, rather than competitive and open—where authority rather than freedom is the guiding principle. Lest, however, we leap too quickly to the inference that communism is nothing but rank hypocrisy, let us see how this divergence of operating principle from expressed objective has been developed and maintained.

The Adaptation of Marxism

When the Russian revolution of March, 1917, occurred, Russian Marxists were placed in a puzzling situation. By the logic of Marxian historical theory, the revolution was not the one that was to usher in the age of communism. It was, instead, a "bourgeois" revolution, which would bring their country to the threshold of the capitalist era. Russia at the time was only starting its industrialization; it was not "ripe" by any standard other than that there were communists with a following among the industrial proletariat who were in a position to capture the revolution for communism. The question of proper course of action was even debated, with some Marxists holding that it was their duty to help the bourgeoisie win their revolution and have their day, with the communist revolution to be staged when capitalism had done its work!

The Bolshevik [1] seizure of power in November, carried through at the insistence of V. I. Lenin, who had hurried home from exile in Switzerland to lead it, faced the new rulers with a situation not covered by Marxist theory. They proceeded nevertheless to attempt or to permit (so anarchical was the condition of Russia from 1917 to 1921 that it would be false to suggest that the Bolsheviks intended much that was done) a wholesale conversion of formerly mixed capitalist and feudalist Russia into an egalitarian and cooperative State. Land was seized by the peasantry; factories were taken over and run (and often mismanaged) by workers' councils (soviets). Pay was equalized in many occupations, and amid the chaos, government orders were issued nationalizing the land, requisitioning grain for the cities, and taking other steps deemed appropriate to the establishment of the new society. To add to the confusion and strain, remnants of the displaced aristocracy with army elements loyal to them maintained a stubborn if ill-organized resistance, aided by a number of the Allied powers after the Bolshevik government made peace with the Germans in 1918. [2]

[1] The term, *Bolshevik*, merely signifies majority. The designation was given to the Leninist faction of the Russian Social-Democratic party at its convention in 1903, which met in exile in Brussels and London. The faction was left in full control in 1912, when the Menshevik (minority) faction formed a separate party. Historians have pointed out that the majority-minority designations were not especially accurate.

[2] This aid, very badly organized, was intended primarily to assist the reopening of the second front against the Germans in order to bring the World War more swiftly to a conclusion. It is regarded by the Russians, however, as clear evidence of the capitalist nations' hostility and warlike intentions toward the Soviet regime. Britain, France, Japan, and the United States participated in it.

In time, Lenin called a halt to the headlong rush into communism. Recognizing the impossibility of gaining peasant cooperation to wholesale communization of agriculture, and alarmed at a fearful drop in productivity that had taken place in both agriculture and industry, he permitted a limited return of capitalism in farming, small industry, and trade. His New Economic Policy (NEP), instituted in 1921, succeeded in restoring productivity to something approaching prewar levels and gave the State the opportunity to concentrate on the more limited problems of dealing with banking, heavy industry, and transportation. It also permitted the new regime a breathing space in which to consolidate its position, review its doctrine and, as it happened, work out the change of leadership required by Lenin's death in January, 1924.

In the West, there was some jumping to the conclusion that the NEP represented an abandonment of communism—that the new rulers of Russia were going to evolve into good bourgeois capitalists after all. Within a few years, however, the small capitalists so recently permitted to flourish were made the object of a campaign of vilification, quickly succeeded by a new expropriation. Communist doctrine was evidently still very much alive in Russia. With the institution of the forced collectivization of agriculture in 1928 to 1929, and the first Five-Year Plan in the former year, the general outlines of the new Soviet political economy took shape. Private ownership, except of consumer goods, was substantially eliminated. Intense State direction of the economic order, oriented to forced growth and to the creation of a heavy industry base for military, as well as for growth purposes, became the clear pattern of the new communist order, later to be repeated in Communist China and in the satellite nations. A new, powerful, and absolutist State was a-building!

That this, "the strongest and the most powerful form of government of all that have existed," [3] could be the proud construction of men who proclaim themselves still to be followers of a theory that bespeaks the "withering away of the State" is a paradox, but one not entirely without warrant in Marxist theory. Modern communism is based firmly upon that theory, but with modifications of the Marxian analysis appropriate to the circumstances of the only countries in which communist revolutions have occurred. To understand this we must return for a moment to Karl Marx. As we have seen, Marx was both a scholar and a prophet, and his work reflects this duality. The analyses of the processes of decay in capitalism and of the forces leading to revolution, which attracted his scholarly attention, were in great detail. His vision of society after the revolution—the prophet's revelation—was misty and indistinct. To connect the two, he and Engels had suggested that there would be a transitional stage, which they called the "dictatorship of the proletariat," but

---

[3] These words are Stalin's, addressing the Sixteenth Congress of the All Union Communist party, 1930, as translated and quoted by Adam B. Ulam in *The Unfinished Revolution: An Essay on the Sources of Influence of Marxism and Communism* (New York: Vintage Books, 1964), p. 201. Ulam's is one of the finest analyses of the Marxist basis of current communist theory.

which they defined no better than they had defined the ultimate stage of communism. Lenin and his followers, having carried their movement past the revolutionary stage, and having found that the precipitate rush into communism was bringing only economic disaster, were obliged to supply the detail for the transition that Marx and Engels had omitted. Thus a relatively minor part of the theory—a part that evidently held little interest for its originators— has been expanded and interpreted to become the main grounding for the present communist system. By the same means, however, the leaders of the movement have been able to preserve the vision of the "pure" communist society intact simply by proclaiming that the time for it to be realized has not yet arrived. In this fashion the ultimate objectives of the movement were kept alive and not tarnished by the harsh realities of the immediate present. At the same time, the Soviet theoreticians sought to justify and explain in Marxist terms the circumstances of their own revolution and their departure from the Marxist schedule. This required additions and revisions to the theory of the decay of capitalism—that is, to the earlier and more detailed part of the theory—that were justified on the grounds that Marx himself had not lived long enough to observe the forms capitalism would take in its final convulsions.

The doctrines that have been enunciated from time to time in the development and elaboration of communist theory do not fall neatly into the categories suggested here, and not all are relevant to our purposes in seeking to understand the political economy of communism. A brief discussion of the more important of them will perhaps suffice to show their tendency.[4]

The fundamental doctrines are those concerning the transitional phase. In the immediate aftermath of their own revolution, the leaders of Soviet Russia had expected other revolutions to break out in the advanced nations of the West. In part, this had justified their own attempt to achieve full communism in the so-called *War Communism* years, 1917 to 1921. When this hope had to be abandoned, and its abandonment had been formerly symbolized by the victory of Stalin over Leon Trotsky,[5] Stalin announced the policy of building "socialism in one country." [6] This meant, in effect, both completing the work of industrial development that capitalism had not been allowed to carry out in Russia *and* bringing the entire economy back into public ownership. Upon

[4] Most present doctrines were given their initial statement by Lenin and have been elaborated on by Stalin, Khrushchev, Mao Tse-Tung, and others. The general body of doctrine was largely complete in the works of Stalin, but because of his posthumous fall from grace, it is referred to as Marxism-Leninism. For precise analyses of the contributions of the various spokesmen of communism, see Ulam's book, already cited, and R. N. Carew Hunt, *The Theory and Practice of Communism: An Introduction,* 5th rev. ed. (New York: The Macmillan Company, 1957).

[5] Trotsky, with Stalin one of the chief contestants for the mantle of leadership upon Lenin's death, had become identified with a policy of primary emphasis on fomenting a world-wide revolution as opposed to consolidating the gains at home. That this is not an entirely accurate portrayal of his position is of no importance in terms of the symbolic meaning of his defeat.

[6] In communist terminology *socialism* is an intermediate stage in which the State still exists and is succeeded by communism proper after the State has withered away.

this were based the famous series of five-year plans for rapid industrialization [7] and the campaign against the new capitalists who had been allowed to flourish during the NEP.

This massive effort of social reorganization was carried out under the totalitarian rule of the Communist party, whose role in it had been prepared by Lenin even before the revolution. He, seeking to mold the party into a strong instrument for revolutionary action, had promulgated the doctrine of "democratic centralism" and had pronounced the party to be the "vanguard of the proletariat." The former applied to the internal rule of the party, and asserted the necessity of disciplined obedience once the leaders had reached a decision. (The term, *democratic,* supposedly applied to the freedom of discussion that might precede a decision, but this freedom was very much eroded as leadership became more firmly entrenched.) The latter built upon Marx' and Engels' description of communists in the *Manifesto* as "the most advanced and resolute section of the working-class parties of every country" and established for the party a monopoly of representation of the workers' interests.

Building "socialism in one country" was, in effect, an extension of the concept of the "dictatorship of the proletariat" that Lenin had been careful to describe on the very eve of the revolution as a period of uncertain length. The dictatorship was to prevail so long as remnants of the former exploiting classes remained as a threat to the new regime. It was pronounced "democratic" on the grounds that it was a dictatorship of the majority (the proletariat) over the minority (the bourgeois and feudal remnants). In 1936, Stalin announced that the socialist victory had been achieved and presented a new constitution that was, on paper, an extraordinarily liberal document. In fact, however, autocratic rule continued, this time under the designation "dictatorship of the workers." (It was asserted that, the older classes having been eliminated, it was no longer appropriate to refer to the workers by their old class name.) The "dictatorship of the workers" was in turn succeeded in 1952 by the "Socialist order," until in October, 1961, Nikita Khrushchev declared that the work of "socialist construction" had been completed, and that the "dictatorship" was over. Nevertheless, the doctrines regarding the party and its role remained in effect, and nothing more remarkable was noticeable than that a new period, "building communism," had now been added to the transitional phase. [8]

Two additional doctrines will be mentioned that affect principally the

---

[7] It is a part of the paradox, as pointed out by Professor Ulam, *op. cit.,* pp. 44–57, that this involved communists doing precisely what Marx had depicted among the harshest cruelties of capitalism: Dispossessing the peasants, "breaking in the worker to factory discipline," and taking surplus value from the workers and putting it into investment. As Ulam indicates, however, Marx himself had suggested that some of these would be necessary in the case of a premature revolution.

[8] Khrushchev rather rashly predicted the achievement of full communism by 1980 in statements to the Twenty-second Congress of the Communist party. His successors, speaking to the Twenty-third Congress in 1966, were more cautious, suggesting a rather indefinite prolongation of the process.

present international posture of communist countries. They are important because they justify revolutions in backward countries (including those in the Soviet Union and China) and because they compel the maintenance of communist economies on a war basis, instead of allowing them to be turned fully to satisfaction of consumer wants, as Marx evidently expected. These are the doctrines of "capitalist imperialism," with its corollary "law of uneven development," both developed by Lenin,[9] and Stalin's contribution of the doctrine of "capitalist encirclement." The former asserts that, in its final stages, capitalism must turn to the exploitation of backward and colonial peoples to maintain itself. Nations develop at an uneven rate, and the fact of exploitation makes the workers of even the most backward or apparently precapitalist States slaves of capitalism and, therefore, inclined to revolt. In the search for raw materials and markets, capitalists in effect carry the class struggle in its most intense form to peoples whose own economic systems would not alone produce a clear opposition of classes. Thus the revolution becomes possible in any country, and not only the most advanced.[10] Through this doctrine the class war is made the basis of international conflict, a conflict that is sharpened in the idea of an "encirclement" of proletarian states (that is, the Soviet Union and other communist countries) by capitalist ones bent on eliminating the class enemy. Doctrinal changes in the Soviet Union since Stalin's death, especially the Khrushchev pronouncement of "peaceful coexistence," have lessened somewhat the militaristic posture displayed there, as the current Sino-Soviet disputes show. However, the doctrines of communism still prescribe a state of military preparedness for a communist nation both for defense against an anticipated capitalist attack and for the support of communist revolutions elsewhere.

To summarize, the developments of communist theory that have occurred since communists have held power have had no significant effect on the long-range objectives of the movement, as expressed in the Marxian vision, but have simply walled them off and projected them into the future. In this, the communists have behaved quite unlike the democratic socialists who, as we have seen, did modify their expectations to conform more nearly to present reality. Equally, the statement of the means by which communists expect to achieve power has been altered only slightly. It is true that recent statements made by Soviet Russian leaders have expressed the belief that advanced Western nations might evolve peacefully into communism, but this view is not shared in China. Nor do either Russian or Chinese communists expect a peaceful transition in underdeveloped areas. The chief change in this segment of the theory is the express attention given to promoting communism in Asia, Africa, and Latin America, as opposed to Marx' and Engels' expectations of

[9] Set forth in his *Imperialism, the Highest Stage of Capitalism,* written in 1916, and largely taken from the work of the English economist, J. A. Hobson.

[10] And thus, also, appears the emphasis in Communist foreign policy in promoting "wars of national liberation."

revolution in Western Europe and North America.[11] Where the theory has shown its most remarkable flowering is in its application to existing communist regimes. Here its effect has been to establish an economy of command with heavy overtones of military preparedness in the context of a totalitarian political order as the characteristics of communism in practice. Precisely what forms this economy can take will be examined in a later section. At this point, we shall turn to the statement of the objectives and principles of communism as they are now reflected in the communist movement.

The Objectives of Communism

As a result of the manner in which communists have dealt with their problem of theory revision, the relationship between the political and economic orders in communism may be viewed as guided by either of two partially related sets of objectives: The ultimate ideals and the more immediate goals of a communist-controlled State. Although the former will be described, our attention will be focused principally on the latter, because we are interested in the actual practice of communism in its existing manifestations.

Unlike socialism and capitalism, the goals of a communist State are not directly derived from the idealized picture of a future communist society. This fact stems directly from the theory itself, for logically, a communist *State* cannot achieve communism; it must disappear for the ideal to be realized. It might, however, create the *conditions for* communism: The fully developed industrial system; the destruction of the "enemies of the proletariat," both domestic and foreign; and the self-conscious unity of the workers that prepares them to live in harmonious cooperation without compulsion, once the instruments of compulsion—the State and its appurtenances—have disappeared.[12] Its goals, therefore, may entail elements that are quite at variance with the ideals of freedom and self-determination that lie at the heart of the moral justification for communism as envisioned by its founders.

Does it seem strange to refer to communism as a moral system? It should not, for it must be remembered that Marx and Engels wrote their *Manifesto* and other works in a spirit of moral revulsion against the evils they saw in capitalism. Their entire theory rests on the premise that a just and moral world

[11] There are a few passages in Marx' and Engels' writings that admit the possibility of revolution in backward countries and of peaceful transition in developed ones, but the central and repeated thrust of their work runs contrary to these occasional observations.

[12] Thus, Mao Tse-Tung could declare on the eve of the establishment of his regime in mainland China: "We . . . openly declare that we are striving with all our might precisely to create the conditions that will hasten the end of [classes, state power, and parties]. The Communist Party and the state power of the people's dictatorship constitute such conditions." From *On People's Democratic Dictatorship* (1949), quoted in *Communism, Fascism and Democracy: The Theoretical Foundations,* Carl Cohen, ed. (New York: Random House, Inc., 1962). p. 205.

will emerge from the processes of history. Despite the form that it has taken in practice, communism springs from an impulse toward reform, inspired by the highest ideals of nineteenth-century economic and social thought.[13]

What are the objectives of communism expressed in its ideal form? As set forth by Marx, and substantially unchanged since his time, they combine what may be termed the most attractive features of both capitalism and socialism. Marx wholeheartedly accepted the capitalist dream of abundance; his enthusiastic praise of the work of capitalists rests precisely on his admiration for their material accomplishments. His theory was designed to show how all of the "mighty works" of the capitalist system would be turned one day to bring affluence to the whole of mankind. Equally, he expressed a belief in personal freedom, which carried to the furthest extreme the capitalist wish to minimize the interference of the State in economic affairs: He had the State disappear altogether! From the traditions of socialist thought he accepted the ideas of voluntary cooperation and equality (expressed in his ideal of the "classless society"), the abhorrence of private economic dominion, and the necessity of economic planning. Here is the very essence of an industrial-age utopia: A society that is abundant in material things, that is free, cooperative, equal, and operating at maximum efficiency through a system of planned production and distribution of goods and services in which all members work together harmoniously and voluntarily because there is literally nothing that would motivate men to do otherwise.

The ultimate goals of communism, then, are not radically different from those espoused in one combination or another in various countries of the West. The understanding of this point helps to explain both communism's failures and its successes in various countries, for communism combines these ideals with a "catastrophic" view of history. Its message is at the same time flagrantly optimistic and darkly pessimistic—optimistic about what might be achieved with the new instruments that industrialization has placed in man's hands, and pessimistic about the likelihood of society's ever realizing these possibilities without revolutionary upheaval. Its appeal lies to those who share the values and hopes of Western industrial culture, but who feel that they are not being and cannot be fulfilled by the existing ordering and tendencies of Western society. It is not among the hopeless (those who have no expectation of betterment) that communism can make its inroads, but among those who have been taught to expect better things and have been frustrated, or feel themselves to have been frustrated, in achieving them.

The conditions in which these attitudes may arise include those that accom-

[13] This point is often difficult for Americans and other Westerners to grasp, accustomed as we are to a rather simple "black and white" picture of the communist-Free World struggle. Yet we should recognize that when communists reproach us and call us hypocrites, oppressors, and imperialists these are moral condemnations that, however mistaken they may be, are offered by men who conceive themselves not as bent on evil, but as infinitely superior to us morally.

pany the start of industrialization (Marx himself wrote the *Manifesto* in just such circumstances in Germany) and at other stages of industrial development that produce frustration on the part of substantial elements in the population. Both rapid industrial growth (common in the early stages) and a marked slowing or reversal of the rate of growth may increase the tendency to seek an extremist solution.[14] In particular, the social upheavals that accompany the period of rapid initial industrialization have a tendency to raise expectations well before they can be fulfilled. New workers flock to the cities and are at once cut off from the stabilizing and familiar influences of their old rural environment while being subjected to the unaccustomed hardships and unpleasantnesses of urban life and dependency on a wage for existence. It is this that makes the occurrence of communist revolutions in Russia and China less surprising than they seem when viewed simply from the perspective of Marxist theory. The explanation is that Marx, writing when he did, described the conditions of *early* industrialization and assumed that they would worsen over time. In fact, these conditions ameliorate as the economy approaches maturity, so that the only truly Marxian revolutionary situation is found under immature, rather than mature, capitalism.

However well the ultimate ideals of communism may serve or may have served as the basis for its appeal to the alienated and distressed in noncommunist nations, and in leading Soviet Russia and Red China into their revolutions, they have little function in terms of shaping the politico-economic systems of communist *States*. For this, a distinctly more limited and pragmatic set of goals exists, which includes *the creation of a modern industrial economy; the development of military supremacy over potential capitalist enemies;* and *the reorientation and indoctrination of the population to full participation in the communist movement.*

Creation of a Modern Industrial Economy.   Because communist revolutions have only occurred in relatively backward economic societies, the first necessity for the achievement of the conditions for communism is to complete the work that capitalism had left incomplete: The full development and application of industrial technology to the processes of production and distribution. It is an essential part of communist theory that communism can only come into existence after the economy has been fully "socialized"—that is, after individual, small-scale effort has been replaced by organized social effort characteristic of large-scale industrial production. Capitalism does this, accord-

[14] This has been well demonstrated in studies by political sociologists who have compared the groups that have accepted democratic socialism (which requires that social change occur but accepts the ability of the existing political order to achieve that change) with those that cleave to communism. See, for example, Seymour Martin Lipset, *Political Man* (New York: Doubleday Anchor Books, 1963), ch. 4, and the same author's "The Changing Class Structure and Contemporary European Politics," *Daedalus,* XCIII (Winter, 1964), pp. 287–293.

ing to Marxist theory, by the process of competition and industrial empire-building in the manner described in Chapter 3. If industrialization has not been carried out fully both in industry and agriculture by the time of the revolution, it must be done in the period of "building socialism."

The pursuit of this goal, naturally, is in harmony with the national aspirations of countries under communist rule, just as it is of backward nations generally, but the vigor with which it is pursued goes well beyond sheer nationalism. For example, the forcible collectivization of agriculture, which is a nearly universal feature of communist practice, is an extremely disruptive process. As we saw in the case of the English enclosure movements, which were somewhat comparable in their economic effect, it produces great unrest and places severe burdens on the political system to compel compliance and preserve order while the job is being done. It is a commonplace to accuse the rulers of communist nations of being merely interested in their own power and in the perquisites of rulership, yet they have regularly made their rule more difficult by their intense pursuit of industrialization. Had they not been devoted to something more than the maintenance of their own power, they might well have followed the guidance of autocracies throughout the ages and disturbed the existing economic and social order as little as possible.[15] So deeply imbedded in communist thought is the idea of industrialization, however, that it is pressed with what must sometimes be described as fanatical dedication.

The relationship of this intermediate goal of communism to the ultimate goals ought to be clearly understood. Communists anticipate a "withering away of the State," but they do not expect society to operate altogether without central direction. They expect the State to be replaced by *central planning,* and this, they believe, will not be possible under any other form of economic organization than that of large-scale industrial production. The economic order must be built to its *highest level of perfection* before it can replace the political order in its functions.

Development of Military Power. As Professor Rostow showed in his study of *The Stages of Economic Growth,*[16] the start of economic growth is frequently stimulated by nationalistic feeling, and that feeling may continue to mark the growth process. It is expected that the national pride that spurs industrialization will also manifest itself in attempts to display military strength to the outside world. In Professor Rostow's analysis, however, intense economic effort and intense military effort during the period of rapid industrialization tend to be alternatives. The striking aspect of communism is the extent to which these are carried out simultaneously. This is most clearly

[15] That the English enclosure movements were allowed to disturb the social order is attributable in part to the *absence* of central autocratic control capable of preventing individual landowners from pursuing their economic self-interest with such ruthlessness.

[16] Walt W. Rostow, *The Stages of Economic Growth: A Non-Communist Manifesto* (Cambridge: Cambridge University Press, 1960), ch. 8.

marked in the present dual effort in Communist China. The communist belief in the internationalization of the class struggle, expressed in the doctrine of capitalist encirclement, and the communist nations' assumption of responsibility for leadership in the world-wide revolution are the ideological bases for making military preparedness an important goal. The Allied adventures in attempting to re-establish the eastern front in the First World War and the German invasion of Russia in the Second World War, as well as recent and current confrontations of American and other Western forces with Chinese and allied forces in Korea, Vietnam, and the Formosa Straits have tended to reinforce these doctrines, which compel the direction of a considerable part of the production arising from economic growth into materials of war. As in the case of promoting industrialization, then, communist ideology demands a somewhat exaggerated emphasis beyond what would be expected in a country at an equivalent growth stage, but it is otherwise reasonably conformable to the value-expectations of a late-developing nation.

Reorientation and Indoctrination of the People. An important part of the Marxist analysis of history is that which attempts to relate the whole cultural "superstructure" to the social relations of production that, in turn, are determined by the requirements of the existing stage of technology. According to Marx, it is not just the political order that is determined by the present organization of the productive process. Religious beliefs, social attitudes, and the like are also related to the needs of maintaining the subjection of one class to another in capitalism, and these will change when the communist productive process supplants the capitalist one:

> "Does it require deep intuition to comprehend that man's ideas, views, and conceptions, in one word, man's consciousness, changes with every change in the conditions of his material existence, in his social relations and in his social life?" [17]

As Lenin saw, however, it would take time and effort to retrain people who were raised and trained under capitalism. Communist leadership must "begin to build Socialism not with imaginary human material . . . but with the human material bequeathed to us by capitalism. . . . [The] function of the proletarian vanguard . . . consists in training, educating, enlightening, and drawing into the new life the most backward strata and masses of the working class and the peasantry." [18] This is the third objective of the communist State. It is related to economic functions in that included in the retraining is the inculcation of a work ethic, the "equal obligation of all to work," cited in the

[17] Karl Marx and Friedrich Engels, *The Communist Manifesto,* Samuel H. Beer, ed. (New York: Appleton-Century-Crofts, 1955), pp. 29–30.
[18] *"Left Wing" Communism: An Infantile Disorder,* 1920, quoted in Carl Cohen, ed., *Communism, Fascism, and Democracy: The Theoretical Foundations* (New York: Random House, Inc., 1962), pp. 229–230.

Manifesto among the other tasks to be faced during the period of the dictator-ship of the proletariat. Despite this tie to original Marxism, the use of the political order to achieve cultural and social change constitutes an essential inversion of Marx's analysis, but it again conforms to the necessities of forced-draft industrialization in a backward State. It can serve to induce the popula-tion to set the needs of the community ahead of private wants—to accept the deprivations that are necessary in order to devote most of the output of pro-duction to investment and growth. In communist theory, however, the justifi-cation is even broader: Its ultimate purpose is to abolish all traces of class feeling and to prepare the workers for willing and enthusiastic participation in the future communist society.

To state the matter in foregoing fashion is, of course, to put the most favor-able interpretation on it. The instruments of this retraining are propaganda, terror, and indoctrination of the young, all of which serve to suppress opposi-tion to the regime. The suppression of opposition is a thread that runs through communist theory. It has the function of ensuring that the work of rapid devel-opment and social reconstruction will proceed without interruption, but it also establishes a kinship between communism and other forms of totalitari-anism. And, indeed, communist propaganda and terror do go beyond the pro-tection of the regime to seek to instill uncritical devotion to its leaders and strong nationalistic fervor, both of which are natural to totalitarianism, but alien to communist theory.[19]

The Operating Principles of Communism

In communism the political and economic orders are so conjoined that to discuss one as if it were acting upon the other is, in a sense, a distortion. Yet for purposes of comparing communism as an economic system with socialism and capitalism, some such separation must be attempted analytically at least. In embarking on a description of the economic operating principles of com-munism, therefore, we should bear in mind that the political order that owns the means of production and directs the planning process is an autocratic one, lacking the competitive democratic practices found in the systems so far sur-veyed. The principles that guide the communist economy are, on the whole, familiar ones: *Social ownership of the means of production and distribution, total government planning and control of the economic order,* and *a system of rewards (and punishments) to maximize productive effort.* Because all three

---

[19] In a now-famous "secret" speech to the Twentieth Congress of the Soviet Com-munist party, Nikita Khrushchev denounced the "cult of personality" that had grown up around Josef Stalin. Nevertheless, there was considerable evidence that a similar tendency to glorify the leader was beginning to develop in his favor up to the time he was deposed. Much more impressive is the adoration of Mao Tse-Tung in China, and other national leaders in satellite nations. In regard to nationalism, one may simply note that in Soviet Russia, the Second World War is dubbed "the Great Patriotic War."

have been discussed in connection with socialism and capitalism, it is not necessary to review them in detail here, but only to show the specific aspects of their meaning in communist ideology.

Social Ownership. The communist view of social ownership of the means of production and distribution differs from the socialist in that cooperative and State ownership are not deemed equally acceptable. Property relations hold a very special place in communist theory. Under the Marxist doctrine of materialist determinism, they are the source of social attitudes and feeling. Private property is not merely a means by which some gain an unequal and unearned share of the social product; it is the source of class consciousness. The capitalist, by his exclusive possession of the means of production, can compel others to accept inferior status and work for the wages he pays.[20] Collective property, although it avoids "wage slavery," still sets the collective owners apart from the rest of society, and is therefore inferior to property owned utterly in common. A true community cannot emerge until all bases of particularist thought and feeling are eliminated, and this requires the transfer of all ownership to the whole community. For the transition period the community is represented by the State, and after it disappears the distinctive function of property will disappear also, and the means of production will become the generalized possession of the entire community, belonging to everyone and to no one. Freed of the distorting influence of property relations, production will become a purely social process,[21] and individuals will lose their impulse to seek their own particular interests.

In sum, although State ownership is fostered under communism for the purpose of gaining control over the economy and to assist the planning process, it is intimately related to the goal of creating the conditions for communist society as well. As we shall see, some concessions to private ownership are made in communist States, and collective ownership is extremely important in agriculture, although less so in productive and distributive enterprise. These are concessions and compromises of a transitional nature, however, and may be expected to disappear gradually in countries adhering fully to communist principles.

Government Planning and Control. We saw in the case of socialism that government planning and control were intended originally to promote rationality and social justice in the production and distribution of society's output, and that it came later to be used also to stimulate economic growth. In com-

[20] For this reason, individual artisans in the Soviet Union are not allowed to own more than the tools of their own trade or to hire others to work for them.

[21] It is to be remembered that, according to Marxist theory, the process of "socializing" production is largely completed by capitalism. The capitalist himself destroys the meaning of property by depriving all but himself of it, and he makes production a social process by his development of the large industrial enterprise.

munism, the promotion of economic growth and industrialization—bringing the economy to a level adequate for the transition to communism—is the prime purpose of planning and control during the transitional stage. Social justice is subsumed, but it is only secondary as a conscious purpose until the final stage is reached. While the communist State exists and maintains its duties of reshaping society, protecting and fostering the revolution and building the economic conditions for communism, those duties or purposes are the standard by which the economy is to be guided. The method used is *command,* expressed in comprehensive planning and a control system embodying both compulsion and rewards—the "carrot and the stick." The market, with its standard of value, is largely *supplanted*. Although market mechanisms are used, they are used only to fulfill the purposes of the plan—to clear the shops of consumer goods produced, for example—or to regulate aspects of the economy that the leaders do not wish to or have not found it feasible to plan.

The significance of this should not be underestimated. Under communism, planning replaces nearly all of the functions of the market in most sectors of the economy: Stimulating innovation, causing expansion, making decisions on variety and choice of product, distributing incomes, allocating resources to investment and production, promoting efficiency, and eliminating undesired and unneeded types of output. Communism replaces economic pluralism with centralized decision-making,[22] or at least attempts to do so within the limits posed by technology, administrative and political feasibility, and human capacity. We shall see later how these considerations have left the market standing in some fields.

It is intended by communists that planning should carry over into the phase of true communism, but without its coercive aspects. The planning organization would be able to carry out its central directing task without the coercive power of the State to back it up because it would not be exploitative in nature. No one, in consequence, would have any reason to oppose it except some deviant few who might retain a "capitalist mentality"—that is, those who would resist because *they* desired to impose exploitation on others (by hiring them to work for them, and so on). They could be dealt with easily by the local community in the same way that mental defectives are handled everywhere. Planning itself would become essentially a routine accounting operation, ensuring an efficient and equitable arrangement of social production and distribution.

Rewards and Punishments to Maximize Effort. So well known is Marx' phrase, "from each according to his ability, to each according to his needs,"

---

[22] In some of the countries of Eastern Europe experimentation with decentralized decision-making within the framework of central planning is being attempted, and some recent slight moves toward this have been made in the Soviet Union. The decentralization involved, however, is of operative decision within the context of a central plan; it does not revive pluralism in the sense that lower-echelon decisions may be made counter to the intent of the plan.

that the presence of differential material rewards in communist countries is often regarded as a clear proof that communists have abandoned their doctrine. It is true that current practice in this respect does differ from Marx' teachings, but not to the degree that is often supposed. For in the same treatise in which the foregoing phrase appears,[23] Marx indicated that payment during the transitional phase would be proportional to hours of work accomplished. The present official principle governing material incentives is phrased, "from each according to his abilities, to each according to his work." By "work" is meant not merely hours on the job, for communists are anxious to publicize a work week at least as short as that obtaining in capitalist countries and so cannot afford to allow workers to work unlimited hours. Payment, therefore, is according to skill, to rate of output, and to type of work performed. In short, this principle has much in common with incentive rewards used in socialist and capitalist countries, although unlike the latter, it is employed for its instrumental value rather than sought as a value in itself. It is still expected to be replaced by reward according to need in the distant future.

A further difference from the capitalist idea of reward is the fact that the principle is supposed to apply only to "socially useful" work. Entrepreneurial profits are excluded, at least technically (there are premia paid to managers for overfulfillment of quotas, and so forth), and interest and rent do not exist, except in the payments made on personal savings accounts, which are intended to induce the people to refrain from spending and putting pressure on the supply of consumer goods.

Finally, the material incentive system under communism is designed to do more than promote self-seeking. As described in the draft program of the Soviet Communist party presented to the Twenty-second Congress in October, 1961, reward according to work reinforces the workers' identification of their personal interests with those of society, an identity which is possible because there are no capitalists to "exploit" them:

> This principle insures that the members of society have a material interest in the fruits of their labor; it makes it possible to harmonize personal and social interests in the most effective way and serves as a powerful stimulus for increasing productivity of labor, developing the economy and raising the people's standard of living.
>
> The awareness that they work for themselves and their society and not for exploiters inspires the working people with labor enthusiasm; it encourages their effort for innovation, their creative initiative and mass Socialist emulation.[24]

It should hardly be necessary to add that communist States have found it necessary from time to time to supplement the reward system with forced labor and

[23] *Critique of the Gotha Program* (1875).

[24] *The New York Times,* August 1, 1961, p. 13. The translation is that of Tass, the official Soviet press agency. One should bear in mind the meaning of "Socialist" in this context—it applies to the transitional period.

legal penalties for slackness, tardiness, and absenteeism, although these have been largely replaced by social sanctions in the Soviet Union since the general easing after Stalin's death.

Closely allied with the material incentive system, and having a similar purpose of reindoctrination as well as stimulation of effort, are what might be called the "psychic" rewards and punishments under communism. These include propaganda, agitation, public commendation of outstanding workers, and systematic terror. The first three are intended to inspire the workers constantly to devotion and hard work and to condition them to identify themselves with the cause of building a communist society. The last, which has eased considerably in the Soviet Union and Yugoslavia, and to a lesser degree in some of the European satellites, seeks the same end by instilling fear that one's efforts will be regarded as insufficient and indicative of lack of enthusiasm for the cause.

Of the three operating principles of the communist State, the third is the only one that is to undergo substantial revision in the ideal future. Once the people have become accustomed to striving for the common good—so goes the theory—and the economy has become so productive that all reasonable needs can be met with a minimum of human effort, material incentive rewards will be no longer needed and will be abolished.[25]

The Practice of Communism

With the relaxation of Soviet Russian control over the satellites that followed the death of Josef Stalin in 1953 and with the appearance of distinct nationalistic aspirations in the leadership of some communist States, notably Yugoslavia and the People's Republic of China, divergences in practice have emerged in the communist part of the world. For our purposes, however, the Soviet Union may be regarded still as the prototype of communism, and our attention will focus on a description of practice there, occasional mention being given to significant deviations from the prototype as may be necessary. Besides its innate importance as the oldest and most successful communist regime, the Russian model displays some of the modifications that might be expected in a well-established, highly industrialized communist State, while still maintaining its adherence to the goals of revolutionary communism. In this it falls somewhere between the extremes of aggressiveness and accommodation represented by China and Yugoslavia, respectively.

The Soviet Political System. Before launching into a description of the operation of the Soviet economy, it would be well to have in mind an outline of the political order that controls it. Formally organized as a democratic

[25] Concurrent with this belief is the idea that the nature of various presently distinct types of work—work "by hand and brain"—will gradually grow to resemble one another, removing any need for incentives to lead people into one or another type of task.

federal State, the USSR has actually a highly centralized and autocratic governmental structure. Its highest elected legislative organ, the Supreme Soviet, exists principally for the formal ratification and publicization of official decisions, and its court system has the duty of applying the law in accord with the currently declared policy objectives of the State. Both administrative and judicial structures operate to ensure conformity within each of the fifteen federated republics (states) to the plans and decisions of the central political authority. The chairmen of the councils of ministers of the several republics, for example, are members of the All-Union Council of Ministers, which body brings together the top planning and administrative officers of the government. The two largest and most representative bodies in the governmental structure, the Supreme Soviet and the All-Union Council of Ministers, are directed in their work by much smaller executive committees or *presidia,* and these in turn are dominated by the leadership of the Communist party.

Superior to the governmental structure, and paralleling it down to the lowest governmental unit, and even beyond, into factory, neighborhood, and block organizations, is the party. The party nominates all candidates for public office, permeates, supervises, and checks all political, economic, and social organizations, and exercises, in its capacity as "vanguard of the proletariat," directing power over the whole. Organized in hierarchical fashion, the party uses a system of elections at each level to choose the members of the next higher level, but these elections are actually controlled from above, so that the selection process works in reverse and central control is maintained. (This is the practical application of the principle of "democratic centralism.")[26] Thus, in practice, the highest ruling bodies in the Soviet Union are the Party Central Committee and its Politburo and Secretariat. For many years Josef Stalin ruled the Soviet Union as General Secretary, a post now held by Leonid Brezhnev.[27] By interlocking memberships, the Politburo and the Party Central Committee dominate the All-Union administration, and the same pattern ensures party control at lower levels of government. As the only legal political organization, the party is assured of its primacy. It sees itself as the guiding and motivating force of the whole society, actively urging, persuading, propagandizing, and, when necessary, threatening and punishing workers and officials at every level to work toward the objectives it proclaims.

The party being the controlling body, and having access to and power over

[26] There has been some recent discussion of increasing "inner-party democracy," including especially a relaxation of the control exerted over the very lowest level of party elections. The changes in party rules adopted at the Twenty-third Congress in 1966, however, operated principally to strengthen party discipline, tighten admission requirements, and permit longer tenure for party officials, all of which should increase central control.

[27] After the death of Stalin, the title of the top party leader was changed to "First Secretary," apparently as part of the de-Stalinization reform. The old title was revived at the 1966 Party Congress, as was also the name of the Politburo, which had been renamed Presidium from 1952 to 1966.

organizations of every sort in Soviet society, it is not necessary for the organs of government to have legal authority in each instance where central direction is desired.[28] Control can be exercised directly by the party instead. This is of importance in the case of enterprises such as the collective farms, which are not officially run by the State, as we shall see. In sum, the Soviet political system (and all other communist political systems as well, despite their superficial variations) is noncompetitive, autocratic, and organized in two interlocking structures that supplement each other to ensure control. Through these structures society as a whole is regulated with all of the instruments common to totalitarian regimes, and, more specifically for our purposes, the economy is directed to the achievement of the objectives of a communist State.

Under ordinary circumstances this structure operates in monolithic fashion, but there are occasions and circumstances in which one may detect some loci of power that have a degree of leverage against it. First of all there are two enforcement arms of the State, the army and the police. These are assumed to be under the direction of the Politburo, but in times of stress, especially during a change of leadership, they may become important semi-independent powers. Nikita Khrushchev found it useful to have the support of the Minister of Defense, Marshal Zhukov, in the 1957 leadership crisis, and rewarded him with full membership in the (then) Party Presidium for a brief period before dismissing him. In an earlier crisis, it was the head of the secret police, Lavrenti Beria, who seemed to hold the controlling position. So great was his power that the successors to Stalin found it necessary to liquidate him shortly after the dictator's death.[29]

Certain other holders of top ministerial offices appear at times to be powerful, but it is not clear whether their power is derived from their posts or from their position in the party hierarchy. The Politburo membership overlaps with the membership of the Council of Ministers, and the influence may run in either direction. There are also some hints that the formal constitutional structure has become a potential source of power, at least in crisis. It is significant that on the morrow of Stalin's death, the titular headship of the Soviet Union, the position of Chairman of the Presidium of the Supreme Soviet, was given to the aging Klimenti Voroshilov, who was regarded as outside the power struggle for succession and would, therefore, serve to neutralize that part of the organizational structure.

At another level, there seem to be some strata of the population upon which the regime relies for support and that, in consequence, receive favored treatment. These include the intelligentsia, highly skilled workers and foremen, and possibly some members of the collective farms.[30] It is also apparent that

[28] It is perhaps significant that the five-year plan directives are adopted at the Party Congresses.

[29] Merle Fainsod, *How Russia Is Ruled,* rev. ed. (Cambridge: Harvard University Press, 1963), pp. 161–175.

[30] Alex Inkeles, "Social Stratification and Mobility in the Soviet Union: 1940–1950," *American Sociological Review,* XV (August, 1950), pp. 465–479.

the regime does not feel able or willing to act in utter disregard of popular feeling, because it not only takes great effort to propagandize its people, but refrains from carrying out its policies to an extreme of logical consistency. It has abandoned labor controls and rationing; it permits free markets for a part of agricultural and some other types of production; it has shown recent concern for the expansion of consumer goods industries; it still allows peasants to till private plots; and it leaves a great part of agriculture in collectives, despite its active effort to implement its preference for State farms and a fully socialized agriculture.

A form of economic power does, in fact, exist in the ability of the mass of peasants and workers to defeat the purposes of the regime by their failure to maintain a high standard of performance or by actively destroying their own product. Peasants have used the device of burning their crops and killing their cattle on a number of occasions to force the regime to relent in its efforts to subdue them. In a sense, this power becomes translated into political power in the form of struggles in the party hierarchy, in which leaders are called to account for the economic failures of the system.[31] Malenkov and Khrushchev both fell from power at least ostensibly on economic issues.

By and large, however, the party is the dominant force in the Soviet system, and it is to be noted that, so far, the party Secretaryship has been the only position capable of giving preeminence to a single man within the leadership of the country. The party leadership does have its factions, but it has usually succeeded in presenting a common front and has never allowed popular participation in the settlement of leadership differences. We may assume, then, for most purposes of describing the direction of the economy, that a description of the system as monolithic will not involve substantial error.

The Drive to State Ownership. In perhaps no other area of Soviet Russian policy has adherence to dogma been more in evidence than in respect to the question of the ownership of the means of production. With the brief exception of the New Economic Policy, Soviet government actions have consistently favored collective over private ownership, and State ownership over collective.[32]

Manufacturing, trading, and financial institutions were largely taken into State ownership in the aftermath of the revolution during the "war communism" years. Some return to private enterprise in light industry and trade was permitted during the NEP, but discriminatory taxation and other measures were used to induce private manufacturers to join producers' cooperatives.

[31] See Adam B. Ulam, *The New Face of Soviet Totalitarianism* (Cambridge: Harvard University Press, 1963), especially ch. IV.

[32] This favoritism has been in evidence even in the distribution of social welfare benefits. Until 1966, for example, collective farmers were excluded from the State pension plans that applied to employees of State farms and industrial enterprises. There is still discrimination against private artisans in welfare and tax policies of the Soviet government.

The campaign of vilification and persecution that signaled the end of the NEP—a campaign that was directed principally against the Kulaks (wealthy peasant farmers)—spilled over on capitalists, the "NEP-men," in industry also. Since 1928, as a result, the area of private enterprise has been reduced to insignificance in Soviet industry. Individual artisans are permitted to exist, but they may not employ workers for hire. As of 1959, the total number of them in existence was reported to be only 174,000.[33] In their turn, producers' cooperatives in light industry were subjected to tax discrimination and other disabilities and they, too, have substantially disappeared, as shown in Table 15. At present cooperation appears only in rural retail trade and in the agricultural cooperatives, the *Kolkhozy*, which are still the mainstay of Soviet agriculture.

Table 15 Industrial Output in the Soviet Union
by Forms of Ownership, 1928–1960
(in per cent)

Form of Ownership:	1928	1937	1950	1959	1960
State	69.4	90.3	91.8	94	97
Cooperative	13.0	9.5	8.2	6	3
Private	17.6	0.2	—	—	—

Source: *Narodnoe Khoziaistvo SSSR v 1960 godu. Statisticheskii Ezhegodnik* (*National Economy of the USSR in 1960. Statistical Yearbook*) Moscow, 1961, p. 213. This is the last year in which this table appears in this source. The presumption is that cooperative industrial enterprise has substantially disappeared.

It was in agriculture that opposition to private ownership took its most violent form.[34] Agricultural production, which had fallen sharply in the aftermath of the revolution, had recovered considerable ground following the institution of the NEP. In 1928 and 1929, however, forcible collectivization of agriculture was instituted against bitter resistance and at fearful cost in terms of cattle and crops destroyed by the rebellious peasants. The annual output of meat, which had stood at 32.7 kilograms per capita on the eve of collectivization, plummeted to 16.7 in the early 1930s (average figure for 1931 to 1934). Per capita milk production dropped from 176.2 kilograms to 111.6 in the same period. Neither of these was to reach 1928 levels again until the 1950s.[35] Collectivization, even at such a price, was entered into because Soviet authorities had been unable to ensure adequate deliveries of farm produce under the requisitioning

[33] Allan G. Gruchy, *Comparative Economic Systems* (Boston: Houghton Mifflin Company, 1966), p. 642. There were also some 92,000 independent peasants.

[34] Legally, title to all land in the Soviet Union belongs to the State, so that in the discussion that follows the difference between collective and State farming is technically only one of ownership of the equipment used and of the organization of the enterprise.

[35] D. Gale Johnson and Arcadius Kahan, "Soviet Agriculture: Structure and Growth," in *Comparisons of the United States and Soviet Economies*, U. S. Congress, Joint Economic Committee, Part I, 86th Congress, 1st session, 1959, p. 210. The Second World War, with its devastation of the Ukraine, delayed recovery enormously, of course, by reducing production below even the 1932 levels.

system used in the war communism years, and because they were unwilling to use price incentives to spur production in private hands, as contrary to ideology. Ideology also demands ultimate replacement of the collective by the State farm, because communists intend to abolish the distinction between rural and urban life—to organize all production on industrial lines. Pursuant to this, the development of State farms (*Sovkhozy*), organized on the pattern of a large industrial enterprise, has proceeded concurrently with the consolidation of collectives into larger and larger units, the latter gradually approaching the *Sovkhozy* in form of operation.

Today the principal survivals of private enterprise in the Soviet Union are privately cultivated peasant plots on collective and State farms which, although not large in area, are a major source of such important foods as eggs (81 per cent), potatoes (63 per cent), and meat, milk, and vegetables (41 to 47 per cent).[36] Because an unregulated market exists for these products they provide a large part of the peasants' income. Each peasant must do his share of the work on the collective or State farm land, and then may cultivate his own plot in whatever time he has available. Yet the private plots are far more intensively cultivated and productive than are the collective and State farm lands. It is evident that the Soviets have not yet solved the problem of conversion of the peasantry to full effort under either form of social ownership, although the drive toward State ownership continues, as indicated in Table 16.

Table 16   Distribution of Total Soviet Sown Land Area
by Type of Farm Holding, 1928–1964
(per cent)

Type of Farm Holding	1928	1940	1953	1964
State farms and other State agricultural enterprises	1.5	8.8	11.6	45.0
Collective farms	1.2	78.3	84.0	52.1
Private subsidiary farming of collective farmers	1.0	3.0	3.5	
Private subsidiary farming of State farm and State industrial workers	—	0.5	0.9	2.9
Private peasant farms	96.2	9.4	*	

* Less than 0.1 per cent.
Calculated from *Narodnoe Khoziaistvo SSSR v 1959 godu. Statisticheskii Ezhegodnik (National Economy of the USSR in 1959. Statistical Yearbook)* Moscow, 1960, p. 332 and *Narodnoe Khoziaistvo SSSR v 1964 godu. Statisticheskii Ezhegodnik,* Moscow, 1965, p. 272.

Soviet communist practice for the management of State-owned enterprise is distinctly unlike that found in Britain. In place of the semiautonomous board, there is a single director in charge of each enterprise (most industrial enterprises are rather large, encompassing several distinct plants or work sites), who is appointed by the governmental authorities of the community,

[36] Joseph W. Willett, "The Recent Record in Agricultural Production," in *Dimensions of Soviet Economic Power,* U.S. Congress, Joint Economic Committee, 87th Congress, 2d session, 1962, pp. 112–113. The Soviet Union has been unable to abolish these plots so far because of the economy's dependence on their produce.

region, or state in which the enterprise is located. In a few cases the appoint-ment is made directly by the All-Union ministry. The enterprise stands, then, as part of a hierarchical structure that runs ultimately to the All-Union Min-istry charged with the particular sector of the economy the enterprise serves.[37] Collective enterprises are in theory governed by elected managers and com-mittees chosen by a general meeting of the members, but the Communist party dominates the selection of key management personnel, so that they, too, are endowed with very limited autonomy. Public ownership in the Soviet Union, therefore, is associated with the lodging of economic power in the hands of the central authorities. Unlike capitalism and socialism, ownership and power remain linked, but the linkage is supplied not by the legal definition of title, but by the organizational structure that translates title into control.

There are some significant departures from the Soviet pattern of public ownership and control in both China and Yugoslavia (and to a lesser degree in other Eastern European nations). Perhaps profiting from Russia's experi-ence under war communism, China did not rush immediately into confiscation of all private enterprise. Anxious to take advantage of the skills and energies of native entrepreneurs, the Red Chinese, as it were, moved directly into the equivalent of the NEP. They distinguished between "national" capitalists and those whose strong adherence to the defeated Kuomintang regime defined them as "bourgeois." The former were allowed to remain in business and even were aided with government orders until the new regime had become reasonably well established. Commencing in approximately 1952, however, a campaign of vilification against them (the five "antis") was undertaken, and their capital systematically eroded by heavy fines for bribery, profiteering, and similar charges. Those who survived this were forced to accept the State as a partner in joint enterprises. They were finally to be edged out with a gurantee of a continuation of fixed interest on their investment for a period of ten years, after which State ownership would be total.[38]

The Chinese communists' treatment of the peasantry was rather different. Having come to power in 1949 promising agricultural land reform, they carried through this promise with an extensive land redistribution. Shortly thereafter (toward the end of 1953), they turned to collectivization, which meant, at first, the voluntary joining together of peasants, with each receiving a share of the earnings of the cooperative proportional to the amount of land he con-tributed. This was accelerated in 1956, with the pattern of the cooperative changed to one similar to the Soviet model, with earnings no longer divided in relation to contributions of land. By the end of 1956, 88 per cent of the

---

[37] In 1957, control was decentralized with the establishment of regional organizations, *sovnarkhozy,* to coordinate management. These were abandoned and the ministries re-established in a reform announced in September, 1965, which also granted more free-dom of decision to plant managers and changed aspects of the planning and incentive system that are discussed at a later point in this chapter.

[38] There have been repeated postponements of the final step.

peasants had been brought into the new form of cooperative, and another 8 per cent were in the older type.[39] In a radical experiment, the "Great Leap Forward," undertaken in 1958, this was suddenly changed again, and a form of agricultural organization far in advance of that attempted by the Soviets was begun. Enormous agricultural communes, characterized by barracks life and military-type organizations of "production brigades" (each about the size of an old-style cooperative), were created. Reward closely approximating the communist ideal of "need" was established. These changes, intended to bring agriculture fully under industrial discipline (and to destroy the strong family ties characteristic of pre-communist Chinese society) appear [40] to have had a most destructive effect on work incentives. Combined with severe drought and flood conditions, they reduced agricultural production to starvation levels, and there has been a subsequent "backing off," reducing the size of the communes, increasing the independence of the production brigades, and reintroducing incentives in the form of shared earnings of the brigades.[41]

Very nearly the reverse of Soviet and Chinese treatment of agriculture has been the pattern presented in Yugoslavia. Starting under the influence of the Soviet Union, Yugoslav communists commenced collectivization of the peasantry but returned to private enterprise after Marshal Tito's break with Stalin in 1948. At present, the Yugoslav agricultural sector is almost entirely private. In industry also, the pattern differs. Even though State ownership is the characteristic form, Yugoslav doctrine asserts that the "withering away of the State" is a continuous process from the time of the Communist Revolution. In consequence, there has been a gradual devolution of responsibility for factory management upon workers' councils. Although there remains considerable supervision by the League of Communists, by local governments, and by superior organs of the economic hierarchy, the authority of the workers' councils is apparently increasing. The councils not only play a part in the selection of the managerial personnel, but decide (subject to possible pressure from party committees and other bodies) on the use of profits from their enterprises, choosing between reinvestment and increased remuneration. Among other communist countries only Poland has followed Yugoslavia in decollectivization of agriculture and institution of workers' councils. Poland's agricultural sector is even less collectivized than is Yugoslavia's, but her workers' councils are far behind in autonomy.

[39] Ta-Chung Liu and Kung-Chia Yeh, *The Economy of the Chinese Mainland: National Income and Economic Development, 1933–1959* (Princeton: Princeton University Press, 1965), p. 14.

[40] The only real proof that the huge communes were failures in themselves lies in the fact of their being abandoned. So severe were the drought and flood conditions at the time that the disastrous crop failure is almost entirely accounted for by weather factors alone.

[41] Another feature of the "Great Leap Forward" was the attempt to use surplus labor in the communes for rural steel-making industries and the like. This proved extremely wasteful and was also abandoned.

Soviet Planning. In the broadest sense, all economies respond in some measure to each of two sets of preferences: preferences of consumers and State preferences.[42] The decision on the allocation of resources may respond primarily to individual choices for particular consumer goods and services, as it does in a market economy, or it may respond more often to collective choices made through the political order. In the Soviet Union, the latter type of choice or preference is by far the dominant one and extends not only to goods and services used, provided, or distributed by the government—such as arms, government employees' labor, roads, public education, and health services— but also to the major part of private consumption. That is, government preferences determine the supply and distribution of most consumer goods and services, overriding consumer preferences wherever these conflict. Why so? Because the politically determined objectives of the Soviet Union are so demanding of the existing supply of resources that they must needs override other demands. The intensive drive for industrialization and growth, the necessity for military strength, and the pressure to show spectacular achievements in science as a basis for international prestige and power require that private consumption be restrained both in amount and variety to minimize the resources that go to private satisfactions.

The instrument for the imposition of State preferences is the Soviet system of *administrative planning*. Through it the output of all significant goods and services is directed, the rate of investment in each sector of the economy is controlled, and even the rate of introduction of new technological processes into production is regulated. The magnitude of this task is astonishing—as much so as the idea of a market economy was to the representatives of traditional economic society depicted in Heilbroner's anecdote in Chapter 1. Of some 20 million commodities produced in the Soviet Union, some 18,000 are controlled by central decisions that attempt to balance the supply with the intended uses of them, and many more are governed by state, regional, and local planning agencies.[43] Planning and administrative bodies

> . . . must coordinate the activities of over 200,000 state industrial enterprises and over 100,000 construction sites. In addition, the national plans (1962) integrate the activities of 8,570 state farms, 39,700 collective farms, 2,900 state repair-and-service stations, several hundred thousand state warehouses and retail trade establishments, a vast transportation network, and a large complex of financial institutions, foreign trade organizations, scientific institutions, and cultural and educational establishments.[44]

[42] This "dual-preference" concept is derived from Jan Drewnowski, "The Economic Theory of Socialism: A Suggestion for Reconsideration," *Journal of Political Economy,* LXIX (August, 1961), pp. 341–354.

[43] Leon Smolinski and Peter Wiles, "The Soviet Planning Pendulum," *Problems of Communism,* XII, No. 6 (November–December, 1963), pp. 21–34, at p. 24.

[44] Gruchy, *op. cit.,* pp. 652–653.

Soviet plans are of two essential types: long-range and annual. The long-range plans (formerly five-year but now covering various periods up to twenty years) set goals toward which the planners aspire and are not in this respect markedly different except in their specificity of detail from those employed elsewhere. The annual plans, however, are in the nature of directives: They include specific output goals that are commands to the operating units within the system; they fix prices; they establish wage levels and the total wage bill; they allocate materials; they define the investment resources to be used by each industry; they specify which industries are to introduce new productive techniques; and, in their detailed implementing commands, they determine which industry shall obtain its supplies from which supplier, how much, and of what quality. In short, the Soviet planning system attempts to do by plan what the market does by bargaining, competition, and trial-and-error.

It would be utterly beyond possibility within the scope of this book to describe the way in which planning and plan implementation are carried out or the administrative machinery that does the job. The Soviet planning system is, moreover, continually being changed to improve its operation or to respond to new objectives developed from time to time.[45] Sufficient for our purposes will be to look at what is done, and at some of the problems and consequences.

Perhaps, however, it would be best to start with what is *not* done. Despite the extensive control exercised over the economy, the Soviet government has left certain areas relatively free of regulation. Although the supply of consumer goods is restricted, rationing has been employed since the end of the NEP only during the conversion to "socialism" (1928 to 1936) and during and immediately after the Second World War. Demand is restricted by wage controls and taxation instead. Price control, which applies to substantially all State enterprises and consumer and producer cooperatives, is absent from the market for foodstuffs produced on peasant plots, surplus collective farm produce, and the output of individual artisans. Labor controls, which were used to direct workers into employment, were dropped largely in 1956. Finally, not all commodities are planned. Many resources obtainable locally, such as sand and gravel, are left to negotiation between user enterprisers and supplying enterprises.

For the rest, however, the mechanisms of planning and plan implementation are supposed to ensure that, in each year, a specified amount of each good and service is produced. To do this, each producer in turn must be supplied with the correct amounts of the materials that go into the making of his product, an adequate supply of labor with the right skills (this is difficult in the absence of labor controls, but it is partly solved by the amounts and types of training given in the educational system and by the adjustment of the planned wage rates), and adequate investment funds and materials to bring production to the planned level. Furthermore, there must be means of checking to see that targets are met, and incentives must be developed to induce workers and

[45] Some aspects of recent changes will be discussed, however.

managers to meet them. (It would be to no advantage to set targets if there were not rewards and punishments for fulfillment and failure—another matter that the market under private ownership handles more or less automatically.)

Is it all as well integrated and organized as this sounds? Not really. Partly because of certain ideological commitments, and partly because of the sheer administrative impossibility of detailing things to the last kopeck, Soviet planning has never succeeded in defining exactly the output of each enterprise. The thrust of the planning effort has been mainly in two directions: Careful accounting for and planning those raw materials and semifinished products that are so essential to most types of production that their lack will seriously disrupt the economy, and intensive campaigns to solve problems of shortage and maldistribution as they arise. Adjustments and revisions of plan targets are made frequently, and the consumer goods sector is often made to accept reduced targets and reduced allocations in order to permit the achievement of targets in basic industries. For various reasons, not the least of which is the attempt of plant managers to conceal the actual productive capacity of their plants so that output goals will be set low enough to be feasible, the targets do not fix rigidly what the production will actually be. Because incentive rewards apply not only to fulfillment, but to overfulfillment, production in various lines is frequently higher than planned, and this excess provides some slack in the system. Targets, moreover, do not usually specify all of the attributes of a product. They may be set in terms of number of items, total tonnage, total value, and so forth, but they may fail to prescribe accurately the "mix" of products of varying weight, quality, and price. An enterprise manager, therefore, operates within a framework of requirements that gives him some leeway. He will have been allotted a certain sum in investment credit; his product prices will be fixed, as will his wage scales (but not the number of workers at each wage grade); and his output goals will be stated by some measure of quantity, volume, weight, or value, with possibly other specifications. He will receive allocation certificates to indicate from whom he may purchase supplies, and in what qualities and quantities, and he will have a profit target estimated in terms of his costs of production (based on the State-fixed prices for his output, less the prices for his labor, his raw materials, and his taxes, and so on).[46] It is then possible for him to try to adjust his output, costs, deployment of labor force, and other factors to meet his targets. If his enterprise makes shoes, for example, and his output target is stated in terms of number of pairs, he may give most of his production to low-quality shoes, with just enough expensive ones to meet his required profit margin.

The enterprise manager, therefore, has some freedom of decision, but not remotely the equivalent of managers of private enterprise in other systems. He may not undertake new projects and new investment without credits from the State banking system, which are allotted in accordance with the plans. He is allowed to retain and use a portion of the profits of his enterprise, but most

---

[46] The recent reforms to be discussed in a later part of this chapter have changed the treatment of some of the matters discussed in this and the ensuing paragraphs.

are siphoned off in taxes to be plowed back into his and other enterprises on the decision of the central planning authorities. In sum, his freedom amounts to a freedom to maneuver within the limits of his various targets and allocations, with the objective of maximizing his rewards under the incentive system, which is tied to those same targets. To this freedom may be added another characteristic of the Soviet system, the use of influence, or *blat,* which is a sort of lubricant to the system not contemplated by the planning mechanism. Through *blat,* a manager may get hold of extra supplies of needed materials that some other manager has succeeded in concealing from the planning authorities in order to fulfill or exceed his quota. The freedom of a manager, then, is not economic power in a real sense. It resembles more the condition of a boy with both chores and an allowance: He may attempt to minimize his fulfillment of the former while retaining full measure of the latter.

Of necessity, the effectiveness of planning depends on the perfection of control mechanisms that see to it that not only are orders transmitted downward, but information about performance, available resources, and needs is transmitted upward. The planners do not plan in a vacuum. They base their work upon information available to them. Because it is always in the interest of an enterprise director or plant manager to understate the capacity of his plant and the supplies of inventories he has (so that he may receive a low output target that will be relatively easy to fulfill), a full apparatus of government and party organs is employed to check on the work of the enterprises. The information received is used both to determine eligibility for bonuses and to serve as the basis for each succeeding annual plan and for the longer-range plans. A considerable staff, then, is engaged in checking and overseeing as well as in planning and directing, so that independence of action at each succeeding lower level of administration is restricted by an overlapping network of control.

Because, however, there is maneuvering room within the system, discrepancies and bottlenecks can and do occur. This calls forth a type of effort dear to the hearts of Soviet leaders: An intensive campaign to induce greater exertion. Over the years, Soviet planning has resembled less an orderly planned progress, with each necessary element accounted for, than a series of grand offensives in one sector after another, each to the accompaniment of a drumfire of exhortations from party agitators, "self-criticism," and rewards for "Heroes of Soviet Labor." All of this is more congenial to the communist purpose of inspiring workers to sacrificial participation in building communism and to the ideal of the party as a "vanguard" of an army in battle than would be some kind of orderly, mechanical planning brought to perfection by the use of high-speed computers, but without the human element that has been present in the great campaigns.[47] To assist this, party and union organizations are oriented to the

[47] It has been remarked that Soviet planners have generally lagged behind even Western economic and mathematical theoreticians in developing and using computer techniques for planning. Some of the satellites are well ahead of Russia in this respect. See Gruchy, *op. cit.,* pp. 676–679.

promotion of the goals of the State, rather than to the representation of workers' needs. Labor unions do not bargain or strike in the Soviet Union; they exhort the workers and chastise them for production failures. Similarly, the court system has been employed to punish not only derelict and dishonest managers, but lagging, tardy, and delinquent workers as well.[48]

Material Incentives. The planned incentive system in the Soviet Union deserves special attention because of its relation to the achievement of plan targets and its involvement in the recent changes that have occurred in Soviet and satellite planning arrangements. There are essentially three bases upon which material rewards are calculated: First, there are the differential rewards offered to persons in occupations requiring different skills; secondly, there are worker incentives to higher individual productivity; and thirdly, there are managerial incentives designed to ensure fulfillment of output targets.

Differential rewards on the basis of occupation and skill were reinstated in Russia even before the end of the war communism period. After Stalin's explicit disavowal of egalitarianism in 1931, the spread between high and low incomes was allowed to increase greatly, although it has begun to narrow again in recent years in conformity to the trend in all maturing economic societies. Communist doctrine may partly account for some of the specifics of the narrowing,[49] but it seems to have little noticeable effect on the choice of skills receiving the highest rewards. Although the pattern differs from that obtaining in the West (notably in the much higher rewards given to intellectuals and teachers), one finds a rather typical pattern of low pay for the ordinary worker and high pay for managers and, surprisingly (because they are not, in a material sense, productive workers), performing artists. Some typical pay ranges are shown in Table 17, which also suggests that over-all income differentials in the Soviet Union may well be greater than those found in the West.[50] The rewards given intellectuals, scientists, and teachers reflect the emphasis on these skills in achieving rapid development, rather than any doctrinal considerations directly applicable to such activities.

---

[48] The use of judicial punishments has declined since Stalin's day.

[49] See Gertrude Schroeder, "Industrial Wage Differentials in the USSR," *Soviet Studies,* XVII (January, 1966), pp. 307–308.

[50] Comparisons of the carefully calculated sort discussed in Chapter 3 (pages 140–141) are not available. To suggest but one example, however, Gertrude Schroeder (*op. cit.,* p. 308) has reported recent wage changes in the Soviet Union to have reduced the discrepancy between the basic pay of skilled and unskilled workers to a ratio somewhere between 1 to 1.8 and 1 to 2.6 in most industries. By comparison, reported median wages for skilled and unskilled male workers in the United States in 1959 were at a ratio of 1 to 1.78, or slightly below the minimum range calculated by Schroeder (*Statistical Abstract of the United States,* 1965, pp. 231, 233). It is probable that the two different means of calculation understate the difference between United States and Soviet differentials, for the United States figures include foremen's wages, whereas the Soviet ones do not.

Table 17 Selected Salary and Wage Ranges in the USSR, 1960

	Monthly earnings, 1960 (in rubles *)
Scientist (academician)	8,000–15,000
Minister (head of government ministry or department)	7,000
Opera star	†5,000–20,000
Professor (science)	6,000–10,000
Professor (medicine)	4,000– 6,000
Docent (assistant professor)	3,000– 5,000
Plant manager	3,000–10,000
Engineer	1,000– 3,000
Physician, head	950– 1,800
Physician, staff	850– 1,000
Teacher, high school	850– 1,500
Teacher, primary school	600– 900
Technician	800– 2,000
Worker, skilled	1,000– 2,500
Worker, semiskilled	600– 900
Worker, unskilled	270– 500

* The official rate of exchange, as fixed by the Soviet government, is four rubles = U.S. $1. The actual purchasing power of the ruble, however, is more accurately represented by the official tourist rate of exchange of ten rubles for U.S. $1.
† The top salary at the Bolshoi Theater has been reported as 5,000 rubles a month. Outside appearances increase the artist's income.
From Edmund Nash, "Purchasing Power of Workers in the USSR," *Monthly Labor Review,* LXXXIII (April, 1960), p. 362.

Within the general scheme of different basic pay rates by occupation, the Soviet Union provides productivity incentives, but these are different for workers and for managers. For workers in industry and on State farms, basic pay rates are usually calculated in relation to a piecework norm. That is, pay is calculated not by hours of work, but in terms of units produced, with the basic or normal pay being the amount a worker would earn if he produced the exact quantity fixed as the normal unit output for a worker in his particular job and grade. His actual earnings would be higher or lower depending on his own output, with double or triple piecework rates sometimes given for exceeding the norm.[51] This method of payment, which is bitterly opposed by labor organizations in noncommunist countries as exploitative, is used to stimulate regular increases in output by increases in the output norms. With each such increase, a worker must produce more simply to maintain his income.

Managerial incentives, which descend to the level of foremen, consist of bonuses paid or penalties imposed on a fixed basic salary for each grade. In addition, successful enterprises may be allowed to make payments into an "enterprise fund" that may be used to provide amenities for the workers, such as housing and free meals at the plant. Unlike those in a capitalist economy, where rewards may accrue to entrepreneurs for the successful exercise of initiative in any direction, Soviet incentive rewards have been tied directly to the plans. The planned output targets serve as "success indicators." Fulfillment

[51] Pay scales in collective agriculture, which are used to determine the distribution of the net income of the collective, are calculated somewhat differently; but the basic unit, the *trudoden,* or conventional workday unit, is similar in character to a piece-rate unit.

or overfulfillment of the targets is the basis for determining the award of bonuses. Essentially, this means that the success indicators cannot account for radical departures from established practice. The rewards are given not for initiative in general, but for initiative and high performance *according to the plan*. If, for example, a production improvement required the shutdown of a plant for retooling, and thus a failure to meet plan targets in a given year, it might well be foregone even though its effect in subsequent years would be to increase production greatly. Innovation, then, must be planned, and indeed, each annual plan designates those industries that are to introduce production changes, labor-saving machinery, and other technical improvements.[52]

Propaganda, Indoctrination, and Terror.   Systematic indoctrination as a means to inspire a high level of performance under communism is a major function of many institutions and organizations in the Soviet Union.[53] The media of mass communication are entirely State-owned and consistently promote the goals of the State, giving attention to the particular slogans and campaigns that are important at the moment. These media include many specialized journals aimed at particular audiences, as well as newspapers, magazines, radio, and television. Soviet literature and art have been harnessed in the cause of propaganda by the requirement that writers and artists portray themes of "socialist realism," that is, themes stressing the glories of communist life. Youth organizations—the Komsomols and the Young Pioneers—see to it that the recreational activities of children include training in the ideals of the communist movement and also serve as preparatory bodies for admission to membership in the party—party membership being a privilege conferred only upon those whose loyalty is not questioned. The educational curriculum at every level includes courses in communist doctrine, and for those at work, the Agitation and Propaganda section (*Agitprop*) of the Party Central Committee provides adult classes to instruct and exhort. Finally, honors, public recognition, and very tangible material rewards are given to outstanding workers, the "Heroes of Soviet Labor" and the like, as symbols of their contribution to Soviet production and of their status as models worthy of emulation.

In an intermediate role that includes indoctrination and surveillance are most of the social and professional organizations of the Soviet Union and the lower ranks of the Communist party itself. Professional organizations are supposed to ensure the ideological "correctness" of their members' work, while labor unions both exhort and discipline workers whose productivity is below the norm or who are persistently laggard or absent. Party members are stra-

---

[52] Another side effect of the incentive system recently revealed is the quarterly cycle of Soviet production. Because bonuses are calculated quarterly, production booms in the last month of each quarter to meet targets and then subsides when the next quarter begins.

[53] Most of these are described in Alfred G. Meyer, *The Soviet Political System: An Interpretation* (New York: Random House, Inc., 1965), ch. XIV.

tegically placed in social, economic, and governmental organizations to guide and supervise them.

Finally there is terror. The function of terror is partly to protect the regime by making it too dangerous to organize against it, but it also serves to create uncertainty and insecurity so that individuals will be inclined to display their loyalty by their application to their tasks and acceptance of the goals of the State.[54] The communist regime is now so well entrenched and accepted by the Soviet people that terror is much less in evidence than it was in Stalin's day, but it is still prominent in China and some of the satellites. It is more than likely that terror is less an aid than a bar to economic efficiency. As Carl J. Friedrich and Zbigniew K. Brzezinski suggest,[55] the continued use of terror tends to cause those surrounding the ruling elite to refuse to give them true information about the state of affairs in the nation, lest in so doing they be accused of disloyalty. This, then, deprives the leaders of their ability to check and correct mistakes. It is notable that the Soviet Union has established the device of self-criticism (*samokritika*), by which even the humblest citizen is urged to report unfavorable information to those in authority. How safe it actually is in the Soviet Union to engage in *samokritika* is not known, but it is certainly safer than the great "Hundred Flowers" campaign in China was for those who were so unwary as to "bloom."[56] Terror also, by the personal anxiety it arouses, may impair worker performance and efficiency, so that its decline in Russia may easily prove to be advantageous to the system itself as well as to the sense of well-being of the people.

Recent Changes in the Soviet Union and Elsewhere. There are a number of drawbacks to the planned incentive system in the Soviet Union (besides its dampening effect on initiative) that have led to recent modifications in the whole planning process there and that have led a number of other communist countries to adopt different arrangements. Success indicators based on measures of physical output are the cause of much of the maneuvering and *blat* described earlier. Concentration upon output goals has led to the ignoring of cost factors, and where quality is not sufficiently specified in the plans, it has often suffered by being subordinated to other considerations for which bonuses were given.[57] Other deficiencies in Soviet planning, including some rather

[54] See Raymond A. Bauer, Alex Inkeles, and Clyde Kluckhohn, *How the Soviet System Works: Cultural, Psychological, and Social Themes* (Cambridge: Harvard University Press, 1956), ch. VII.

[55] *Totalitarian Dictatorship and Autocracy* (Cambridge: Harvard University Press, 1956), ch. XVI.

[56] In May, 1956, Mao Tse-Tung invited criticism of the regime with the statement, "Let hundred schools of thought contend and let hundred flowers bloom." Such a storm of criticism was unleashed that the terror was resumed unabated, and many who had spoken out were executed.

[57] A fuller discussion of the "success indicators" is given in Alec Nove, *The Soviet Economy: An Introduction* (New York: Frederick A. Praeger, 1961), pp. 155–181.

unrealistic policies derived from ideological positions (such as a long-time refusal to calculate interest on capital investment), have hampered the development of adequate gauges of efficiency for planners to use and have lent strength to a movement toward new methods of planning and directing a communist economy.

In brief, the 1965–1966 reorganization of the Soviet economy restates the targets for managers in terms of the output they are able to *sell* (as measured by the profits made by the firm), rather than in terms of the physical quantities they *produce*. Targets are still fixed centrally, but greater room for managerial decision is given, such as the right to make small investments in new equipment, to change production methods, to contract with suppliers, and to determine the product mix, so that managers may have more control over the efficiency of their production and the saleability of their product. Correspondingly, reforms in the system of fixed prices are to be made in order for those prices to be a more realistic reflection of costs, and interest charges have been introduced on investment capital.

Some have hailed these reforms (a bit prematurely) as "creeping capitalism," and indeed there are some surprising new words being used in connection with them, such as *profit* and *entrepreneurial freedom*. Yet we would be in error to discount too much, in the Soviet Union at least, the intention of the planners to maintain control over the economy. The Russian reform seeks to call forth greater and more useful effort from managers by imposing upon them a new criterion—the acceptability of their product to those who will buy it—and by giving them greater discretion in fulfilling their plans.

But perhaps we should allow Professor Yevsei Liberman, long-time advocate of these changes in the Soviet Union, whose leadership in them is recognized by their being dubbed "Libermanism" by Western observers, to speak on this point himself:

> These methods fit in well within the framework of a centralized planned economy. There is no need for us engaging in economic hypocrisy and claiming that we can solve, by methods of direct administration, tasks which can best be solved by methods of economic stimulation. Scientific prognostication and optimal planning, effective stimulation of production through profitability—such is our economic weapon, and we are confident that it will bring us victory.
>
> Make no mistake, you Western observers, this will not be a step back to capitalism, but a step forward, to the consolidation and development of socialism. There is not even a hint here of distribution by capital [i.e. profit-making in the capitalist sense], it is only a more efficient distribution by labor, i.e., compensation of each enterprise for genuine services to its only boss—society.[58]

[58] Yevsei Liberman, "Mr. Alsby, You Are Mistaken . . ." *Literaturnaya Gazeta*, March 5, 1966. Mimeographed translation furnished by the Soviet Embassy in Washington, D.C., p. 8. Minor typographical errors corrected and American spellings substituted.

In Czechoslovakia, Poland, and some of the other Soviet satellites, even more managerial discretion is allowed than under the Liberman reforms in Russia, among the more important examples being the scheme of target-setting. Enterprises are allowed to set their own targets, with incentives being given for aiming at and achieving high goals, rather in the fashion of earning points in contract bridge.[59] Special incentives are used to spur ambitious planning in those industries deemed important in the central plans. The chief advantage here lies in the avoidance of the Soviet manager's tendency to seek the lowest possible targets.

Of all of the communist economic systems, the Yugoslavian is the most distinctive in its departure from the Soviet model. Profit, in Yugoslavia, is not used as a success indicator or as a measure of the fulfillment of the national plans; it is an actual reward that is shared, within limits, by all of the workers in an enterprise. Called *market socialism,* the Yugoslav system bears a family resemblance to cooperative socialism, with an overlay of central planning and controls governed by the communist State. The State sets the general goals and targets, rations investment credit, and controls prices and materials allocations where necessary to preserve stability and ensure a balanced supply. Production plans, however, most prices, and the decision to employ profits either for reinvestment or for employee compensation are made by the enterprises themselves, which are becoming more and more effectively governed by their workers' councils. The enterprises look to the market, rather than to State-fixed output goals to determine how much they should try to produce. This is not to say that the worker-run agencies are entirely free in their pursuit of profit. The State takes a large proportion of earnings through taxation, which it then may lend back to the same enterprises or to others for major investments. Party and governmental supervision and union organizations restrain attempts of workers to dip too heavily into profits for their own compensation, and other controls prevent profiteering from monopolistic positions. Still further relaxations of central controls, first instituted in 1961, and given decisive restatement in March, 1966, have enlarged the autonomy of individual enterprises and even permitted them to seek foreign private capital to carry out investment plans. It is apparent that Yugoslavia is on a different road from the one that the Soviet Union may be expected to follow in the predictable future.

Evaluation of Communism

How well has communism worked? After a half century of experience in the Soviet Union, one can only conclude that communism is clearly viable and at least partially successful. The immediate objectives have in large measure been achieved, however distant or unlikely may still remain the realization of the ultimate ones. A modern industrial economy has been built in the Soviet

[59] The analogy is made by Nove, *op. cit.,* p. 243.

Table 18 Estimated Gross National Product Indexes,
Western Alliances and Sino-Soviet Bloc,
1950–1965, Selected Years

	Index 1950 = 100					Per Cent of Total			Average Annual Growth Rate (%)	
	1950	1955	1958	1959*	1965†	1950	1959*	1965†	1950–1959	1959–1965†
Canada	100	125	133	137	175	3	2	2	3¾	4¼
European NATO	100	128	141	152	200	23	23	23	4¾	4¾
OAS, SEATO, and Bilateral Allies	100	125	145	155	207	12	12	12	5	5
United States	100	124	126	134	171	39	34	32	3¼	4¼
Total, U. S. and Allies	100	125	134	143	185	77	71	69	4	4½
European Satellites	100	142	167	179	246	5	6	6	6½	5½
Communist China	100	147	193	216	342	5	7	8	9	8
USSR	100	139	175	185	262	13	16	17	7	6
Total, USSR and Satellites	100	141	177	190	275	23	29	31	7½	6½
Grand total	—	—	—	—	—	100	100	100	—	—

* Preliminary estimates.
† Projections.
From U. S. Congress, Joint Economic Committee, *Comparisons of the United States and Soviet Economies,* prepared by the Central Intelligence Agency in cooperation with the Department of State and the Department of Defense, 86th Congress, 2nd session, 1960, p. 48. The 1959 to 1965 projections of growth rates in this table were somewhat high for the Soviet Union and somewhat low for the United States, as things turned out.

Union, substantially without foreign assistance and despite a devastating war. Russia fought that war to a successful conclusion, demonstrating a military potential that has since become even greater by the addition of nuclear weapons and sophisticated delivery systems. Communist leadership has trained a backward population to industrial life and, if it has not made every Russian an enthusiastic communist, it has at least held and developed the loyalties of its people to the extent that it faces no significant internal unrest or underground movement—a fact that is more apparent now, with the relaxation of terroristic control, than it was in the years of Josef Stalin's rule. Of course, the Soviet Union is the most successful of the communist regimes to date, but there is no present reason to believe that its success is accidental.

Communism as an Economic System. The most impressive record of communism has been written in the statistics of economic growth. By concentrated effort, the communist bloc generally has maintained a growth rate in excess of that in the Western Alliance, as shown in Tables 18 and 19. Yet it is difficult to avoid either overstatement or understatement of the communist economic achievement. Customary comparisons of the Soviet Union with the United States tend to stress either the rate of growth (which has tended to be higher in the Soviet Union than in the United States, although not in very recent years), or to point to the time lags—the number of years by which the Soviet Union lags behind the United States in reaching a given level of total output or per capita output. One comparison gives the advantage to the Soviet

Table 19 Estimated Industrial Production Indexes,
Western Alliances and Sino-Soviet Bloc,
1950–1965, Selected Years

	Index 1950 = 100					Per Cent of Total			Average Annual Growth Rate (%)	
	1950	1955	1958	1959*	1965†	1950	1959*	1965†	1950–1959	1959–1965†
Canada	100	133	142	150	200	3	3	3	4¾	5
European NATO	100	141	161	172	243	24	24	24	6¼	6
OAS, SEATO, and Bilaterial Allies	100	150	186	193	286	7	8	8	7¾	7
United States	100	129	125	141	183	48	40	35	4	4½
Total, U. S. and Allies	100	135	141	155	211	82	75	70	4¾	5¼
European Satellites	100	157	198	215	323	7	8	9	9	7
Communist China	100	266	516	640	1,400	1	3	5	23	14
USSR	100	168	211	229	380	10	14	16	10	8.6
Total, USSR and Satellites	100	171	223	247	414	18	25	30	10.5	9
Grand total	—	—	—	—	—	100	100	100	—	—

* Preliminary estimates.
† Projections.
From U. S. Congress, Joint Economic Committee, *Comparisons of the United States and Soviet Economies*, prepared by the Central Intelligence Agency in cooperation with the Department of State and the Department of Defense, 86th Congress, 2nd session, 1960, p. 49.

Union, the other to the United States. Each, however, tells only part of the story. Russia began her industrialization later than the United States, so that a lag is to be expected. Furthermore, she has yet to apply the full range of modern technology to all parts of her economy, which means that a higher rate of growth is to be expected while that process is still going on. A long-term comparison worked out by G. Warren Nutter encompassing both Czarist and communist Russian experience suggests that the communists have, in general terms, managed to maintain a pattern of growth that, although differing in many respects of detail, has tended to parallel that of the United States in the long run (Figure 3). The period of communist rule began with a disastrous loss of production, but this was made up at the same time that the United States was suffering the effects of the Great Depression (a phenomenon that did not occur in the Soviet Union, where there has never been significant unemployment). The Second World War had opposite effects in the two countries, because Russia suffered invasion and the United States did not, but Russian production recovered speedily thereafter. In the period from the institution of the five-year plans until the Second World War, and again after the war, Soviet growth was markedly faster than that of the United States, although there has been another retardation in Russia and a speeding up by the United States in the period since 1959 (not shown in Figure 3).

The analysis by Professor Rostow lends further support to the view that Soviet industrialization has proceeded at a pace not markedly different from that displayed in other countries—neither faster nor slower—and also points out some of the more important differences between the Soviet and American

Figure 3. Industrial Production: Tsarist Russia, Soviet Union, and United States, 1870–1959

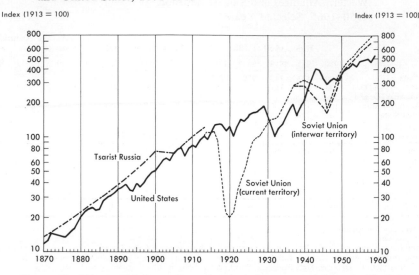

Index (1913 = 100)   Index (1913 = 100)

From G. Warren Nutter, *Growth of Industrial Production in the Soviet Union* (Princeton, 1962), p. 228. Reprinted by permission of the Princeton University Press. Copyright © 1962 by National Bureau of Economic Research. All rights reserved.

Note: Soviet index interpolated for 1913–1928 and extrapolated for 1955–1958 by industrial materials index. For 1913, output in Tsarist territory taken as 118 per cent of output in interwar territory; for 1940–1959, output in the latter taken as 90 per cent of output in postwar territory.

experience.[60] In the first place, the Soviet regime had to cope with a far more entrenched traditional social system than ever existed in the United States— a severe disadvantage for an industrializing country. Secondly, and with opposite effect, the Soviet industrialization came later and had the advantage of a large existing pool of unused technology; there was no need to await invention. To Professor Rostow's analysis may be added the fact that the United States enjoyed a massive immigration during its industrialization, a major advantage when it is considered that immigrants are a form of "human capital"—already educated and mature, posing no burden on the educational system and on the economy for support during their unproductive nonage. And the United States had a further advantage in that it was receptive to foreign private investment— a resource from which the Soviet Union was cut off for ideological reasons.

If the conditions for industrialization differed, so also did the manner in which it was carried out. Soviet industrial growth has been achieved through

[60] W. W. Rostow, *The Stages of Economic Growth* (Cambridge: Cambridge University Press, 1960). The comparison with the United States, which includes Nutter's analysis, is in ch. 7; the comparison with other countries is in ch. 2–5, *passim*.

the deliberate suppression of consumption and through the direction of growth into selected sectors of the economy (notably heavy industry and military-support industries). It has been accompanied by a repression of political and social freedom as well as of economic freedom and private initiative.[61]

In short, communism has proved to be one way to achieve industrialization, and a way that has its own distinctive advantages and disadvantages. Among the former are the ability to compel social change, to "go it alone," and to concentrate on areas of growth that further national purposes. Soviet Russia, with approximately half the Gross National Product of the United States, has a modern military potential at least as great as the latter's. She has fostered scientific development in selected areas with spectacular results, especially in missile and space technology. She has surpassed the United States in the production of coal, iron ore, and cement, and is fast approaching United States levels in many other areas.

To accomplish this, communism has created a substitute for the drive of the capitalist entrepreneur. In place of a multitude of individuals each seeking in his own way and for his own advantage to develop resources, to create new enterprises, to save, to invest, and to build, communism provides the zeal of a dedicated elite and a hierarchical apparatus for control and ideological exhortation by which that zeal can be transformed into the actions of an army of workers, managers, planners, and administrators. The motivation is supplied from above, rather than from within the system, but it is both effective and capable of being concentrated on a narrow range of objectives. With the experience of past errors and successes now available upon which to build, there is little reason to doubt that communism offers the best instrument yet devised for rapid economic development and the swift achievement of military strength.

Growth and military power, however, are not the only functions of an economy. An economy, even that of the Soviet Union, exists at least partly for the welfare of the members of society, and here the record is less favorable. The single-minded pursuit of rapid industrialization has seen two generations pass without their members sharing appreciably in the increased material wealth. Only recently has there been a shift toward distributing the benefits of production to the people in the form of more and better consumer goods and services. Russia devotes an even smaller proportion of her resources to individual consumption than the socialist countries reviewed earlier. According to one calculation, the share of the Gross National Product going to private consumption expenditures (including government free services, pensions, and such) was 55.9 per cent.[62] Similarly, the communist Chinese have reduced

[61] It should be noted that forced labor was used extensively in the Stalin period, but whether or not this was a net advantage in terms of growth is doubtful. Its origin and purpose were more political than economic.

[62] Stanley H. Cohn, "Soviet Growth Retardation: Trends in Resource Availability and Efficiency," in Joint Economic Committee, *New Directions in the Soviet Economy,* 89th Congress, 2nd session, 1966, p. 129. Compare the figures in Table 11, p. 133.

private consumption from 71.2 per cent of Gross Domestic Product in 1952, to an estimated 56.7 per cent in 1962.[63] The consequence of this is that the amenities of life are not very much in evidence in Russia, despite an economic capacity to produce them. Most striking is the situation with regard to housing: The average city Russian in 1963 had 6.18 square meters of living space, or .27 square meters *less* than he had had in 1923. United States per capita living space in 1963 was nearly 19.5 square meters.[64] Some other indications of different levels of living are given in Table 20. It is to be noted that the only consumer durable that was as widely available in Russia as in most European countries was the radio, an important instrument of the Soviet domestic propaganda system.

Table 20   Consumer Durables Per Thousand Population and Per Capita Nonindustrial Use of Electricity, USSR and Selected Noncommunist Countries

Country	**Consumer Durables in Use per 1,000 Population**				Nonindustrial Use of Electricity, Kwh per Capita, 1964
	Passenger Cars *	Radio Receivers *	Television Sets *	Telephones †	
EEC countries ‡	131	265	131	118	625
United Kingdom	158	294	242	171	1,590
Norway	112	289	110	228	3,815
Sweden	219	331	255	420	1,880
Canada	264	NA	255	349	2,055
United States	360	1,143	334	443	2,530
USSR	4	313	52	29§	440

* January 1, 1965.
† End of 1963.
‡ Includes the Federal Republic of Germany, France, Italy, Netherlands, Belgium, and Luxembourg.
§ January 1, 1964.
Source: Statistical Office of the European Communities, *Basic Statistics of the Community*, 1965, pp. 146, 149, 150.

The delay in giving attention to consumer wants is not accidental under communism and cannot be lightly dismissed. It derives partly, as has been shown, from the Marxist view of what capitalists do to achieve industrial growth. Communists exploit their people because they believe exploitation to be economically necessary for growth. This may well be true for a nation that cuts itself off from the rest of the world by the adoption of a fighting ideology, but there are ways open to those that do not take so aggressive and antithetical a posture. Professor Rostow's calculations indicate that Canada, for example, began her industrialization at approximately the same time as Russia and achieved maturity also at about the same time.[65] Because she was an integral

[63] Calculated from figures given in Yuan-Li Wu, *The Economy of Communist China: An Introduction* (New York: Frederick A. Praeger, 1965), p. 91.

[64] U. S. Congress, Joint Economic Committee, *Current Economic Indicators for the USSR*, 89th Congress, 1st session, 1965, pp. 146–147.

[65] Rostow, *op. cit.* chart facing p. 1 and pp. 38, 59.

member of the Western community, she received foreign investment on a scale permitting her people to develop and maintain a far higher level of personal consumption than exists in the Soviet Union.[66] Yugoslavia's recent change of policy to admit foreign investors is evidently a recognition of the advantages that flow from cooperative economic relationships between nations.

If private consumer choices and the gadgetry of modern civilization have been neglected, the same has not been true of all aspects of consumer welfare. The Soviet Union has devoted a comparatively large proportion of its re-sources to a number of communal services that operate to maintain the health and strength of the people, to educate and train them, and to provide them with some comforts and a high degree of economic security. There are at least two reasons for this: In the first place, communists display an "ideological bias toward communal consumption," [67] largely because communal services repre-sent the principle of reward according to need toward which they aim. Secondly, they have been concerned with the development of human resources and energies. They have given attention to the health and education of their people to ensure their ability to fulfill the tasks demanded of them, and they have sought to develop and maintain morale by various free services such as vaca-tions, cultural activities, and pensions. The results are impressive. Communal services represent nearly 17 per cent of the total expenditure for private con-sumption.[68] The share of the Soviet State budget allotted to social and cultural measures has risen steadily from 23.5 per cent of the budget in 1940, to 28.2 per cent in 1950, and 36.1 per cent in 1964.[69] The most recent Five-Year Plan calls for further increases by 1970 equalling 40 per cent of present expenditures for these purposes.[70] The educational system has virtually eliminated illiteracy, and although it does not offer as wide a variety of choices as does that in the United States, nor accommodate as large a proportion of the population at the higher secondary and university levels, it does give training to the many appro-priate to the employment opportunities they will find. To a few it offers ad-vanced scientific and technical education fully comparable to that in the West.[71] Free services available to Soviet citizens include medical care, nurseries for children, and places at vacation homes. Pensions for some classes of worker are 100 per cent of wages. To show the effects of the communal effort in the

[66] Canada also was favored by a considerable immigration.

[67] I am indebted to Professor Charles K. Wilber of The American University for this phrase.

[68] Calculated from Cohn, *loc. cit.*

[69] *Narodnoe Khoziaistvo SSSR v 1964 godu. Statisticheskii Ezhegodnik* (*National Economy of the USSR in 1964. Statistical Yearbook*), Moscow, 1965, p. 771. These figures should not be compared with similar expenditures in the budgets of other coun-tries, because the budgets are not comparable in scope.

[70] *23rd Congress of the Communist Party of the Soviet Union* (Moscow: Novosti Press Agency Publishing House, n.d.), p. 373.

[71] See Nicholas DeWitt, "Education and the Development of Human Resources" in *Dimensions of Soviet Economic Power,* Joint Economic Committee, pp. 233–268.

realm of health and nutrition, the same countries listed in Table 20 are compared in Table 21, with respect to the provision of doctors, hospital beds, and calorie intake of food. Here the Soviet Union compares favorably indeed.

Table 21 Doctors and Hospital Beds Per Hundred Thousand, and Calorie Food Consumption Per Capita Per Day, USSR and Selected Noncommunist Countries

Country	Doctors per 100,000 Pop. (End 1963)	Hospital Beds Per 100,000 (End 1963)	Calories Food Consumption Per Person Per Day, 1963–1964
EEC Countries	139	970*	2,900
United Kingdom	107	1,022	3,280
Norway	126	1,090	2,970
Sweden	101	1,591	2,950
Canada	117	981	3,060
United States	149	900	3,090
USSR	205	903	3,200†

* Estimate.
† 1962. This figure taken from Joint Economic Committee, *Current Economic Indicators for the USSR,* 1965, p. 121.
Source: Except as noted, Statistical Office of the European Communities, *Basic Statistics of the Community,* 1965, pp. 143, 151.

To what extent may we expect that Soviet concern for communal services will be paralleled in the future by a reorientation of the remainder of the economy toward production of consumer goods and services? There are certainly some indications of change, especially in the 1966–1970 plan, yet too much hope should not be held out for a radical and immediate change. Party General Secretary Brezhnev, in announcing the plan to the Twenty-third Congress made it quite clear that the increased emphasis on consumer production was subordinate to the main goal of maintaining growth in heavy industry. The implicit likelihood still remains that any failure to fulfill the new plans will be registered first in the consumer sector:

> . . . The Party will continue to give priority to the development of heavy industry, continue [to] provide a faster growth of the production of the means of production. At the same time, due to the successes that have been scored in developing heavy industry, we have the possibility in the new five-year period of investing much larger resources into industries producing consumer goods.[72]

Central planning has been in operation in the Soviet Union for a long time, and one of its basic characteristics is its ability to block the direct transmission of raw consumer preferences back through the economic system to influence the allocation of resources. Such preferences are mediated by the planning authorities and the political order; there is no established habit of responsive-

[72] *23rd Congress of the Communist Party of the Soviet Union, op. cit.,* p. 76.

ness to consumer demand in the production sector. Equally important is the fact that planning has so shaped the economic structure that neither the facilities nor the market-oriented techniques for consumer service exist, and these will take a long time to build, even given the intention to do so.[73] It is not

Table 22 Professional Graduates with Completed Higher Education in the USSR and College Graduates in the United States, 1926–1960

Field	USSR	United States	Comparison and Notes
Engineering	1,244,000	695,000	USSR trained 1.8-fold as many as United States. Soviet reporting is inflated, in comparison with U. S. figure, by about 15 per cent by inclusion of some other science fields (about 10 per cent) and graduates in economics (about 5 per cent) normally reported elsewhere in U. S. practice.
Medical doctors	462,000	196,000	USSR trained 2.4-fold as many as United States. Physicians only (medical doctor equivalent) were included in USSR's figure.
Agricultural specialists ...	437,000	177,000	USSR trained 2.2-fold as many as United States.
Science majors, total	485,000	795,000	United States trained 1.6-fold as many as USSR. The category includes chemistry, physical sciences, and mathematics, earth sciences (geology, etc.), and biology. In the USSR some of the majors in these fields are also found among engineering specialties above.
Total, engineering, applied and theoretical science fields	2,628,000	1,863,000	USSR trained 1.4-fold as many as United States.
All other fields: humanities, social sciences, teacher training in nonscientific fields, arts, etc.	1,897,000	5,787,000	United States trained 3-fold as many as USSR. There was greater diversity of training in the United States, with heavy emphasis on business and commerce, social sciences, and jurisprudence.
Grand total	4,525,000	7,650,000	United States trained 1.7-fold as many as USSR.

From Joint Economic Committee, *Dimensions of Soviet Economic Power,* 87th Congress, 2d session, 1962, p. 261.

merely a matter of the construction of light industries and trading establishments, but of training persons in the skills of trade and distribution. Soviet education has been extensively and rightly praised for its accomplishments, but its planned weighting has been heavily to the engineering, physical, and medical sciences to the neglect of nearly everything else, including the humanities, the law, and commercial skills, as indicated in Table 22. Despite the

[73] It is noteworthy that in one consumer field in which the Soviets apparently do plan to make good, they have decided to purchase the entire production facility abroad. In May, 1966, it was announced that a contract had been made with the Italian Fiat auto makers to construct a plant in the Soviet Union that will quadruple existing Russian automobile production.

general trend toward higher levels of consumption in the Soviet Union since Stalin's death, there is little evidence that there has been a reorientation of the goals or the capabilities of the Soviet economy that would place the consumer in anything approaching the position he enjoys in non-communist nations.

One further question remains about the economic capabilities of communism, and that is its ability to operate a complex advanced economy under centralized administrative planning. For most of the history of communist rule, the planning problem has been simplified by the ability to concentrate attention on a limited number of growth sectors. As maturity is approached, the number and variety of industries using the resources of the country multiplies, and the calculations necessary to allocate resources become more demanding. There has been a recent slowing of the Soviet growth rate (Table 23) that may be attributable at least in part to the stultifying effects of central planning in a maturing economy.[74]

Table 23 Annual and Period Growth Rates of Soviet Gross National Product (Percentages)

Year or Period	Rate
1958	9.4%
1959	4.9
1960	5.2
1961	6.2
1962	5.1
1963	2.6
1964	7.9
1950–1958 average	7.1
1958–1964 average	5.3
1960–1965 average	4.9

Adapted from Stanley H. Cohn, "Soviet Growth Retardation: Trends in Resource Availability and Efficiency," in Joint Economic Committee, *New Directions in the Soviet Economy,* 89th Congress, 2d session, 1966, pp. 104, 127. The 1964 rate of 7.9 per cent is not indicative of a new upturn. Presently available figures suggest that the 1965 rate was again low.

Where innovation itself must be planned, and does not come from individual initiative, the burden of foresight and flexibility on the planners is great indeed.[75] The recent turn to "Libermanism" in the Soviet Union and the more far-reaching changes in the European satellites and Yugoslavia seem to represent a sentiment on the part of communist planners that some sort of limit has been reached so far as the old methods are concerned. Nevertheless, there is

[74] See Robert W. Campbell, "The Postwar Growth of the Soviet Economy," *Soviet Studies* XVI (July, 1964), pp. 15–16. The disappointing performance of the Czechoslovakian economy under communism suggests the same explanation, for Czechoslovakia was far more advanced industrially than Russia at the time of the communist takeover.

[75] Gregory Grossman, "Soviet Growth: Routine, Inertia, and Pressure," *American Economic Review,* L (May, 1960), pp. 62–72, discusses many of the problems involved and the Soviet attempts at their solution. See also his "Innovation and Information in the Soviet Economy," *American Economic Review,* LVI (May, 1966), pp. 118–130, for the effect of recent changes in the Soviet planning arrangements on the problem of innovation.

general agreement among observers that there are few prospects of Soviet abandonment of central planning altogether. If Soviet planners continue to balk at the large-scale use of computers while insisting upon retaining central control of the planning process, it is possible that their system of economic organization will perform less well in the future than it has so far. This, however, should not be taken as a prediction. There is no inherent reason to assume a refusal to change on either point, given the adaptability that they have shown so often in the past.[76]

Political and Economic Power Under Communism. Although the communist pattern of economic growth displays many points of similiarity to capitalism and socialism, its pattern of economic and political power does not. The Russian, Chinese, and most of the satellite economic systems are so organized that there is no locus of economic decision-making power adequate to challenge the overriding power of the State or to act independently of it. This is a consequence partly of the economic logic of a centrally planned economy, and partly of a political choice made by the communist rulers. Were the cause solely in the planning mechanism, it might have become possible for highly placed managers, or managers of important or basic industries to exercise strong bargaining power within the planning process. This would have been especially possible had there been a competitive, rather than a monolithic political system. Managers of important employing industries or unions representing their employees might have been able to appeal over the heads of the planners to the political process. There is no inherent reason why command of organizations affecting large aggregations of people cannot be translated into political power in a planned system. Indeed, such is the basis of the power of the Communist party itself. But the Leninist doctrine of democratic centralism, the role assumed by the party as vanguard of the proletariat, and the party's demonstration of the coercive implications of both have precluded the development of independent managerial power. The party's permeation of unions, workers' councils, factory managements, and other political structures and its monopoly of the electoral process have reinforced the dual controls of State ownership and State planning over all major types of economic organization. Thus, the despotic nature of communist systems cannot be ascribed to the economic aspects of communism alone. Rather, it springs from the totality of communist ideology and practice.

Whatever the cause, the concentration of power within Communist countries is immense, and its employment has been often ruthless, leading Milovan Djilas, one-time Vice-President of communist Yugoslavia, to describe the interlocking membership of party and bureaucracy as a "new class of owners and

[76] Equally, there is no assurance that computers could do the job of comprehensive planning adequately. See Egon Neuberger, "Libermanism, Computopia, and Visible Hand: the Question of Informational Efficiency," *American Economic Review,* LVI (May, 1966), pp. 141–143.

exploiters," that is "voracious and insatiable, just as the bourgeoisie was." [77] We must be cautious in accepting Djilas' statement of the matter, because his definition of class is explicitly Marxist; he defines the ruling group in terms of its relation to the means of production—as the effective holders of the rights of ownership in the collective property. It would not be correct to describe the communist social structure as class-ridden in the traditional sense of displaying rigidity and a lack of social mobility. There are wide differences in income and in the prestige attaching to different occupations, and there are the inevitable differences in advantage between the children of the rich and powerful and the children of the poor. Moreover, the educational system tends to fix career patterns at an early age, selecting those who are to receive training that will enable them to reach the top and substantially condemning the remainder to less prestigious occupations.[78] Nevertheless, even casual observation of the Soviet system reveals the humble origins of substantially the entire leadership group. The little firm information that exists on Soviet occupational and social mobility confirms the presence of a mobility rate at least as high, and most likely higher, than that in other countries at a comparable level of industrialization.[79] By the very fact of revolution, and by the later terror of the great purges, vacancies were created in the upper echelons of Soviet society that had to be filled from below. In mobility terms Soviet society is "classless," and the same is probably true subjectively. The Soviet people have been heavily indoctrinated with the concept of "classlessness"—they are taught to call their leaders "comrade," and they doubtless entertain aspirations for their children that envision them rising to greater heights than they did. But this is the classlessness of a *striving* society; not the egalitarianism of a Marxist one. It has much, in fact, in common with the classlessness of the United States.[80]

Yet the Djilas argument remains. Concentrated economic and political power has been placed in the hands of an identifiable ruling group, and it is exercised by them without the necessity of referring to popular choices to affirm or reject the policies made. This in itself denies the Marxist vision. The elite thus empowered has committed spectacular excesses of brutality: In Russia under Stalin, in China under Mao Tse-Tung, and in the various satellite repressions of the 1950s. Although it may not be possible to prove that the actual degree of

[77] Milovan Djilas, *The New Class: An Analysis of the Communist System* (New York: Frederick A. Praeger, 1957), pp. 54, 60.

[78] See Warren W. Eason, "Labor Force" in *Economic Trends in the Soviet Union*, Abram Bergson and Simon Kuznets, eds. (Cambridge: Harvard University Press, 1963), p. 69.

[79] See S. M. Miller, "Comparative Social Mobility," *Current Sociology*, IX, No. 1 (1960), pp. 28–58.

[80] This is clearly indicated in much of the Soviet children's literature, which abounds in Horatio Alger-type stories. It should be marked in passing that communist sociology does admit to the existence of classes, although not in the sense of higher and lower classes. There are two "friendly" classes—the workers and the peasants—and one "stratum"—the intelligentsia. There is no admission that the intelligentsia might constitute a class.

brutality practiced follows inevitably from the nature of communism,[81] it can be argued, first, that the absence of competing and mutually restraining power centers facilitates the *extended* abuse of power, and secondly, that the communist view of the world and of history—its own value scheme, in fact—inclines a communist regime toward brutality. The former point has been so well argued by political philosophers from Aristotle to Acton (with intermediate stops in the rest of the alphabet) that it needs no elaboration here. The other has to do with the communist preoccupation with industrialization. Industrialization is never a comfortable social process and has yet to be carried out without dislocation, hardship, and deprivation. To force the matter autocratically, however, as the communists have done consistently, exacerbates these conditions. Some of the most inhumane of the communist repressions have been employed for the purpose of reconstructing the social order—a necessity for industrialization. The collectivization of agriculture is a case in point. Communist ideology with its emphasis on historical forces leaves little room for the kind of regard for human dignity that socialists display, just as the monolithic nature of the communist State destroys the sanctuaries of humane dissent that so characterized even the most rapacious periods of capitalism.

Whither the Millennium? We may conclude this evaluation with a consideration of communist prospects for the achievement of the ultimate goals of the movement. How near is the Soviet Union to that condition of freedom, abundance, equality, and cooperativeness that its leaders proclaim as their objective?

On some counts, there are apparent indications of progress. The goal of abundance is within sight, if only the leadership will allow the people to share it, and the increased allotment of resources to consumer goods, the narrowing of income disparities, and the enlargement of communal services all give hope that they will. These same trends offer some encouragement to those who seek for evidences of growing economic equality. The easing of severe repressions since the Stalin period is also regarded by some as evidence of a gradual growth of liberty in the Soviet Union and of offering a hope for the ultimate emergence of at least a liberal regime, if not the stateless one of Marxist theory.

Yet the distance covered toward the ultimate goals is very slight in comparison to that yet to go, and there is little assurance that the trends so far will continue. It is sometimes stated that liberty once granted cannot be taken away again, and that a return to terror in Russia is therefore unlikely. But to so assert is to ignore the history of totalitarian regimes generally and of Russia in particular. Some years ago Barrington Moore, Jr., observed that there has

---

[81] But see, for some arguments, Calvin B. Hoover, *The Economy, Liberty and the State* (Garden City, N.Y.: Doubleday Anchor Books, 1961), ch. 3, 4, and the article "Was Stalin Really Necessary?" by Alec Nove, *Encounter*, XVIII, No. 4 (April, 1962), pp. 86–92, and his subsequent exchange of letters with Leopold Labedz in the August and November issues.

been a cyclical alternation of heightened and loosened autocratic control in the Soviet Union,[82] and the recent resurrection of the titles of General Secretary and Politburo, with their implicit partial rehabilitation of Stalin are disquieting. Certainly the terrible reversion to terror that followed the NEP leaves no assurance that another reversal will not occur, although one can detect no present reason at least why a new terror should become necessary. Bound up in this question are all of the imponderables that surround the possible Soviet reaction to future disappointments and difficulties. The Russian leaders from Khrushchev on, for example, have expressed a faith that they will "bury us" economically. Khrushchev himself predicted Russian surpassing of the United States economic achievement by 1980. In the same Twenty-third Congress of the Communist party of the Soviet Union in which the old Stalinist party titles were revived, however, the specific date of catching up was omitted and Khrushchev, who was in many respects a symbol of both relaxed relations with the West and eased internal control, suffered growing criticism of his policies, although he was not specifically named.

The fact seems to be that, even though communism is probably capable of achieving the economic goals set for it, it is not likely to approach the social and political ones. Leaving aside the broad question of whether or not an industrial society without a political government is possible under any conditions, the evidence so far indicates that the conditions for a free society do not exist and are not developing in Russia. The unhappy fate of Boris Pasternak and the trials of Andrei Sinyavsky and Yuli Daniel serve to underscore the illiberalism that continues and the inability of the Soviet leadership to tolerate criticism.[83] Without free expression no regime can be or become politically free, and the claims of communist doctrine to "scientific objectivity"—the incredible references to "correct" doctrines that permeate the leaders' statements—militate absolutely against this essential of democratization and liberalization. For related reasons there is at least as great a prospect that the present social inequality will gradually harden as there is that social equality will grow. The present tightening of entrance requirements into the party bodes ill in this respect. Russia's social mobility is partly a product of past revolution and terror. Continued consolidation of an elite dictatorial regime should slow it, even though income differentials may continue to decline.[84]

[82] *Soviet Politics—The Dilemma of Power* (Cambridge: Harvard University Press, 1950), p. 403.

[83] Pasternak, recipient of the Nobel Prize for his novel, *Dr. Zhivago,* was denied permission to receive the award and died in disgrace shortly after. Daniel and Sinyavsky were tried in early 1966 and given severe sentences for writing critical works that were smuggled out and published outside of Russia. In April and May, 1966, Communist China broke out on a new campaign to compel conformity and even demanded self-abasement of Kuo Mo-Jo, septuagenarian "grand old man" of the Red Chinese intelligentsia.

[84] Inkeles, *loc. cit.,* gives many evidences of just such a hardening of the class structure, not the least of which was the abolition of the inheritance tax in 1942. Because the Soviet income tax is quite low and is, in fact, being gradually abolished, this affords considerable opportunity for well-to-do parents to pass on advantages to their children.

The problem of the ultimate goals of communism is the old one of discovering if ends can be achieved by means that are essentially incompatible with them. This is the underlying difficulty in Marxist theory, and it has not been resolved in communist practice.

Communism and the Developing Nations

Because the major part of this chapter has dealt with communism at least tangentially in the context of economic underdevelopment, it would seem hardly necessary to add to it with reference to the as yet uncommitted underdeveloped part of the world, but some observations should be made because of the distinctive situations many of these nations face. As we have seen, communism is a politico-economic theory intended to be applicable in a fully developed industrial country, but it has fitted far better the conditions of economic backwardness and a feudal or semifeudal social pattern. In some respects the underdeveloped nations present analogous conditions, but they are in others rather different from both Germany at the time of Marx's writing, and Russia and China at the time of their revolutions.

The fundamental differences lie in the fact that most of the newer underdeveloped nations are not at this time up to the level of economic and social development that characterized even Russia and China at the time of communist accession to power. China, although low in per capita income, had made an important start in native industrialization, and Russia, according to Rostow, had actually completed its take-off into sustained economic growth. Few of the new nations have reached take-off, although many in Latin America have done so and since stagnated. Both of the major Communist countries had traversed many historical stages beyond tribalism, whereas a number of the new nations are only slightly removed from it, with tribal loyalties dim, but present. Communist doctrine, even with the addition of Lenin's theory of imperialism, is ill-equipped to serve as a framework for the organization of a society in which economic classes are at best rudimentary, and other types of social division are stronger. The rejection of the Marxist idea of classes has already been discussed with respect to Africa, and the experience of the most active apostles of communism—the Chinese—in Africa and Indonesia in the winter of 1965–66, when they found themselves summarily ousted and even slaughtered, underscores the problem of gaining acceptance for their methods and their doctrine.[85]

By the same token, the prospects for communism are better in Latin America than elsewhere. Latin America has a European cultural heritage, a class structure, and the beginnings of industrialization. Here the chief bar exists

[85] Of course, the Chinese communist slaughter in Indonesia (which struck down many noncommunist Chinese as well) had its origins in racial as well as in ideological tensions. What part race played in the ouster of the Chinese from Ghana is not clear, but it seems to have been minimal.

in the visible record of communist rule in Eurasia and in Cuba. Alike in Latin America, Asia, and Africa, the communist history of oppression is not overlooked. The fact that economic advance under communism has been regularly accompanied by extreme coercion, forced labor, and the police state is known to the leaders of the Left in these nations, and a number have made clear their intention to avoid a system that produces such practices.[86] Equally, the suppressions in East Germany, Poland, and Hungary were costly for the communist image, as has been the older communist nations' failure to sustain their economic aid to Cuba.

The communists' record, then, is their own worst obstacle, but it does not mean that they will not succeed in extending their domination. The very backwardness of many of the underdeveloped nations means that they will be undergoing the strains and frustrations of preindustrial social reorganization and industrial growth for a long time. Opportunities for fomenting "wars of national liberation" will present themselves repeatedly, especially if the free world does not recognize the herculean nature of its task of aid. This will present no small problem to the West, for as indicated in earlier chapters, the amount needed to bring along industrialization without forcible suppression of consumption is very great. It will be difficult to maintain the effort for as long as will be required.

For the underdeveloped nations, a communist take-over carries dangers beyond those of repeating the ordeals of Russia and China. Communism has proved so far to be a one-way road; once a communist regime has consolidated its position neither revolution nor voluntary return to freedom need be expected—the instruments of the police state and the strategy of terror are too highly developed and scientific in their application for the former,[87] and the communist will to control is too strong for the latter. Yet there is no certainty that communism can or would bring economic growth to these areas. There are many pitfalls. Too rapid a shift to public ownership or collectivization, as the Russian and Chinese examples showed, could produce a sharp drop in production—one that a country at the subsistence level simply could not afford.[88] There is also the question of aid and foreign investment. Communist leaders may have the will to suppress popular aspirations for consumer goods —a will that Western leaders appear to lack—but so low is the starting level of

[86] Chandler Morse, "The Economics of African Socialism," in *African Socialism,* William H. Friedland and Carl G. Rosberg, Jr., eds. (Stanford, Calif.: published for the Hoover Institution on War, Revolution, and Peace by Stanford University Press, 1964), pp. 37–38.

[87] See Hannah Arendt, *The Origins of Totalitarianism,* 2nd enlarged ed. (New York: Meridian Books, 1958), Part Three, especially ch. XIII.

[88] M. Bronfenbrenner, "The Appeal of Confiscation in Economic Development," *Journal of Economic Development and Cultural Change,* III (April, 1955), pp. 201–218, makes a convincing argument for the economic benefits of confiscation of private capital, but he skims over the transitional period during which incentives are destroyed and resentment is high—a period that, as argued here, could be fatal.

economic well-being and industrial life in a number of the countries in question, and so rapid is the new surge of population growth, that even with repression aid will probably be required, and outside investment will certainly be most helpful. A "bootstrap" operation like the Russian one may be very satisfying to national pride, but it is unnecessarily costly. It may be actually impossible under present conditions, where the gap between the rich nations and the poor nations is so much greater than at any previous time in history, and is getting wider. It seems rather more than likely that the chief and perhaps sole source of such aid and investment would have to be found among the existing communist nations because of the polarizing tendencies of the cold war. These, however, are the nations least able and willing to afford external aid, being still in the process of modernizing themselves. The decline of both Russian and Chinese aid to Cuba and the largely token nature of the aid given other nations suggests this. Worse yet, the experience of the European satellites in their relations with the Soviet Union leaves room for doubt that the relationship would in fact be beneficial to the weaker nation. There is at least an equal chance that it would be exploitative instead.

But if there are dangers there are also possibilities for underdeveloped nations under communism, just as under the other two systems. Communist leaders have been effective in reorganizing traditional societies, in pressing vigorously for growth in the most useful and basic sectors of the economy, and in forcing an extraordinarily high level of saving and investment. They are practitioners of the art of economic development. They have shown their ability to learn from and correct their past mistakes. With the instruments and power at their disposal there is no inherent reason why they should fail, if they are willing to pay the cost. This is the advantage that their alternative offers to nations still facing a choice.

5 / Fascism

A survey of the major politico-economic ideologies of the twentieth century would not be complete without a discussion of that one that produced the disaster of the Second World War, yet there is some warrant for treating it somewhat differently from the systems described before. Fascism was not so much a theoretical system as a *happening* for which an ideology was developed to provide justification. This is not to say that it was an isolated or accidental phenomenon, but merely that its philosophical roots were not only slight, but largely manufactured as rationalizations after the fact. It was characteristically opportunistic in outlook, and although both apologists for and serious students of the movement have found in it many reflections of philosophical ideas reaching back to as far as Plato, its ideological content was drawn principally from contemporary currents of popular thought.[1] Rather than describe it as theory and practice, we shall try to understand what brought it into being and what it was, for its historic significance does not lie in the manner in which it distributed power between the political and economic orders and organized the forces of production. What is important was its demonstration of the possibilities of irrational action when both the political and economic orders cease

[1] See Dante L. Germino, "Italian Fascism in the History of Political Thought," *Midwest Journal of Political Science,* VIII (May, 1964), pp. 109–126. Representative of the scholarly literature on the philosophical ancestry of fascism are: Carl Cohen, ed., *Communism, Fascism, and Democracy: The Theoretical Foundations* (New York: Random House, Inc. 1962); William Montgomery McGovern, *From Luther to Hitler: The History of Fascist-Nazi Political Philosophy* (Boston: Houghton Mifflin Company, 1941); and Karl R. Popper, *The Open Society and its Enemies,* rev. ed. (Princeton: Princeton University Press, 1950). A somewhat different approach, looking at sociological currents as expressed in political ideas, is given in J. L. Talmon, *The Origins of Totalitarian Democracy* (New York: Frederick A. Praeger, Inc., 1960).

to function adequately to serve the needs and wants of men. As the declared enemy of communism, socialism, and capitalism alike, fascism offered no real economic alternative,[2] only a political one. Yet it was accepted by millions of people in relatively advanced industrial nations, not only in Italy and Germany, but in a score of other countries where fascist movements, large and small, were founded.

But what was *fascism?* The term is widely used, but its meaning is far from fixed. Originating with the *fasci di combattimento* of Mussolini in 1919, the name Fascist was rapidly applied to movements of a similar character throughout Europe. When Japan joined the Axis Powers in the Second World War, her system was identified with theirs, despite some obvious differences in origin and structure. Since that time, fascism has come to refer to almost any type of noncommunist dictatorial or totalitarian system. Yet there was a special quality about the German and Italian movements and their counterparts in the period 1919 to 1945 that renders them worth distinguishing from others, and we shall confine our attention principally to them.[3] As such, we can define fascism as *a revolutionary nationalistic movement of an economically distressed middle class against both the collectivist and internationalist ideology of Marxism and the tendencies toward concentration in a capitalist economic society.* It is a form of *extremism* born of acute social unrest, leading to the creation of an antidemocratic, totalitarian State.[4]

A Brief History of Italian and German Fascism

The earliest of the fascist movements to achieve power was that in Italy, led by Benito Mussolini. Prior to the First World War, Mussolini had been an ardent and active socialist, but he broke with his party in 1914 over the issue of participation in the war, which he had come to favor. In 1919 he founded his fascist movement and seemed for a while to continue his espousal

[2] That a reorganization of the economic order did take place under fascism is somewhat beside the point. In Italy, this reorganization was devised after the seizure of power, and in Germany the economic program of the Nazi party was never made a major part of its propaganda before seizing power. See Franz Neumann, *Behemoth: The Structure and Practice of National Socialism* (New York: Oxford University Press, 1942), p. 232.

[3] Ernst Nolte, whose study, *Three Faces of Fascism,* (trans. by Leila Vennewitz (New York: Holt, Rinehart and Winston, 1965), is by far the best in terms of historical and philosophical analysis, defends the designation of the period 1919 to 1945 as the "era of fascism" with considerable cogency. See his ch. 1 and appendix A.

[4] For other definitions, see *Ibid.,* pp. 20–21, Seymour Martin Lipset, *Political Man* (Garden City, N.Y.: Doubleday Anchor Books, 1963) ch. 5, and David J. Saposs, "The Rôle of the Middle Class in Social Development: Fascism, Populism, Communism, Socialism," *Economic Essays in Honor of Wesley Clair Mitchell* (New York: Columbia University Press, 1935), pp. 393–424.

of a proletarian revolution, but with a strong nationalistic appeal instead of the internationalist bias of his former Marxism.[5] Leadership of the labor movement, however, remained with the socialists. Shortly after the failure of the workers' occupation of the factories in 1920,[6] Mussolini turned on his former comrades, leading his movement in organized violence against them. Armed fascist bands attacked socialist leaders, beating and killing them and burning their property, all with the acquiescence and even connivance of the police and military authorities, who were glad to see the "Red Menace" thus disposed of. With his movement gaining strength in the lower middle class and attracting the support of short-sighted industrialists bent upon destruction of the Marxist workers' movement, he then turned on the government itself, ordering a great march on Rome. The government capitulated, and on October 30, 1922, Mussolini was installed as Prime Minister by King Victor Emmanuel III.

The next few years were spent in establishing the fascist dictatorship and developing an ideology, which it had never really had as a movement seeking power. Then followed the only period in which the attention of the regime can be said to have been fixed rather clearly upon the economic system. Intense effort was given to agriculture and to industry, and the structure of the economy was reshaped by the creation of what was called the *corporative State*—an organization of the various sectors of the economy into large associations of enterprises, called corporations, for the purpose of giving coordination and the power of direction to the State and to the Fascist party, which dominated the State. In the early part of this period the reputation of fascism was at its height. All the world was to know that "Mussolini made the trains run on time." Land reclamation projects, social welfare services, public works programs, and business expansion were among the proud accomplishments of the regime. Yet these rested on an insecure basis. A part of the success was attributable to a law—the so-called *Charter of Labor*—that forbade strikes and lockouts, and much of the increased productive effort was ill-planned and excessive for the available markets. Even before the laws creating the corporative State had been implemented, a recession struck, becoming worse after the American crisis of 1929. A good part of the reorganization involved in the creation of the corporations was in fact related to the effort to counteract depression. While it was a device for increasing the State's powers over the economy, the

[5] Mussolini's nationalism owed something to an extraordinary episode that occurred that same year. The city of Fiume, which many Italians felt should belong to Italy, had been placed under Allied occupation after the war. On September 11, the wartime hero and poet, Gabriele D'Annunzio, led a small band of rebels and army deserters into the city and captured it, remaining in power for over a year before Italy herself was compelled to drive them out and retake the city. Mussolini pledged his movement to D'Annunzio and supported him throughout the affair.

[6] Faced with a lockout in the metal-working industries, workers seized many of the plants and attempted to run them themselves. The effort failed in part because of their lack of managerial skills.

corporative State was equally a vehicle for cartelization and concentration in Italian industry.

The failure of the economic measures of fascism to provide real relief and strengthening of the economy brought the fascist movement into its last phase, the turn to military adventure. War would not only stimulate production, but would turn the people's attention from domestic problems. To this end the dream of the mediterraneaum as *Mare Nostrum* was revived, and fascist Italy set out to recapture the Roman Empire, first by its invasion of Abyssinia (Ethiopia) in 1935 and finally by its distastrous alliance with Nazi Germany in the Second World War.

The German version had a somewhat different history and Nazi racist doctrine both differed from the statist doctrine of Italian fascism and was much more fully developed in the preaccession period. Yet there were important elements in common. Both movements offered themselves at first as nationalistic versions of socialism, opposed to international Marxism, and the nationalistic component of their appeal became increasingly dominant with time. Both were led by men supremely adept at demagogic persuasion. They both found their initial strength in a miscellaneous group of malcontents composed of former soldiers, students, and petty-bourgeois intellectuals. Both attracted support among the "little men" of the middle class—artisans, shopkeepers, and the like—and both gained assistance from at least a portion of the large industrialist class after they had demonstrated that they had a following and that they were ardently anti-Marxist. Both used private armies to shake the foundations of public order and weaken the democratic State. When transformed into governing regimes by accession to power, both employed systematic terror to ensure compliance and docility in the population, and finally, both forsook the domestic solution of economic problems and turned to war, partly as a means of solving them by expansion, and partly as a way of diverting popular attention from them.[7]

Adolf Hitler's National Socialist German Workers party (Nazi party) was much slower to gain control of the State than were Mussolini's fascists. Hitler's movement was hurt by a premature attempt to seize power in Bavaria in 1923, but it revived with the depression and, by the time of its victory in 1933, had gathered a far larger army of voters than Mussolini had at any time prior to the march on Rome. After a series of elections in 1932 which failed to produce a workable democratic majority in the Reichstag (the German legislature), Hitler was called by President Paul von Hindenburg to form a government as Chancellor of the Republic. Once in office he moved swiftly to consolidate

---

[7] In the German case the effort to find an economic solution through war was embodied in the slogan of *lebensraum,* or "living space," which symbolized a plan for the extensive resettlement of Germans in land seized from Germany's neighbors to the East. This was to assist in enlarging the agricultural basis of the economy and in rendering Germany agriculturally self-sufficient.

his position and to turn the German economy toward production for war. He, too, established a corporative State, slightly different from the Italian one, but similar in broad outline. Substantially his entire effort, however, had war as its premise: A war internally against the Jew, whom he pictured as the racial enemy of the German *volk;* a war externally against the Bolshevik menace to the East; and a war ultimately against the entire civilized world that would dare to deny the superiority of the "Master Race" and its demands for land and for domination over the Eurasian heartland.

The Conditions for the Rise of Fascism

How are we to explain these histories? To attribute them to some unique irrational qualities in the German and Italian people is to ignore the extent to which fascist doctrines spread during this era. These were not the only countries in which substantial proportions of the population adopted fascism; little Estonia has the dubious distinction of having given her fascists the majority of the vote in a free election (they were prevented from taking power by a coup). Belgium had her Rexists, Britain her British Union of Fascists, France her *Croix de Feu,* and even the Scandinavian countries had small fascist movements, albeit too small to gain more than one or two per cent of the vote. A variety of fascist movements occurred also in the United States.

Equally weak is the Marxist interpretation of fascism, according to which fascism was the last gasp of a dying capitalism attempting to defend itself against a rising working class. There is good reason to dispute this. We may note it in the peculiar origins of the fascist movement. Fascism drew its first major leader from the ranks of the socialists and its voting support from the middle class. It was from the beginning anticapitalist and proclaimed itself to be a new, nationalistic version of socialism.[8] The membership was drawn not from the industrial rulers of the two countries, but from among the middle class and workers, with a larger proportion of the latter in the Italian movement, apparently, than in the German. A report of the Fascist party Secretary, giving the occupations of 152,000 of the party members in November, 1921, indicated that about 62,000 could be classed as workers and 90,000 independent or professional. An analysis made of the Nazi party in 1933 showed that it overrepresented the self-employed, domestic servants, and nonagricultural family helpers, white-collar workers, and civil servants, while underrepresenting peasants and urban workers. Perhaps more to the point is the fact that financial support from industrial leaders to the Nazis was not forthcoming until after their movement had grown to considerable proportions in 1932, and that even then it did not involve more than a minority of the Ger-

---

[8] Mussolini's socialist origins have been noted, as has also been the name chosen for Hitler's movement: the National *Socialist* German *Workers'* party. Partly, of course, the German nomenclature was simply propaganda, but Mussolini's socialism had been genuine enough.

man industrial class, at least until after power was seized.[9] Italian industrialists probably jumped on the bandwagon sooner, although to what extent has never been confirmed.[10]

The Marxist explanation, then, involves only a half-truth. There must have been something else in Italy and Germany that permitted a war-dislocated rabble of ex-soldiers, students, and radicals led by a demagogue, even a highly skilled one, to gain both a following and substantial immunity to police and army repression. Most countries have had to deal with such problems, and most have maintained public order against them and denied them respectable support.

To approach this analysis, we need to know something about the state of economic society in the West at this point in time. The First World War marked the end of one era and the beginning of another. Economic development had reached the point at which large industrial combinations (many of them stimulated by the war effort) were replacing the small, individually owned businesses of earlier capitalism. Increasingly the small proprietor, the small agriculturalist, and the small merchant found themselves in competition with giants of far greater economic power. At the same time, strong organization had spread among the workers, and a rising tide of votes seemed to speed the ultimate victory of socialist collectivism. The smaller bourgeoisie found themselves faced with the loss of their identity as a result of forces from above and from below. To add to their distress (and incidentally to create great uneasiness in the wealthy industrial-capitalist class), the victory of communism in Russia inspired a fear of communist revolutions elsewhere. The "Red Menace" had shown its ability to conquer. The behavior of the labor movement did little to assuage these fears. In Europe especially, workers raised in the class-conflict tradition of Marxist socialism were aggressive, and their actions were often tinged with violence. In Italy, Mussolini's activities as a socialist before the war were only slightly less offensive than those his fascist squads carried out afterward. Where socialists were in control of local government in Italy (as they were in large sections of the country), their oppressions and exactions against the small merchants were feared and resented. In Germany the socialists were more firmly democratic and moderate, but a separate communist party maintained the violent image of the Left.[11]

There was thus created in the lower middle class a readiness to welcome either relief or escape from insecurity and fear. Fascism offered both. The relief was in the form of fascism's proclaimed anti-Marxism and anti-capital-

---

[9] It was naturally unwise for them to withhold contributions once the Nazis were in, because to do so might invite retribution. After all, the Nazis did nationalize a number of industries.

[10] For more thorough analyses of this question see Lipset, *op. cit.,* pp. 131–173 and Nolte, *op. cit.,* ch. 2.

[11] The division of the old-line socialist parties into communists and Socialists had not occurred in Italy by the time Mussolini gained power.

ism, and in the fascists' active warring upon labor organizations in particular; the escape was a new identity: An active nationalism, an identity with a cause, that of the Nation or the *volk*.[12]

But even this would not have been enough, and was not enough in most countries, to bring fascism into power. If the basis of fascism lay in economic and social insecurity, the facilitating conditions were the weakness of the economic and political orders. In this respect Italy and Germany differed. Italy fell to fascism not so much because its economic system had ceased to function, but because its political system did. Italy was suffering economic difficulties caused by readjustment after the war, and these difficulties were intensified by labor agitation, but there was by no means an economic collapse.[13] Her political system, however, failed utterly to suppress the fascist bands, and her army and police even aided them. At no point was Mussolini brought to task for his treasonous utterances (such as his declaration in 1919 that he would not recognize the government of Italy as his own, but only that of the rebellious band which had seized Fiume), nor was action taken to halt the March on Rome. In the face of such weakness, it is not to be wondered that a people would flock to the only evidence of strength that displayed itself upon the Italian political horizon.[14]

The political system of the Weimar Republic was stronger, but not strong enough to cope with the Nazi movement after the economic system broke down in the depression of the 1930s and added the unemployed to the other groups of discontented and fear-ridden to whom the movement appealed. In the 1920s attempted coups (including the one by Hitler in Bavaria) had been put down successfully and their leaders jailed. It was in the general disaster of the depression that the political and economic systems failed together, and Nazi bands were allowed to create violence in the streets while voters rallied to their cause. If a good word may be said for the Weimar Republic in comparison to pre-fascist Italy, the former did not fall as the latter did to a party of a mere 300,000 members represented by less than seven per cent of the seats in the legislature. Hitler's followers were the largest party in Germany, with nearly 34 per cent of the seats in the Reichstag. He himself had obtained over 13 million votes in an election for the presidency, only 6 million fewer than the number cast for President Hindenburg. Nevertheless, political as

[12] Mussolini's appeal was to the greatness of the Italian State, whereas Hitler's was to the mystical German *volk,* or race, which he declared to be superior to all others and the bearer of the only true culture. For a full development of the thesis of escape in psychological terms, see Erich Fromm, *Escape from Freedom* (New York: Holt, Rinehart and Winston, 1941).

[13] Gaetano Salvemini, *The Fascist Dictatorship in Italy* (London: Jonathan Cape, 1928), pp. 44–52, presents some evidence in defense of this point.

[14] The explanation of the weakness of the Italian political system requires far more space than can be allowed here. For some interpretations, see Harold E. Goad, *The Making of the Corporate State* (London: Christophers, 1932), ch. 1, and Herman Finer, *Mussolini's Italy* (London: Victor Gollancz Ltd., 1935), part II.

well as economic weakness was displayed in Germany, for the Nazi vote had declined in the most recent election, and the surrender of power to Hitler can be regarded as a confession of impotence.[15]

As a final condition facilitative of fascism, there must be mentioned the neutrality or active connivance of the military. The military in most political systems where democracy has not been firmly established is a force that can strongly influence the course of events. In both Italy and Germany it aided the fascists in their rise to power. To a large extent this was because of the connection between the military and a group that has escaped mention so far: the aristocracy. In both nations a landed aristocracy had continued down from feudal times far stronger than in most European countries. No friend to the rising forces of democracy, and only slightly less antagonistic to the growing competitive elite of wealthy capitalists, the aristocracy was willing to permit the new foe of both elements to gain power in government—thus the acquiescence shown by King Victor Emmanuel III in signing the appointment of Mussolini as Prime Minister, and the Prussian Hindenburg's acceptance of Hitler.[16] Thus also is explained the failure of the armies of both nations to put down the marauding fascist squads whose disruption of public order contributed so greatly to the crises that brought them to power.

It was the tragedy of Italy and Germany that these *movements,* which captivated the distressed among the population and found political power almost freely handed to them, produced *regimes* that offered no real solution to the problems these nations faced. In the midst of its distress the middle class had given support to a new regime that could not possibly have provided what it wanted. A class that feared both big business and big labor could not have wished to trade these for the big State with its apparatus of terror, but it did. Unemployed workers could not have preferred death on the battlefield or under a rain of bombs, but that is what they received. What happened was that a flight from present economic hardship had led to an irrational refuge in romantic nationalism and bitter anti-Semitism, neither of which was relevant to the needs of the time. The fascist movement had simply seized upon emotional currents which were present. Both nations had suffered humiliation in the First World War and after—Germany as the loser, and Italy as the winner who felt deprived of the fruits of victory—and Germany had for long harbored anti-Semitism. Lacking any real program, these were the issues most ardently pressed by fascists. Once in power and unable to solve the basic problems of

[15] For the story of the Nazi accession to power, see Frederick L. Schuman, *The Nazi Dictatorship* (New York: Alfred A. Knopf, Inc., 1935), ch. 1–5, Neumann, *op. cit.,* "Introduction," and F. M. Watkins, *The Failure of Constitutional Emergency Powers under the German Republic* (Cambridge: Harvard University Press, 1939). The two accessions are compared in Michael T. Florinsky, *Fascism and National Socialism* (New York: The Macmillan Company, 1936), chs. 1, 2.

[16] Hindenburg was of a Prussian landowning family and combined in his name (von Beneckendorff von Hindenburg) two ancient lineages, according to Schuman, *op. cit.,* p. 154.

their nations' economies, these were the supports to which they turned with increasing insistence, until the Fascists, who had begun by draining the Pontine Marshes, went on to attack a helpless African state; and the Nazis, who began with the construction of a great network of highways and the building of an economical small car designed to give each German family the benefits of cheap transportation,[17] ended with the deliberate murder of six million Jews and a war against the world.

The Corporative State

Although as suggested at the start of this chapter the organization of the economic order under fascism was not its most significant feature, it was sufficiently distinctive to warrant a brief description. Both Italy and Germany adopted a politico-economic structure that was called, after the Italian model, the corporative State. The idea for it was imported into Italian fascism from the syndicalist version of socialism, whereas in Germany the pre-Nazi form of business and trade associations seems to have contributed much to its development. Essentially, the corporative State was a grouping of industries, agriculture, and other types of economic activity such that each sector of the economy had its own pyramidal structure of committees ranging from regional organizations at the bottom to a central "corporation" (Italy) or "chamber" or "estate" (Germany) on the national level. At the top, all of the central organizations were joined in one large body—representative of the entire economic organization—dominated by the ruling party and the State. In Italy this central body, the Chamber of Fasci and Corporations, replaced the old Chamber of Deputies to become the chief legislative organ of the State. It thus substituted a form of functional representation for the individual and geographic representation characteristic of most democracies.[18]

Although this organization has been called "representative," control over the selection of members of the governing bodies in fact lay with the governing and party officials at the top. The control was exercised unofficially in Italy, but in Germany it was formalized under the "leadership principle."

Membership in an association or corporation was compulsory in order to do business, so that these organizations served as devices to control entry to every kind of economic activity. They were also organs of propaganda—vehicles through which government orders were transmitted—and frameworks for the reorganization and rationalization of industry, the elimination of compe-

[17] The Volkswagen was one of the few purely constructive products of the regime. The great *autobahnen* (highways) were intended to facilitate wartime transport.

[18] Italy provided separate organizations for workers and for management, uniting them only in the Chamber of Fasci and Corporations; Germany, however, declared the workers and management of each enterprise to be united under the "leadership principle," with the owner or manager in command. Therefore labor was not represented separately, although there was an organization for propaganda and control of labor called the Labor Front.

tition, and the control of production, markets, and prices. Fully merged with the State apparatus at the top (with ministers or other officials heading each corporation, chamber, or estate, rather like the Soviet system of ministries), they gave the deceptive appearance of being structures of business power in the State, while actually functioning as instruments of State power over the economy.

Under the exigencies of depression and war mobilization, State power was increased by all forms of regulation and intervention. The Nazi regime undertook a number of nationalizations and the creation of new State-owned industries. The Italian government found itself increasingly deeply involved in the management of enterprise through extensions of credit, especially during the depression, ultimately leading to the creation of a State holding company, the *Instituto per la Ricostruzione Industriale,* which still exists in command of some 120 enterprises.[19] Credit controls, materials and labor allocations, price and profit controls, licensing of both entry and termination of business, and, finally, rationing completed the network. If industry had hoped for gain and protection under fascism, it got it only in the sense that the movement toward corporate mergers was continued and encouraged. Beyond this, only title to ownership was maintained, and even profits could be taken only with the permission of the State. Perhaps Mussolini best summed up the meaning of the corporative State when he said, "We control the political forces, we control the moral forces, we control the economic forces, thus we are in the midst of the corporative fascist state." [20]

Fascism produced nearly as complete a control over the economic order by the political order as does communism, but with three important differences: In the first place, fascist planning was rudimentary at best. Germany announced two four-year plans, but the first was revealed to have existed only near its termination, and neither was substantially more than a vehicle for State intervention in those aspects of the economy to which the regime wished to devote attention in its drive for autarky [21] and its preparation for war. They were in no sense comprehensive.[22] Secondly, the principal beneficiaries of the use of the economic powers thus concentrated were the members of the ruling

[19] Andrew Shonfield, *Modern Capitalism: The Changing Balance of Public and Private Power* (New York: Oxford University Press, 1965), p. 179.

[20] Quoted in Nolte, *op. cit.,* pp. 218–219. The absolute domination of the State over business in Germany is denied by Robert Koehl, "Feudal Aspects of National Socialism," *American Political Science Review,* LIV (December, 1960), pp. 921–933, who sees a certain amount of self-deception among the Nazi leaders themselves.

[21] Both the Italian and German regimes engaged in considerable efforts to free their economies from dependence upon imports in preparation for war. This condition, called autarky, is obviously less desirable from a purely economic standpoint than is international trade, which permits each participating nation to concentrate on the goods it can produce efficiently and cheaply.

[22] L. Hamburger, *How Nazi Germany Has Controlled Business* (Washington, D.C.: The Brookings Institution, 1943), pp. 12–13.

group itself. Although fascists made a considerable show of social welfare services, State assistance to (and direction of) cultural and recreational groups, and so on, these were in the nature of "bread and circuses" designed to forestall unrest. Certainly the central direction of labor organizations was not used for the benefit of the workers, but to ensure that they would not become power centers capable of competing with the party apparatus. The reality of fascist economic life, especially in Germany, was the development of business empires by members of the leadership clique and the growth of industrial wealth in the hands of those who found favor with the regime. In this there is a sharp contrast to the use of economic power under communism, for there, although the ruling elite may enjoy privileges and incomes that are decidedly above the mean, there is a self-imposed (or perhaps mutually imposed) limit to greed and self-serving. There is very real attention given, as we have seen, to the communal services and benefits for the population at least. Thirdly, and most importantly, fascism's control over the economic order proved ultimately to be for a noneconomic purpose, even an anti-economic purpose. Communist effort has been consistently geared to economic development, with military power as an important concomitant objective but deemed a temporary necessity rather than a goal in itself. Fascism placed military preparedness at the forefront of its objectives from at least 1935 on. Whether or not the corporative State could have served as an adequate vehicle for purely economic purposes is not known, because it was imbedded in an irrational nationalistic ideology that did not permit it to continue its economic function.

Variations on the Fascist Theme: Right and Left Extremism

Our review of fascism has been useful in showing how an economically distressed and insecure middle class can be led to abandon its traditional allegiance to democracy and to accept political dictatorship and an irrational ideology as a means of escape from its condition. But the acceptance of dictatorship and of a set of myths is not confined to the middle class alone. If fascism does nothing else, it demonstrates the linkage between the economic and political orders by showing how dissatisfaction in the one may erupt in the other. In consequence, one would expect that frustration and fear at any level of society might manifest itself in a comparable fashion. Indeed, it is not inappropriate to compare the extremist ideology of communism with that of fascism, identifying the former with discontent and desperation in the working class as the latter relates to the same phenomena in the middle class. Communism, however, is highly specific; it has a fully developed doctrine that has the merit of approaching the causes of discontent more directly than does fascism, although it has its share of irrationality, too. It does not exhaust the possibilities of a politics of desperation in the working class.

That other possibilities exist was demonstrated by the rule of Juan Perón in Argentina and the continued existence of a strong peronist movement there even after the dictator's deposition and the revelation of his moral and financial corruption. Perón's government, which was often called fascist, was actually a labor-based *authoritarianism* [23] that succeeded an earlier conservative autocracy in a country that had never fully established the institutions of democracy. Conservative army admirers of fascist practice had overthrown a conservative, but elected, government in 1943. Among those officers, however, was a Colonel Juan Domingo Perón, who was given charge of the National Labor Department in the new regime. Perón soon saw the possibilities of developing a popular following in the labor movement, which had suffered neglect and repression under the earlier conservative governments. By his efforts considerable advances were made in the field of social security and collective bargaining, while at the same time he used the power of government to destroy union leadership unfriendly to him. When the next (and for many years the last) free elections were held on February 24, 1946, Perón ran for and won the presidency with the largest popular vote in the history of Argentina.[24]

There was nothing essentially irrational in the popular choice of Perón, but there is in the existence of a continued peronist movement now that his regime is over. Perón not only curbed civil liberties, including freedom of the press, but he mismanaged the Argentine economy while collecting a vast fortune for himself—a fact which was revealed after his overthrow by the combined military forces in 1955. His regime was not so oppressive or so characterized by terror as were the true fascist regimes, but his reforms and his aid to labor were superficial in the sense that they were given at the expense of the permanent development of a healthy Argentine economy, upon which any real advances for the workers depended.

Just as there is a parallel to fascism in the form of an extremist politics of the Left, so also is there one on the Right,[25] the examples of Franco's Spain

[23] It is important to understand the distinction between totalitarian regimes, of which the communist and fascist States are examples, and authoritarian ones. The former are antipluralistic, that is, they attempt to erase all social institutions that cannot be made into integral parts of one monolithic social and political system. Thus their attacks on churches (Mussolini was an exception to this) and other independent social structures, their organization of satellite social and youth groups (Young Communists, Hitler Jugend), and their insistence upon universal acceptance of an all-encompassing ideology. Authoritarian regimes, by contrast, have a characteristically incomplete ideology, and their permeation of the social order is far from total. They may copy the repressive measures of totalitarianism to suppress opposition, but do so only to the extent necessary to forestall resistance. An excellent analysis of this distinction is contained in a paper presented at the 1963 convention of the American Political Science Association in New York City, by Juan Linz, entitled, "An Authoritarian Regime: Spain." See also Gabriel A. Almond, "Comparative Political Systems," *Journal of Politics*, XVIII (August, 1956), pp. 391–409.

[24] Robert J. Alexander, *The Peron Era* (New York: Columbia University Press, 1951), p. 51.

[25] The class basis of "Right" and "Left" extremism is not so much argued as assumed in this discussion. For further elaboration and the justification for this position, see Lipset, *op. cit.*, ch. 5.

and Salazar's Portugal being most obvious. Like peronism, these regimes are more nearly attuned, at least superficially, to the needs of the classes supporting them, and they are not aggressively militaristic [26] in the pattern of true fascism. Also, like peronism, they are authoritarian rather than totalitarian— they do not permit free criticism of the regime, and they attempt to inspire uncalculated devotion. However, they neither have a full-fledged ideology nor attempt to control the whole of society. Rightist extremism is probably the least irrational of all forms from the point of view of the supporting classes, although not by the standard of developing a strong and healthy economy. Unlike the other two forms, rightist extremism does not seek change. Its support comes from a conservative class, often more aristocratic than capitalist, merely wishing to prevent new social and economic developments from robbing it of power. It is driven to use some methods common to totalitarianism to ensure this, but only because a people with some slight history of or acquaintance with democracy is less easy to govern autocratically than one still under the influence of a nondemocratic tradition. Some restraint of free communication and some terror are needed. The conduct of the economic system under a right-wing extremist regime is as unsatisfactory as under the other forms. It permits economic development to lag, if it does not actually impede it. It wastes resources on grandiose monuments to the ruler [27] and by its prideful tenacity to economically unproductive colonial empires, which cost more to keep in subjection than they return in revenues. Rightist fascism may not be aggressive, but it is possessive of remnants of national glory.

The Future of Fascism

Benito Mussolini described fascism as "a new departure in history," and called the twentieth century "a Fascist century." [28] In some ways he was correct, as we have seen. Fascism was a phenomenon that arose at a certain point in time, and in its massive oppression and terror it was indeed a new departure in the arts of political domination. Having once been put down, however, has it a future?

The specific conditions that permitted fascism to come to power in Europe were unusual and may well not be repeated there. With the passage of time

[26] That is, they do not seem expansionist despite their emphasis on militaristic trappings (but perhaps this is because they are also relatively small and weak nations).

[27] Franco's monument to (and intended tomb for) himself in the Valley of the Fallen has been described as "one of the most costly and stupendous monuments ever built." See Herbert Matthews, *The Yoke and the Arrows,* rev. ed., (New York: George Braziller, 1961), p. 229. Portugal's Dr. Salazar is, fortunately, more modest.

[28] Benito Mussolini, *Fascism: Doctrine and Institutions* (Rome: "Ardita" Publishers, 1935–XIII), pp. 25–26. Note that this volume, published in Italy, bears two dates, one being the normal year and the other signifying that it was published in the thirteenth year of a new era—the fascist era. Characteristically, the latter date is in the numerals of ancient Rome.

the labor movement has become more attached to democratic methods and the landed aristocracy has declined to impotence. Causes for unrest may still arise, but the many factors that combined to usher Hitler and Mussolini into office do not seem likely to present themselves again. In other parts of the world, however, there may still be occasions of danger.

The danger seems greater in Latin America than elsewhere, for many of the same conditions are present. There the army is still a force of major proportions in politics, and it is closely tied to a land-based aristocracy. There are weak foundations for democracy, a middle class of no inconsiderable size, an awakened nationalism, and labor movements still inadequately integrated into the social and political structure. Although most of the existing Latin American dictatorships are of the traditional *caudillo* (militarist-authoritarian) type, and a number of outstanding examples of working democracy can be found, there is no guarantee that either will survive an economic or political crisis in their present form.

In Africa and Asia the situation is somewhat different. Power there is already in the hands of the Left, and the old rural aristocracy is far too weak to play its necessary role in the process.[29] A substantial middle class has yet to emerge, and large industry is not, for the most part, privately owned by a native industrial class. It is either public, or foreign. A strong and sometimes irrational nationalism does exist, but this is not of itself a sufficient condition. Authoritarian regimes do exist, and totalitarian ones may arise, but their nature and their class basis are likely to be rather different than those of fascism.

It may be that the conditions for a resurgence of fascism will not occur, and it is to be hoped that they will not. But fascism is only one representation of a danger that is presented whenever the political and economic systems fail to perform adequately, or when a considerable segment of the population is rendered insecure and fearful by their operation. Fascism was a flight from economic reality into an idealized politics, and thence to war, which is the negation of politics and economics equally. One must be sanguine indeed to believe that other forms of political irrationality do not lie ahead if the economic problems of Asia, Africa, and Latin America remain unsolved.

[29] A much fuller analysis, to which most of that contained here is owed, is to be found in John H. Kautsky's excellent essay on the politics of development in John H. Kautsky, ed., *Political Change in Underdeveloped Countries: Nationalism and Communism* (New York: John Wiley & Sons, Inc., 1962), pp. 90–113.

6 / Concluding Observations

The Political and Economic Orders

If the nineteenth century was the heyday of separation of economics from politics, the twentieth has seen them brought together again. But the new relationship between the economic and political orders in each nation is a far more deliberately chosen one than most of those found earlier in man's history and reflects more closely a conscious effort to achieve goals held important by the nation or its leaders. In each of the four systems we have surveyed here, we have seen how the pursuit of specific objectives has produced a distinctive role for the State in the economic affairs of society and how that role has been extended to and reflected in the larger social functions of the State.

In communism and fascism the role of the State is comprehensive, or nearly so. The political order dominates economic activity by command and attempts to direct almost every aspect of human social life as well. These systems differ, however, in the purposes the State tries to serve by its totalitarian involvement. For communists the ultimate goal is both economic and social: The forcible construction of a new economic society. To do this, the State undertakes to operate the economic system as if it were one gigantic firm and seeks by exhortation, command, inducement, and sometimes terror to reshape the habits and attitudes of its people, training them and leading them into a new way of life. For fascists, the direction of the economy is no less complete but is secondary to the major goal toward which the regime aspires: National glory and conquest over "lesser" peoples and nations. Fascism controls the economy because it must in order to prepare for war; it exhorts and terrorizes its people because it is little more than an ideology of incitement. That these two systems, so unlike in philosophical intention, should have proved so similar in practice is an irony, but not a surprising one, given the dogmas of absolute truth to which both have laid claim.

Socialism and capitalism have far more in common with one another than with either of the other two, because both reject the comprehensive role of the State and both have been practiced under political regimes imbued with liberal willingness to doubt and question the validity of received beliefs. For each the choice of proper functions for the State has been more difficult and, because their proponents have admitted to uncertainty, more subject to change with the passage of time. Their differences lie in the nature and scope of the partial role the State is called upon to play.

Under socialism the State is custodian for a larger set of social and economic values than it is under capitalism. In relation to the economy it is likely to attempt more specific direction of production in the nonmilitary and nongovernmental sectors than is a capitalist State. It may be that this tendency arises more now (that is, since the Second World War) from the economic condition of the States that happen to be socialist, especially in their dependence on export trade and its concomitant necessity to promote those sectors that contribute most to exports.[1] It has its roots, however, in historic socialist doctrine, in which the State enjoys a central economic role. More important in this field is the State's commitment to the development of substantial economic equality, which requires intervention well beyond the level required by capitalism. As to the social functions of the State, again the emphasis on equality leads to a higher level of government activity, sometimes economic, sometimes not. Because socialism is not purely an economic doctrine, the demand for equality does not stop with incomes and wealth. It carries into social recognition, the elimination of special and exclusive cultural advantages, and the like. In a larger sense, the State is entrusted with a task of social reconstruction although, unlike communism, by gradual and largely uncoercive means.

In capitalism, the role of the State is smallest, but it is of growing importance. The myth of *laisser faire* can no longer hide the central place that the State holds as framer of the legal structure through which the economy works and by which it is regulated. Although the setting of specific production objectives is left largely to market forces, the State has moved steadily to enlarge the area in which it calls forth production for public services, welfare, science, and, of course, military uses. It has accepted permanently the task of regulating and supplementing market forces in such a way as to ensure full employment and economic growth. And it does not and cannot ignore its responsibilities for some social values that are affected by or find expression in economic behavior. It gives care to the disadvantaged. It seeks to ensure equality of opportunity in the economic struggle through education, retraining, employment services, and assistance to depressed and malfunctioning areas of the economy. More recently, it has moved to prevent social discrimination from

[1] One may note something of the same tendency in the United States when, as in the mid-1960s, a balance of payments deficit develops.

working an economic hardship through "fair employment laws," "open occupancy" laws, and the like. Yet the responsibilities of the capitalist State tend, in theory at least, to lessen when equality of opportunity is approached and the losers are cared for; when a reasonable level of minimum economic welfare is achieved; when a reasonable balance among the powers of the participants in economic bargaining has been reached; and when the forces of the market have been so adjusted that its own regulating forces can do their work of guiding and promoting production without bringing erratic cycles of unstable prosperity and depression. That none of these objectives is ever fully attained or permanently secured in a changing economy assures that the involvement of the political order will be continuous and subject to constant re-examination and debate. Nevertheless, the scope of governmental action contemplated tends to be limited by a presumption akin to the presumption of innocence in Common Law: The effects that the market produces are deemed desirable unless proven otherwise.

Power, Liberty, and the Economic Order

For each of the four systems the problem of power has been a central concern. The two associated with autocratic rule—communism and fascism—have sought to protect the power of the political order by making economic power subservient to it, whereas those operating under a democratic ethos—socialism and capitalism—have seen in concentrated power a danger to individual liberty and the freedom of dissent and action on which democratic politics depends.

Yet as we have seen, power is not easily suppressed and cannot be eliminated from a social system. Organization itself breeds power, and the large-scale organization characteristic of modern society breeds it abundantly. Nor is power necessarily concentrated at the top of an organizational structure; it may be found wherever there is autonomy in the making of decisions that affect the lives and fortunes of men. We have witnessed this in the phenomenon of managerialism: In the transfer of power from the ownership to the management of private corporations and in the independence of the managing boards of the British public enterprises. We have seen it also in the contrary example of the Soviet plant managers, whose limited autonomy made their power relatively slight.

And what of liberty? It is apparent that its preservation is not to be sought in the elimination of power. Liberty must be achieved by limiting the capricious exercise of power, by checking it, and by holding its users accountable—by subjecting power to the rule of law, in short, whether that power is privately-held or public.[2]

---

[2] For a most perceptive discussion of the application of the rule of law to private power, see Abram Chayes, "The Modern Corporation and the Rule of Law," in *The Corporation in Modern Society,* Edward S. Mason, ed. (Cambridge: Harvard University Press, 1959, pp. 25–45.

The autocracies have had in a sense the easier time with the problems of power, for they have sought not to minimize it, but to channel and concentrate it. For this, the instruments of political direction of the economic order have proved highly effective. Clearly recognizing that not mere wealth, but the ability to direct the economic efforts of men, was a source of influence in society, they assumed that direction themselves. In doing so, they have shown that the uniting of these two powers can destroy liberty and sustain the power of the political order beyond any effective challenge from within the society in which it operates.

Whether or not this concentration of power can be continued without severe cost to the effective functioning of the economic order, however, is more doubtful. The answer for fascism may never be known, for its failure was political and it immolated itself in war. The lessening of restraints over managers in the Soviet Union and the satellites does seem to have been a decision forced on the communists by the deadening effects of bureaucratic and political thwarting of economic initiative and there is no reason to doubt their leaders' own admissions that this was the cause. The maintenance of control and the suppression of liberty have an economic cost in terms of the effort spent and the people employed in exerting that control; this much is clear. That the denial of liberty may in itself stunt economic growth has long been claimed by capitalists and is not denied either in theory or practice by socialists. In this they may well prove to be correct, for a mature economy at least.

For a developing economy, however, the communist concentration of power has proved useful and effective, and the absence of liberty has seemed to offer no bar to rapid advance. It should also be said that there is no inherent certainty that communists will not some day achieve a successful marriage of the computer with decentralized initiative in a mature economy as well. Westerners have erred more than once in the past in predicting failure for them.

If the communists succeed in granting a limited autonomy to their managerial class without actually conferring power and liberty upon its members, they may yet face one more rival to concentrated power that arises from a complex industrial society, and that is the increasing influence of the possessors of technical knowledge. Along with managerialism, technological specialization is one of the hallmarks of the present age, and it is increasingly difficult for political leadership, whether democratic or dictatorial, to understand sufficiently the work of the technological expert to give effective direction to him. Too much should not be made of this so far as communism is concerned. The curious history of the biological theories of Lysenko [3] indicates that com-

[3] Trofim D. Lysenko, a Soviet agronomist, published, in 1948, a theory of heredity that ran counter to all theoretical and experimental work at the time. Because his theory seemed to have useful implications for communist social theory, however, he received the backing of the Party Central Committee, and his theory was for a time the official Soviet line in his science. With changes in personnel in the Soviet political leadership, Lysenko's star has fallen and risen again, suggesting that technical or scientific knowledge is not immune to political prescription under communism.

munist leaders are not always deterred from the exercise of command by any consciousness of their ignorance of the technical or scientific questions involved. It is also doubtful that specialists would be inclined or able to wield effective power outside their chosen fields, so that they need not be regarded as serious challengers for political rule as managers might. What is raised for autocratic government (and for democratic government as well) is the problem of making rational choices in fields in which political leaders are dependent on technical specialists for guidance without in fact allowing the specialists a major voice in the decisions themselves.

Both capitalism and socialism have been concerned to limit and control power for the sake of liberty, although each has tended to regard one form of power as inherently more dangerous than the other. Over time the solutions they have reached have developed considerable similarity, but the original bias with which each started is still displayed.

The power most feared by capitalists was that of the State, for capitalism's origins lay in the emancipation of economic activity from political control. This has caused its bias to be toward the dispersion of both economic and political power so that liberty might be preserved by keeping power centers relatively weak and competitive with one another. Until relatively recently only the powers of government were subjected to any really effective limitation and dispersion. But, as we have seen, the growth of private economic empires led to demands for their control as well, and ultimately the State was granted authority to oversee the power struggle in the economy and to assist the weaker contestants in their development of countervailing power. There has remained, however, a suspicion of State activity in the economic realm that has produced opposition to even such helpful ventures as attempts to cure or prevent economic fluctuations—phenomena which are damaging to capitalism itself.

Thus capitalism's bias in defense of liberty carries with it dangers—dangers to the economy and to the very liberty it seeks to protect. It is possible to risk the survival of a system by diffusing its power too greatly, rendering it incapable of swift and concerted action when the need is great. And it is possible to so weaken the State that private despotism may flourish, especially when individuals have the power to veto community action that would hold them responsible for their deeds. These things have happened under capitalism, but perhaps their danger is less now that the ritual antistatism of *laisser faire* has been largely abandoned and a deeper understanding of the constructive functions of the State has been gained.

Socialists have approached the problem of power from the standpoint of their feeling of repugnance for private economic domination and their longing for equality. This tended to mislead them so far as their early expectations were concerned, for it suggested too simple a solution: If once private economic power were eliminated by the transfer of ownership to the State, then both economic and political equality could be achieved and power would be at the disposal of the community, acting through the democratic process. As it happens, they never put this theory to a test, nor did they even subject those industries that they did nationalize to full and direct political control. Through the device of the public corporation they maintained a dispersion of managerial decision-making power and developed under public ownership something akin to the autonomy of the private corporation. By their adoption of economic planning, however, and the controls by which it is implemented, socialists have expressed and implemented their preference for State control of economic decision-making at the most general level, despite the concentration of power that it entails. They continue to look to the State as a safeguard to liberty against private oppression and to constitutional restraint and the democratic process to keep the State in bounds. The risk that they take is that the democratic decision-making process will prove unequal to the burden laid upon it—that politically unattractive decisions might give way to those that were economically unwise,[4] or that the technical complexity of economic questions will render popular participation meaningless. The strength of socialists' commitment to liberty is demonstrated in their increasing awareness of this problem and their growing unwillingness to concentrate power too greatly lest it become impossible to hold it accountable. As one of them has stated it, "The main task of socialism today is to prevent the concentration of power in the hands of *either* industrial management *or* the state bureaucracy—in brief, to distribute responsibility and so to enlarge freedom of choice." [5] To this statement both socialists and capitalists could subscribe.

Common Ground

Despite the many differences among them, the systems we have studied here are products of the modern age, and as such have many features in common. Perhaps this could not be said of fascism, for with all of its paraphernalia of modern methods of repression, it was an act of rebellion against the tide of history, seeking to recapture an earlier glory, real or imagined. But for the rest, the essential lessons of the Industrial Revolution and of human experience since that time have been accepted. All three display a faith in man's ability to exert rational control over his environment; all give a central place among society's goals to the development of economic well-being for the population as a whole; all are imbued with the idea of progress.

Attachment to the idea of progress, specifically economic progress, is perhaps the most striking common characteristic of all three modern ideologies. Socialism has turned from its preoccupation with the sharing of scarcity to seek

[4] But this, of course, is a risk all democracies take.

[5] R. H. S. Crossman, *The Politics of Socialism* (New York: Atheneum Publishers, 1965), p. 57.

economic growth, while capitalism and communism have maintained and strengthened their commitment to abundance. At times manifested in spectacular competition as in the United States-Soviet race to the moon, the drive toward technological change and advance has become a seemingly permanent feature of modern life throughout the world.

Perhaps equally significant is the extent of agreement in all societies that the well-being of all individuals is a matter of public concern. Although social justice and the welfare of the poorer segments of the community have been prime elements in the program of socialism, and of communism at least ideally, the provision of free public education, public assistance, and more recently comprehensive welfare programs in advanced capitalist countries have proven that concern to be universal.

A third area of agreement, in practice at least, has been the necessity for material incentives to maximize productive effort. The emphasis on material goals that infuses modern industrial society has left its imprint upon the individuals within it. No longer are the sanctions of tradition or command sufficient to call forth personal striving, if indeed they ever were. Nor has any modern society yet succeeded in relying on social recognition, honors, and other symbolic rewards to the exclusion of material incentives. This may be viewed with regret by socialists, dismissed as a passing phase by communists, and embraced as reasonable and natural by capitalists, but all three accept and reflect it in their practice.

Finally, there is the recognition that a complex, interdependent economic society cannot sustain itself without some exercise of rational forethought on the part of the community and some use of the powers of government to control it. Planning is a central article of faith in socialism and communism, but something approaching it is being practiced in capitalist countries, even if without the comprehensiveness and regularity of implementation that characterize the other two. The work of the Council of Economic Advisers in the United States is a case in point. This body does not, like planning agencies elsewhere, establish sectoral targets for production that it is hoped the economy will meet. But it does attempt to anticipate economic trends to aid both government and business in planning their activities, and it occasionally finds its work serving as the basis for intense governmental efforts to control, restrain, or stimulate the economy in line with its recommendations.

An End to Ideology?

The presence of these common elements and the many changes that have occurred in the programs and policies of capitalism, socialism, and communism that seem to have brought them closer together have led a considerable number of writers—scholars and journalists alike—to suggest that we are nearing an end to ideological struggles and approaching a time when all nations and parties will agree on the means to be used to regulate and guide the economic order. We have seen some of the evidence suggestive of this: The great relaxation of central control in the communist satellite economies, their increasing use of market techniques, and the similar, but more modest changes in the Soviet Union; the abandonment of extensive public ownership by socialists; the acceptance by capitalists of forethought, if not of planning. To this may be added even more. The United States, for example, is giving increasing attention to the discussion of national goals—an apparent first step toward planning proper.[6]

There are some forces at work in the modern world that may tend to promote a gradual assimilation of economic systems. International trade is one of these, with its requirements of at least a minimal congruity between trading systems. Another is found in the experiments in economic regionalism, of which the European Common Market is the most prominent. The development of economic ties not only promotes adjustments tending toward uniformity, but it increases cultural contact, which may produce a sharing of values.

Of perhaps greatest significance is the decline in class feeling that has been noted in much of Europe. The antagonisms that gave rise to the great ideological struggles of the past century have weakened under the combined impact of growing affluence, expanded exercise of the suffrage, and increased governmental provision against individual economic hardship. It is this, in fact, in the eyes of many, that signals the end of an age.[7] From one point of view the consequence of the decline of class consciousness may be seen leading to an "Americanization" of European society, making the social structure and possibly the politics of European countries resemble the United States in "classlessness" and lack of ideological cleavage. Professor Lipset, in fact, suggests that the latter, as the nation least encumbered with a feudal past, and the most advanced technologically of any in the world, might be "the image of the European future." [8] Another view is manifested in the increasing interest of American economists, and occasionally politicians, in certain of the con-

[6] See, for example, The Report of the President's Commission on National Goals, *Goals for Americans* (Englewood Cliffs, N.J.: Prentice-Hall, Inc., 1960). This commission was appointed by President Eisenhower and was financed by private sources under the auspices of The American Assembly of Columbia University. More recently, a National Commission on Technology, Automation, and Economic Progress appointed by President Johnson and financed by the Federal government went so far as to recommend the creation of a permanent body to discuss national goals. This proposal is dealt with further in this chapter.

[7] Writings that set forth the "end of ideology" thesis include: Daniel Bell, *The End of Ideology*, rev. ed., (New York: Collier Books, 1961), especially pp. 393–402; Seymour Martin Lipset, *Political Man* (Garden City: Doubleday Anchor Books, 1963), pp. 439–456, and Robert A. Dahl and Charles E. Lindblom, *Politics, Economics, and Welfare* (New York: Harper & Row, Publishers, 1953), pp. 3–18.

[8] Seymour M. Lipset, "The Changing Class Structure and Contemporary European Politics." *Daedalus*, Vol. 93 (Winter, 1964), pp. 271–272. For a related, yet very different view, see R. L. Bruckberger, Image of America (New York, The Viking Press, 1959).

tinental economies, especially that of France, as presenting models of a "middle way," presumably one on which all others might meet.[9]

France, a "Middle Way"?　It is worthwhile to dwell a moment on the French system to test at least partially the strength of the argument for an end to ideology against the propositions set forth in this book. For France *has* a distinctive system, and one that does, in fact, fall somewhat outside all of the categories we have used. In the immediate postwar period she was governed by a coalition of socialists, communists, and reformist-minded Catholics, who instituted an extensive nationalization program and a national economic plan. Given these origins, the intent was apparently socialist, although the need for some kind of planning to restore the French economy after the devastation of war was fairly generally accepted. After control of the government returned to a coalition of "bourgeois" parties, however, the system of planning was continued and there was no denationalization, not even of the limited sort that occurred in Britain. In fact, French governments, especially the conservative government of General de Gaulle, have improved and strengthened the planning mechanism and have enlarged the government's control over the nationalized industries. French planning is now no less complete, and is probably more so, than that found in Britain and Scandinavia. Called *indicative planning,* it is regarded as a voluntary joint effort by representatives of management and labor with professional governmental planners to set growth and production goals toward which both government and industry will direct their efforts. Actually it is somewhat more than that. In the first place, the initiative in planning lies with the professionals, and they tend to dominate, even to the point of chairing, the various planning commissions and other bodies. Furthermore, the implementation of the plans is not wholly voluntary but is assisted by governmental policies that include approximately the same mixture of inducement and coercion that characterize socialist plan enforcement. There is one significant deviation from socialist practice in that the plans are not cast in annual installments along the lines of the Scandinavian "economic budgets." They are of four years' duration and only fix the production targets for the terminal year.[10]

[9] One gains this impression by implication, for example, in comparative studies such as that by Alfred Oxenfeldt and Vsevolod Holubnychy, *Economic Systems in Action,* 3rd ed. (New York: Holt, Rinehart & Winston, 1965), in which three countries are chosen: The United States, the Soviet Union, and France, with the latter described as "The Newest 'Middle Way.'" More direct evidence is provided by Andrew Shonfield, *Modern Capitalism: The Changing Balance of Public and Private Power* (New York and London: Oxford University Press, 1965), pp. 72–73, who discusses the intense interest shown by Chairman Walter W. Heller of the Council of Economic Advisers and others of the Kennedy Administration in European planning, especially French.

[10] Useful, brief discussions of the French system are contained in Shonfield, *op. cit.,* chs. V, VII, VIII, in Oxenfeldt and Holubnychy, *op. cit.,* ch. 4, and in Allan G. Gruchy, *Comparative Economic Systems* (Boston: Houghton Mifflin Company, 1966), ch. 10. A fuller study of the planning system is given in John Hackett and Anne-Marie Hackett, *Economic Planning in France* (Cambridge: Harvard University Press, 1963).

If French planning and plan implementation appear to resemble socialism, French social policy does not. France has one of the most complete systems of social welfare benefits in the world, but it is built on the capitalist model; its purpose is not to bring about a major redistribution and equalization of incomes, but to give protection to the worker and a satisfactory standard of living to those at or near the bottom of the income scale.

Is this, then, a middle way? To suggest that it is, is to intimate that the French system is the outcome of some sort of compromise between those espousing the objectives of socialism and those who favor the goals of capitalism in the French political system. In fact, this does not seem to be the case. There still exists a socialist movement in France that does not regard its objectives as having been met and that did not, in fact, play any significant part in bringing the French planning system to its present state. The socialist influence declined markedly shortly after the Second World War, while the intensity of the planning effort increased. Excepting only its immediate post-war beginnings, French planning is a creature of the business community in concert with the professional planners. It has even been characterized by one observer as a "conspiracy to plan" and as "an act of voluntary collusion between senior civil servants and the senior managers of big business" [11] that did not even gain the full commitment of the political branches of government until a decade after its inception.

Surely we must look deeper than the "end of ideology" thesis invites us to do if we are to find an explanation for this. And indeed we can—we can look into values and attitudes that have characterized French economic behavior and the relationship between the State and the economic order through most of French history. French capitalism has never been as vigorous or self-assertive as have been its counterparts in Britain or America. The French did not give themselves over wholly to the market, or to a drive for aggrandisement in which each firm has seen no limit to the possibility of its expansion. There has even been noted a tendency on the part of a successful competitor to share his secrets with his rivals in order to save them from going under.[12] The characteristic French method of competition is not through price, but quality. Trade associations have been devoted to arranging the appropriate sharing of the market, tending neither to drive prices so high as to exploit the consumer, nor so low as to bankrupt the weakest firm. Of course, these are generalizations too broad to be an accurate description of the behavior of each firm and industry, but they do represent a tendency that made France one of the least competitive and (through the trade associations) most highly cartelized in Europe. Economic freedom, insofar as it meant freedom to compete unreservedly, has never been a high ideal of French industry.

But more important, for the purposes of understanding French planning, is the presence of a statist tradition in economic thinking that runs directly back to mercantile times. The State has been an active participant in economic

---

[11] Shonfield, *op. cit.,* p. 128.
[12] Oxenfeldt and Holubnychy, *op. cit.,* p. 174.

activity through subsidization, protection, regulation, mixed ownership in private enterprise, and planning itself, throughout the industrial period. Although the phrase, *laisser faire, laisser passer* is French, it was uttered only in reaction to an excess of cumbersome regulation; France never subscribed to the view that the sum of unrelated free choices would inevitably work to the common good. One observer has put it this way:[13]

> The essential French view, which goes back to well before the Revolution of 1789, is that the effective conduct of a nation's economic life must depend on the concentration of power in the hands of a small number of exceptionally able people, exercising foresight and judgment of a kind not possessed by the average successful man of business. The long view and the wide experience, systematically analysed by persons of authority, are the intellectual foundations of the system.

Do we, then, attribute the French economic system to compromise? No. It is a continuation, with new and better tools, of traditions well imbedded in French thinking. It relates as surely to the values and attitudes dominant in France as does capitalism to the values of American society or socialism to those of Sweden. It is the uniqueness of the combination of values dominant in France that makes her system differ from both.

An End to Dogmatism. The difficulty with the end of ideology thesis is that it claims too much. It depends too greatly on identifying ideology in general with the class-struggle ideology of original Marxism. It also seems to define ideology too narrowly as a fully integrated system of ideas, all of which are dogmatically held and unvaryingly followed without regard to reality. It is not necessary to define it so narrowly. Certainly some ideologies are like this; there are *weltanschauungen* that purport to provide all of the answers necessary to the solutions of life's problems. But persons and nations may hold generalized views of man, may guide themselves by a common core of values, and may be committed to those values—in short, they may hold ideologies—while seeking to realize their values in the world by pragmatic means.[14] It is true that much of the heat has gone out of the debate between alternative systems; that there is an increasing tolerance for alternative points of view and a waning of class hatred; that there is less intransigent adherence to dogma and more ready acceptance of a pragmatic approach to the solution of political and economic problems. But these solutions still must be related to the values

---

[13] Shonfield, *op. cit.,* pp. 71–72.

[14] This distinction between meanings of the term *ideology* is made by James B. Christoph, "Consensus and Cleavage in British Political Ideology," *American Political Science Review,* LIX (September, 1965), pp. 629–642. Christoph applies the distinction to the differences between the British Conservative and Labour parties in a most illuminating fashion.

of the society employing them. It is upon differences in values—in objectives and goals—that the differences in politico-economic systems are founded. As Professor Berle has put it: ". . . to survive, an economic system must satisfy the community well enough to assure its continued acceptance." [15] That satisfaction must be moral as well as material.

Before a world-wide unanimity could be achieved on a choice of economic system, formidable obstacles of differing values and attitudes would have to be overcome. Consider, for example, the terms in which the United States National Commission on Technology, Automation, and Economic Progress put forth what was probably its most radical proposal—a suggestion for the creation of a permanent body to formulate national goals. The commission represented some of the least doctrinaire and most progressive-minded elements of the American business, labor, and academic communities. Yet its proposal was curiously diffident and characteristically insistent that the body to be set up be both nongovernmental in composition and powerless—not a planning body, but one to "suggest alternatives." What a far cry from the planning system of France:

> . . . the Commission, while not endorsing any specific format, feels that some national body of distinguished private citizens representing diverse interests and constituencies and devoted to a continuing discussion of national goals would be valuable. . . . Its role would not be to plan the future, but to point out what alternatives are achievable and at what costs.[16]

Have we reached an end to ideology? No, not yet. The struggle will go on a little longer, even if greatly tempered by tolerance, pragmatism, and goodwill. Nations will continue to choose separate paths and parties to oppose one another in terms of their values and goals. Can we reach an end to dogmatism, to sloganeering, to rigidified thinking and facile solutions to complex problems? This we should hope, for only through reasoning, honest experimentation, open discussion, and adjustment can any nation hope to achieve its goals and fulfill the values that its people hold dear.[17]

[15] Adolf A. Berle, Jr., *Power Without Property* (New York: Harcourt, Brace & World, Inc., 1959), p. 120.

[16] *Technology and the American Economy*, Report of the National Commission on Technology, Automation, and Economic Progress, Vol. I (February, 1966), p. 106. It is to be noted that this proposal brought dissenting comments from several members of the commission, one of whom felt the proposal went too far and five who objected that it did not go far enough. The one was an industrialist, the five were three union leaders, one academician, and one representative of a civil rights group.

[17] A sharp rebuttal to the "end of ideology" thesis is given by Joseph LaPalombara in "Decline of Ideology: A Dissent and an Interpretation," *American Political Science Review*, LX (March, 1966) pp. 5–16. In his rather puzzled reply (pp. 17–18 of the same issue), Professor Lipset shows what has been noticeable in his writings all along: He, too, sees the continued existence of values as the foundation for political and economic choices, but he still believes that there is a growing consensus on the values themselves.

The Future of the Economic Order

Just as there are grounds for doubting that all nations are reaching toward a common solution to the economic problem, so also may we be assured that man has not exhausted his inventiveness in employing political and economic effort for the fulfillment of society's needs and desires. The ideological struggle is still at white heat in the developing nations of the world and from this furnace there are already emerging new ideas and new variations of old ones. The history of the modern economic order has been largely written in the West. New chapters are even now being inscribed by African socialism, by the *Aprista* parties of Latin America, in the Chinese communes, in the village economies of India, and in the *kibbutzim* of Israel. Each of them owes something to the experience of Europe and North America, and each bears distinctive marks of the culture in which it is found. The older economies, too, will change as they have changed before and so will the role of the political order in them. For the first time in history man seems close to gaining true ascendancy over nature. To what uses and for what goals he will use his power, we can only guess.

Selected Bibliography

An attempt has been made throughout this book to suggest relevant sources for additional reading in footnotes to the text. At this point are listed together works of the most general interest pertaining to each chapter, including some items not previously cited that present either important points of view or good broad treatments of the subjects concerned. As in all brief bibliographies, the selection is a personal one and doubtless omits many items that others might have chosen for inclusion. For the convenience of students, paperback editions have been cited where known to exist.

Chapter 1

The works listed here divide themselves into fairly distinct categories according to the outline of Chapter 1. BEARD and GRAHAM represent two philosophical approaches to the place of economics in political and social life, the former being an historian seeking economic causes of political events and the latter a liberal of the classical school attempting to define that relationship between the economic and political orders which will best realize liberal values. Further approaches to this topic can be found in the bibliography for Chapter 6.

Broad historical and interpretive surveys are to be found in the two items by HEILBRONER and in POLANYI, ROSTOW, and TAFT. More specific coverage of certain periods is given by HERSKOVITS and in the classic writings of SMITH and TAWNEY. The remaining works in this list, including the two excellent collections of readings by FEINSTEIN and by AGARWALA AND SINGH, provide a basis for the understanding of the modern problem of politico-economic development.

Agarwala, A. N., and S. P. Singh, eds., *The Economics of Underdevelopment*. New York, Oxford University Press (Galaxy Books), 1963.

Beard, Charles A., *The Economic Basis of Politics and Related Writings*. Compiled and annotated by William Beard. New York, Random House, Inc. (Vintage Books), 1957.

Feinstein, Otto, ed., *Two Worlds of Change: Readings on Economic Development*. Garden City, N.Y., Doubleday & Company, Inc. (Anchor Books), 1964.

Galbraith, John Kenneth, *Economic Development*. Boston, Houghton Mifflin Company (Sentry Editions), 1964.

Graham, Frank D., *Social Goals and Economic Institutions*. Princeton, Princeton University Press, 1942.

Heilbroner, Robert L., *The Making of Economic Society*. Englewood Cliffs, N.J., Prentice-Hall, Inc., 1962.

———, *The Worldly Philosophers: The Lives, Times, and Ideas of the Great Economic Thinkers*, rev. ed. New York, Simon & Schuster, 1961.

Herskovits, Melville J., *Economic Anthropology: The Economic Life of Primitive Peoples*. New York, W. W. Norton & Company, Inc., 1965.

Polanyi, Karl, *The Great Transformation: The Political and Economic Origins of Our Time*. Boston, Beacon Press (Beacon Paperbacks), 1957.

Rostow, W. W., *The Stages of Economic Growth: A Non-Communist Manifesto*. Cambridge, England, Cambridge University Press, 1960.

Smith, Adam, *An Inquiry into the Nature and Causes of the Wealth of Nations*. 2 vols. With an introduction by M. Blaug. Homewood, Ill., Richard D. Irwin, Inc. (Irwin Paperback Classics on Economics), 1963.

Taft, Philip, *Movements for Economic Reform*. New York, Rinehart & Company, Inc., 1950.

Tawney, R. H., *Religion and the Rise of Capitalism: A Historical Study*. New York, The New American Library, Inc. (Mentor Books), 1954.

Ward, Barbara, *The Rich Nations and the Poor Nations*. New York, W. W. Norton & Company, Inc., 1962.

Chapter 2

The literature on capitalism is abundant and varied and, as might be expected, frequently polemic. Most of the items listed here are by authors favorably disposed toward the system in its broad outlines at least, although many have proposals for reforms of various sorts. More critical literature is to be found in the bibliography to Chapter 3.

General treatments of greatest interest include SCHUMPETER's classic study, the very fine and insightful work by SHONFIELD (which defines capitalism very broadly and thus includes most of the European economies as well as that of the United States) and HACKER, REAGAN, WALLICH, and WRIGHT. Power is most usefully discussed in BERLE's two books, in BRADY (with alarm), in GALBRAITH's *American Capitalism,* REAGAN, WALLICH, and SHONFIELD. Proposals and problems affecting capitalism are the subject of FRIEDMAN, GALBRAITH (*Affluent Society*), and THEOBALD, and also appear in the books referred to earlier. Other works deserving special mention are HANSEN's simplified exposition of Keynesian economics, ROSTOW's equally helpful introduction to the law of capitalism, PALAMOUNTAIN's essay at a group approach to the study of certain economic policy issues in the United States,

Sutton and others' look into the mind of the American businessman, and Lauterbach's pioneering investigation of attitudes of Latin American businessmen, which will have a bearing on the future course of capitalism there.

Berle, Adolf A., Jr., *The American Economic Republic*. New York, Harcourt, Brace & World, Inc., 1963.

——, *Power Without Property: A New Development in American Political Economy*, New York, Harcourt, Brace and Company, 1959.

Brady, Robert A., *Business as a System of Power*. New York, Columbia University Press, 1943.

Friedman, Milton, *Capitalism and Freedom*. Chicago, University of Chicago Press (Phoenix Books), 1962.

Galbraith, John Kenneth, *The Affluent Society*. New York, The New American Library of World Literature, Inc. (Mentor Books), 1958.

——, *American Capitalism: The Concept of Countervailing Power*. Boston, Houghton Mifflin Company (Sentry Editions), 1956.

Hacker, Louis M., *American Capitalism: Its Promise and Accomplishment*. Princeton, D. Van Nostrand Company, Inc. (Anvil Books), 1957.

Hansen, Alvin H., *The American Economy*. New York, McGraw-Hill Book Company, Inc. (McGraw-Hill Paperbacks in Business and Economics), 1957.

Hofstadter, Richard, *Social Darwinism in American Thought*, rev. ed. Boston, Beacon Press (Beacon Paperbacks), 1955.

Lauterbach, Albert, *Enterprise in Latin America: Business Attitudes in a Developing Economy*. Ithaca, N.Y., Cornell University Press, 1966.

Palamountain, Joseph Cornwall, Jr., *The Politics of Distribution*. Cambridge, Harvard University Press, 1955.

Reagan, Michael D., *The Managed Economy*. New York, Oxford University Press, 1963.

Rostow, Eugene V., *Planning for Freedom: The Public Law of American Capitalism*. New Haven, Yale University Press (Yale Paperbounds), 1959.

Salvadori, Massimo, *The Economics of Freedom: American Capitalism Today*. Garden City, N.Y., Doubleday & Company, Inc., 1959.

Schumpeter, Joseph A., *Capitalism, Socialism, and Democracy*, 3rd ed. New York, Harper & Row, Publishers (Harper Torchbooks), 1950.

Shonfield, Andrew, *Modern Capitalism: The Changing Balance of Public and Private Power*. New York, Oxford University Press, 1965.

Sutton, Francis X., and others, *The American Business Creed*. New York, Schocken Books, Inc., 1962.

Theobald, Robert, *The Challenge of Abundance*. New York, The New American Library of World Literature, Inc. (Mentor Books), 1961.

Wallich, Henry C., *The Cost of Freedom: A New Look at Capitalism*. New York, Harper & Brothers, Publishers, 1960.

Wright, David McCord, *Capitalism*. Chicago, Henry Regnery Company (Gateway Editions), 1962.

Chapter 3

Omitted from this listing are the works of the great exponents of socialist ideology, because they are well known and are to be found in any good library in various editions. A most useful collection of excerpts, however, is given by FRIED AND SANDERS, while critical-interpretive and historical writings are represented by EDMUND WILSON's justly famous study, LANDAUER's massive and well-written history, and the histories by the two COLES. Some diversities of outlook within British socialism are provided by ATTLEE, CROSLAND, CROSSMAN, JAY, and HAROLD WILSON, the first- and last-named having led Labour governments. Socialism in Scandinavia is described in CHILDS and in Part Three of GRUCHY; SHANNON gives a good history of the movement in the United States, while FRIEDLAND AND ROSBERG have compiled a very well-balanced collection of writings on the African varieties of socialism. Aspects of nationalization and planning are covered by ROBSON and LEWIS. Finally, two classic attacks on socialism, those by HAYEK and JEWKES, are included.

Attlee, Clement R., *As It Happened.* New York, The Viking Press, Inc., 1954.

Childs, Marquis W., *Sweden: The Middle Way,* rev. and enlarged ed. New Haven, Yale University Press, 1938.

Cole, G. D. H., *A Short History of the British Working Class Movement, 1900–1927.* New York, The Macmillan Company, 1927.

Cole, Margaret, *The Story of Fabian Socialism.* New York, John Wiley & Sons, Inc. (Science Editions), 1964.

Crosland, C. A. R., *The Future of Socialism.* Abridged and rev. ed. New York, Schocken Books, Inc., 1963.

Crossman, R. H. S., *The Politics of Socialism.* New York, Atheneum Publishers, 1965.

————, ed., *New Fabian Essays.* London, Turnstile Press, 1965.

Fried, Albert, and Ronald Sanders, eds., *Socialist Thought: A Documentary History.* Garden City, N.Y., Doubleday & Company, Inc. (Anchor Books), 1964.

Friedland, William H., and Carl G. Rosberg, Jr., eds., *African Socialism.* Stanford, Calif., published for the Hoover Institution on War, Revolution, and Peace by Stanford University Press, 1964.

Gruchy, Allan G., *Comparative Economic Systems: Competing Ways to Stability and Growth.* Part Three. Boston, Houghton Mifflin Company, 1966.

Hayek, Friedrich A., *The Road to Serfdom.* Chicago, University of Chicago Press (Phoenix Books), 1955.

Heilbroner, Robert L., *The Great Ascent: The Struggle for Economic Development in Our Time.* New York, Harper & Row, Publishers (Harper Torchbooks), 1963.

Jay, Douglas, *Socialism in the New Society.* New York, St. Martin's Press, Inc., 1963.

Jewkes, John, *Ordeal by Planning.* New York, The Macmillan Company, 1948.

Landauer, Carl, *European Socialism: A History of Ideas and Movements from the Industrial Revolution to Hitler's Seizure of Power.* 2 vols. Berkeley, University of California Press, 1959.

Lewis, Ben W., *British Planning and Nationalization.* New York, The Twentieth Century Fund, Inc., 1952.

Potter, Beatrice (Mrs. Sidney Webb), *The Cooperative Movement in Great Britain.* London, George Allen & Unwin, Ltd., 1930.

Robson, William A., *Nationalized Industry and Public Ownership*. Toronto, University of Toronto Press, 1960.

Schumpeter, Joseph A., *Capitalism, Socialism, and Democracy*. 3rd ed. New York, Harper & Row, Publishers (Harper Torchbooks), 1950.

Shannon, David A., *The Socialist Party of America: A History*. New York, The Macmillan Company, 1955.

Wilson, Edmund, *To the Finland Station: A Study in the Writing and Acting of History*. Garden City, N.Y., Doubleday & Company, Inc. (Anchor Books), 1940.

Wilson, Harold, *Purpose in Politics*. Boston, Houghton Mifflin Company, 1964.

Chapter 4

Similarly to the treatment given socialism, theoretical writing is represented here not by whole works, but by a selection of excerpts in Part One of COHEN, and by interpretive writing and commentary in HUNT, PLAMENATZ, ULAM (*Unfinished Revolution*), and WILSON. The theory and practice of totalitarianism under communism (and fascism) are given in ARENDT and in FRIEDRICH AND BRZEZINSKI, while the general political system is described in FAINSOD, MEYER, ULAM (*New Face . . .*) and, for China, SCHURMANN. Sociological aspects are described by BAUER, INKELES, AND KLUCKHOHN, and by MOORE; the economic system is explained in a manner suitable for beginning students by NOVE, and in more technical terms by CAMPBELL, BERGSON, BERGSON AND KUZNETS, PEJOVICH, and WU. The critical book by DJILAS is by now a landmark of dissent within the communist sphere, while the question of communism's appeal in developed and developing nations, respectively, is discussed by ALMOND and KAUTSKY.

Almond, Gabriel A., *The Appeals of Communism*. Princeton, Princeton University Press, 1954.

Arendt, Hannah, *The Origins of Totalitarianism*. New York, Meridian Books, Inc., 1958.

Bergson, Abram, *The Economics of Soviet Planning*. New Haven, Yale University Press (Yale Paperbounds), 1964.

————, and Simon Kuznets, eds., *Economic Trends in the Soviet Union*. Cambridge, Harvard University Press, 1963.

Bauer, Raymond A., Alex Inkeles, and Clyde Kluckhohn, *How the Soviet System Works: Cultural, Psychological, and Social Themes*. Cambridge, Harvard University Press, 1956.

Campbell, Robert W., *Soviet Economic Power: Its Organization, Growth, and Challenge*. 2nd ed. Boston, Houghton Mifflin Company, 1966.

Cohen, Carl, ed., *Communism, Fascism, and Democracy: The Theoretical Foundations*. Part One. New York, Random House, Inc., 1962.

Djilas, Milovan, *The New Class: An Analysis of the Communist System*. New York, Frederick A. Praeger, Inc. (Praeger Paperbacks), 1957.

Fainsod, Merle, *How Russia is Ruled*, rev. ed. Cambridge, Harvard University Press, 1963.

Friedrich, Carl J., and Zbigniew K. Brzezinski, *Totalitarian Dictatorship and Autocracy*. New York, Frederick A. Praeger, Inc. (Praeger Paperbacks), 1961.

Hunt, R. N. Carew, *The Theory and Practice of Communism: An Introduction.* 5th rev. ed. New York, The Macmillan Company, 1957.

Kautsky, John H., ed. *Political Change in Underdeveloped Countries: Nationalism and Communism*. New York, John Wiley & Sons, Inc., 1962.

Laqueur, Walter Z., and Leopold Labedz, eds., *The Future of Communist Society,* New York, Frederick A. Praeger, Inc. (Praeger Paperbacks), 1962.

Meyer, Alfred G., *The Soviet Political System: An Interpretation.* New York, Random House, Inc., 1965.

Moore, Barrington, Jr., *Soviet Politics—The Dilemma of Power: The Role of Ideas in Social Change.* New York, Harper & Row, Publishers (Harper Torchbooks), 1965.

Nove, Alec, *The Soviet Economy: An Introduction.* New York, Frederick A. Praeger, Inc. (Praeger Paperbacks), 1961.

Pejovich, Svetozar, *The Market-Planned Economy of Yugoslavia.* Minneapolis, University of Minnesota Press, 1966.

Plamenatz, John, *German Marxism and Russian Communism.* London, Longmans, Green and Company, Ltd., 1954.

Schurmann, H. F., *Ideology and Organization in Communist China.* Berkeley, University of California Press, 1966.

Ulam, Adam B., *The New Face of Soviet Totalitarianism.* Cambridge, Harvard University Press, 1963.

———, *The Unfinished Revolution: An Essay on the Sources of Influence of Marxism and Communism.* New York, Random House, Inc., (Vintage Books), 1964.

Wilson, Edmund, *To the Finland Station: A Study in the Writing and Acting of History.* Garden City, N.Y., Doubleday & Company, Inc. (Anchor Books), 1940.

Wu, Yuan-Li, *The Economy of Communist China: An Introduction.* New York, Frederick A. Praeger, Inc. (Praeger Paperbacks), 1965.

Chapter 5

Literature on fascism, particularly that written during the time of the Nazi and Italian fascist regimes, is not notable for its balance or objectivity. The selection given here includes a few of the better contemporary studies, including ABEL, FINER, FLORINSKY, LOEWENSTEIN, and NEUMANN, and some of the more recent ones that profit from both the distance in time and the availability of materials released by the collapse of the fascist governments. In the latter class are the work of BAUMONT AND OTHERS on Germany, and GERMINO's careful study of the Italian party. Brief treatments and excerpts from relevant documents are given by HALPERIN and WEBER.

By far the best historical and intellectual analysis of fascism is that by NOLTE, who also reviews the *Action Française,* a related movement of similar outlook in France. Efforts to explain fascism in psychological and sociological terms include FROMM's highly acclaimed analysis, KORNHAUSER, and the last two chapters in CANTRIL. The assumed intellectual heritage of the movement is traced through excerpts in Part Two of COHEN, and the history of totalitarianism, especially racism, is given in ARENDT. TALMON strikes a middle ground between an intellectual and a social movement approach. FRIEDRICH AND BRZEZINSKI review totalitarian practice in general and comparative terms, while the remaining items listed present the Argentine and Spanish version of autocratic rule.

Abel, Theodore, *The Nazi Movement: Why Hitler Came to Power.* New York, Atherton Press (Atheling Books), 1965.

Alexander, Robert J., *The Perón Era.* New York, Columbia University Press, 1951.

Arendt, Hannah, *The Origins of Totalitarianism.* New York, Meridian Books, Inc., 1958.

Blanksten, George I., *Perón's Argentina.* Chicago, University of Chicago Press, 1953.

Beaumont, Maurice, and others, eds., *The Third Reich.* New York, Frederick A. Praeger, Inc., 1955.

Cantril, Hadley, *The Psychology of Social Movements.* Chapters 8 and 9. New York, John Wiley & Sons, Inc., 1941.

Cohen, Carl, ed., *Communism, Fascism, and Democracy: The Theoretical Foundations.* Part Two. New York, Random House, Inc., 1962.

Finer, Herman, *Mussolini's Italy.* London, Victor Gollancz, Ltd., 1935.

Florinsky, Michael T., *Fascism and National Socialism: A Study of the Economic and Social Policies of the Totalitarian State.* New York, The Macmillan Company, 1936.

Friedrich, Carl J., and Zbigniew K. Brzezinski, *Totalitarian Dictatorship and Autocracy.* New York, Frederick A. Praeger, Inc. (Praeger Paperbacks), 1961.

Fromm, Erich, *Escape from Freedom.* New York, Holt, Rinehart and Winston, Inc., 1941.

Germino, Dante L., *The Italian Fascist Party in Power: A Study in Totalitarian Rule.* Minneapolis, University of Minnesota Press, 1959.

Halperin, S. William, *Mussolini and Italian Fascism.* Princeton, D. Van Nostrand Company, Inc. (Anvil Books), 1964.

Kornhauser, William, *The Politics of Mass Society.* Glencoe, Ill., The Free Press, 1959.

Loewenstein, Karl, *Hitler's Germany: The Nazi Background to War,* rev. ed. New York, The Macmillan Company, 1940.

Matthews, Herbert L., *The Yoke and the Arrows: A Report on Spain,* rev. ed. New York, George Braziller, Inc., 1961.

Neumann, Franz, *Behemoth: The Structure and Practice of National Socialism.* New York, Oxford University Press, 1942.

Nolte, Ernst, *Three Faces of Fascism: Action Francaise, Italian Fascism, National Socialism,* trans. by Leila Vennewitz. New York: Holt, Rinehart and Winston, Inc., 1966.

Payne, Stanley G., *Falange: A History of Spanish Fascism.* Stanford, Calif., Stanford University Press (Stanford Paperbacks) 1961.

Talmon, J. L., *The Origins of Totalitarian Democracy.* New York, Frederick A. Praeger, Inc. (Praeger Paperbacks), 1960.

Weber, Eugen, *Varieties of Fascism: Doctrines of Revolution in the Twentieth Century*. Princeton, D. Van Nostrand Company, Inc. (Anvil Books), 1964.

Whitaker, Arthur P., *Argentina*. Englewood Cliffs, N. J., Prentice-Hall, Inc., 1964.

Chapter 6

This final list is in the nature of an *envoi,* and no characterization of the various items on it will be attempted. They are left to the reader's own pleasure of discovery.

Bell, Daniel, *The End of Ideology: On the Exhaustion of Political Ideas in the Fifties,* rev. ed. New York, Collier Books, 1961.

Bruckberger, R. L., *Image of America,* trans. by C. G. Paulding and Virgilia Peterson, New York, The Viking Press, Inc. (Compass Books), 1959.

Dahl, Robert A., and Charles E. Lindblom, *Politics, Economics, and Welfare: Planning and Politico-Economic Systems Resolved into Basic Social Processes.* New York, Harper & Row, Publishers (Harper Torchbooks), 1953.

Drucker, Peter F., *The Future of Industrial Man: A Conservative Approach.* New York, The New American Library of World Literature, Inc. (Mentor Books), 1965.

Hoover, Calvin B., *The Economy, Liberty and the State.* Garden City, N.Y., Doubleday & Company, Inc. (Anchor Books), 1961

Hoselitz, Bert F., ed., *Economics and the Idea of Mankind.* New York, Columbia University Press, 1965.

Lipset, Seymour Martin, *Political Man: The Social Bases of Politics.* Garden City, N.Y., Doubleday & Company, Inc. (Anchor Books), 1963.

Mason, Edward S., ed. *The Corporation in Modern Society.* Cambridge, Harvard University Press, 1959.

Myrdal, Gunnar, *Beyond the Welfare State: Economic Planning and its International Implications.* New Haven, Yale University Press, 1960.

Reagan, Michael D., ed., *Politics, Economics, and the General Welfare.* Chicago, Scott, Foresman and Company, 1965.

Shonfield, Andrew, *Modern Capitalism: The Changing Balance of Public and Private Power.* New York, Oxford University Press, 1965.

Tinbergen, Jan, *Central Planning.* New Haven, Yale University Press (Yale Paperbounds), 1964.

Index

A Note on the Type

The text of this book is set on the Linotype in 10 point Times Roman, a highly legible and masculine face, based on the original designs of Stanley Morison. Commissioned by *The Times* of London in 1931, this face has become known throughout the world.